COOK'S COMPANION

COOK'S COMPANION

CONSULTANT EDITOR

Lorraine Turner

BARNES & NOBLE

NEW YORK

Created and produced by The Bridgewater Book Company Ltd
Project editor: Emily Casey Bailey
Project designer: Lisa McCormick
Commissioned photography: Clive Bozzard-Hill
Home economist: Philippa Vanstone

2006 Barnes & Noble Publishing

ISBN-13 : 978-0-7607-8506-5
ISBN-10 : 0-7607-8506-6

Printed in China

1 3 5 7 9 10 8 6 4 2

Notes for the reader
This book uses imperial, metric, or US cup measurements. Follow the same
units of measurement throughout; do not mix imperial and metric. All spoon
measurements are level: teaspoons are assumed to be 5 ml, and tablespoons are
assumed to be 15 ml. Unless otherwise stated, milk is assumed to be whole, eggs
and individual vegetables such as potatoes are medium, and pepper is freshly
ground black pepper. Recipes using raw or very lightly cooked eggs should be
avoided by infants, the elderly, pregnant women, convalescents, and anyone
suffering from an illness. The times given are an approximate guide only.
Preparation times differ according to the techniques used by different people
and the cooking times may also vary from those given. Optional ingredients,
variations, or serving suggestions have not been included in the calculations.

CONTENTS

PART ONE:
INTRODUCTION 8

Healthy eating 10
Health and safety 14
Equipment 16
Preparation techniques 24
Cooking methods 30
Pantries 38

PART TWO:
MAIN COMMODITIES
AND RECIPES 48

1. EGGS AND DAIRY 50

Introduction 52
Eggs benedict with quick hollandaise sauce 56
Eggs florentine 57
Sweet soufflé omelet 58
Spanish tortilla 59
Quiche Lorraine 60
Cheese fondue (blue cheese) 63
Eggplant gratin 64
Crêpes 67
Meringues 68
Lemon meringue pie 69
Crème brûlée tarts 70
Crème caramel 73
Rich vanilla ice cream 74
Chocolate chip ice cream with hot chocolate
    fudge sauce 75
Tiramisù 76
Chocolate milk shake 78
Nectarine melt 79

2. FISH AND SHELLFISH 80

Introduction 82
Salmon coulibiac 86
Fish cakes 87
Broiled trout fillets 88
Broiled sardines 90
Grilled sea bass with stewed artichokes 91
Dover sole à la meunière 92
Paella 95
Traditional Greek baked fish 96
Seafood gratin 97
Shrimp & pineapple curry 99
Squid & red onion stir-fry 100
Tempura whitebait 102
Cod & french fries 103
Crispy baked flounder 104
Smoked fish pie 107
Chargrilled tuna with chili salsa 108

3. MEAT 110

Introduction 112
Roast beef with Yorkshire puddings 116
Beef bourguignon 119
Beef stroganoff 120
Hungarian beef goulash 121
Classic beef fajitas 122

Broiled steak with tomatoes & garlic 125
Mixed grill 126
Glazed ham steaks 128
Lamb kabobs 129
Shepherd's pie 130
Moussaka 133
Rack of lamb 134
Provençal barbecued lamb 136
Lamb shanks with roasted onions 137
Rogan josh 139
Pot-roast pork 140
Citrus pork chops 142
Sweet-&-sour pork ribs 143
Braised veal in red wine 144
Osso bucco with citrus rinds 147

4. POULTRY AND GAME 148

Introduction 150
Traditional roast chicken 154
Chicken biryani 156
Thai red chicken curry 157
Chicken fricassée 159
Roast squab chickens 160
Chicken & ginger stir-fry 163
Duck breasts with chili & lime 164
Peking duck 165
Roast duck with apple 167
Roast turkey with bread sauce 168
Roast pheasant with red wine & herbs 170
Quails with grapes 171
Chargrilled venison steaks 172

5. VEGETABLES AND SALADS 174

Introduction 176
Borscht 182
Leek & potato soup 183
Les Halles onion soup 184
Ratatouille 187
Classic roast potatoes 188
Roasted garlic mashed potatoes 189
Dauphinois potatoes 190
Stuffed baked potatoes 191
Roast summer vegetables 192
Oven-dried tomatoes 194
Crisp noodle & vegetable stir-fry 196
Gratin of mixed vegetables 198
Stuffed red bell peppers with basil 199
Braised red cabbage 200
Baked eggplants 203
Caesar salad 204
Roast chicken salad with orange dressing 205
Greek salad 206
Spicy tomato salad 209

6. HERBS AND SPICES 210

Introduction 212
Pea & mint soup 216
Basil & pine nut pesto 218
Tarragon chicken 219
Omelets with fines herbes 221
Salmon cooked with dill 222
Tagine of lamb 225

7. RICE, PASTA, PULSES, AND GRAINS 226

Introduction 228
Spaghetti bolognese 232
Vegetable lasagna 235
Gnocchi with quick tomato sauce 236
Golden cornmeal, Italian-style 237
Chinese fried rice 238
Risotto Milanese 240

Brown rice vegetable pilaf   241
Vegetable couscous   242
Tabbouleh   243
Cassoulet   245
Chili con carne   246
Chinese noodles   247

8. FRUIT   248

Introduction   250
Berry yogurt ice   254
Orange sherbet   257
Tropical fruit salad   258
Traditional apple pie   260
Stuffed baked apples   261
Tarte au citron   262
Golden baked apple pudding   265
Tropical fruit dessert   266
Apple strudel with warm cider sauce   268
Date & apricot tart   269

9. BAKING   270

Introduction   272
Crusty white bread   276
Whole wheat harvest bread   277
Mixed seed bread   279
Olive & sun-dried tomato bread   280
Banana & orange bread   281
Fresh croissants   282
Chelsea buns   285
Blinis   286
Leek & onion tartlets   288
Steak & kidney pudding   289
Mushroom & spinach puff pastry   290
Vegetable jalousie   292
Potato, beef & leek pasties   293

Profiteroles   294
Cherry biscuits   297
Treacle tart   298
Rich fruit cake   300
Chocolate & almond layer cake   301
Jewel-topped madeira cake   302
Gingerbread   304
Chocolate chip muffins   305
Manhattan cheesecake   307
Crunchy peanut cookies   308
Almond biscotti   309
Chocolate brownies   310

Glossary   312
Index   317

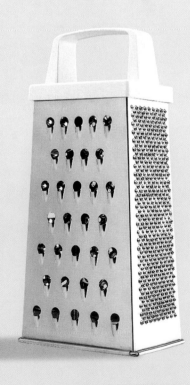

PART ONE

INTRODUCTION

HEALTHY EATING

THE AMERICAN WRITER, MARJORIE RAWLINGS, ONCE SAID THAT FOOD IMAGINATIVELY AND
LOVINGLY PREPARED, EATEN IN GOOD COMPANY, WARMS THE SOUL WITH SOMETHING
MORE THAN MERE CALORIES. WHILE THIS IS TRUE, IT IS ALSO TRUE THAT THE HUMAN BODY
NEEDS A REGULAR AND BALANCED INTAKE OF OVER 70 NUTRIENTS—VITAMINS AND
MINERALS—IN ORDER TO KEEP IT WORKING PROPERLY AND PROTECT IT FROM DISEASE.

The five food groups

A healthy and balanced diet needs to
contain adequate amounts of five major
food groups: protein, carbohydrates, fat,
vitamins, and minerals.

PROTEIN

This food group provides the building
blocks for the body. Everyone's protein
requirement differs, depending on
health, age, and size, but the average
minimum requirement is around
1¾ oz/50 g per day. There are two
types of protein: complete protein,
which is found in foods of animal origin,
such as meat, poultry, fish, eggs, milk,
and cheese, and incomplete protein,
which is found in foods of nonanimal
origin, such as nuts, seeds, grains,
beans, and pulses. Complete proteins
provide the proper balance of amino
acids necessary to build body tissues;
incomplete proteins need to be mixed
with small amounts of complete protein
in order to provide adequate nutrition.

CARBOHYDRATES

The main source of the body's energy
is carbohydrates. No official daily
requirement exists, but a minimum of
1¾ oz/50 g daily is recommended to
avoid an acid condition of the blood
called "ketosis." This condition occurs
when your body has to use fat instead
of carbohydrates to provide its energy.
Carbohydrates can be found in starchy
and sugary foods. There are two types of
carbohydrate: complex carbohydrates,
which can be found in bread, pasta,
rice, cereals, beans, pulses, fruit, and
vegetables, and simple carbohydrates,
which can be found in desserts,
puddings, cakes, chocolate, candies, and
sodas. Complex carbohydrates take
longer to be broken down in the body,
which means they release energy into
the body more slowly and gradually.
These are the best carbohydrates to eat.
The sugary, simple type of carbohydrate
will provide a quick boost of energy, but
this surge is quickly used up; such "highs
and lows" of energy are not good for
maintaining good health and vitality.

FAT

These days we are encouraged to eat a lowfat diet, but to cut fat out completely would be very unhealthy. What we should be doing is eating the types of fat that are good for us, and reducing our intake of the potentially harmful kinds. Saturated fat is potentially harmful in excessive amounts: it can raise our blood cholesterol levels and blood pressure. A good way to remember which foods are high in saturated fat is to think of the fats that stay solid at room temperature, such as lard and butter. It is these kinds of solid fats that clog our arteries and can lead to heart disease. Healthier kinds of fat are polyunsaturated fats, such as sunflower-seed oil and canola oil, and monounsaturated fats, such as olive oil and peanut oil. We also need a regular intake of essential fatty acids (EFAs): these actually help the body to burn off excess fat. Good sources of EFAs include oily fish, sunflower seeds, pumpkin seeds (pepitas), and avocados. So it is not true to say that all fat is bad for you. Restrict saturated fat in your diet by all means, but not the other kinds. Remember also that a lowfat diet is unsuitable for children under 5 years of age.

VITAMINS

This food group comprises organic substances that can be found within the foods we eat. We need only minuscule amounts of these substances in order to be healthy, but a deficiency of even one type of vitamin can cause us to be unhealthy. Vitamins range from the "fat-soluble" kind, such as A (found in green leafy vegetables, liver, and dairy products), D (found in fish liver oils, sardines, tuna, and dairy products), and E (found in soybeans, whole wheat and grains, and eggs), to the "water-soluble" kind, such as C (found in citrus fruits, green leafy vegetables, and tomatoes). Some people think that it is possible to live on vitamins only, but this concept is a myth: vitamins are only one of the five main nutrients necessary for a healthy body. It is always preferable to get your vitamins naturally from the foods you eat, rather than from synthetic materials such as tablets, because synthetic vitamins can sometimes cause toxic reactions. Natural vitamins are much safer.

MINERALS

There are about 18 minerals required for healthy body function, and the six most well known minerals are: calcium (found in milk, cheese, and beans), iodine (found in seafood, kelp, and onions), iron (found in red meat, egg yolks, oysters, nuts, and beans), magnesium (found in figs, lemons, nuts, seeds, and apples), phosphorus (found in meat, poultry, fish, whole grains, eggs, nuts, and seeds), and zinc (found in steak, wheat germ, brewer's yeast, eggs, and pepitas). Minerals are essential for maintaining good health. For example, a deficiency of calcium can lead to rickets or osteoporosis, and a deficiency of iron can cause anaemia.

Making the right choices

It is vital to make good food choices and eat sensibly. Did you know, for example, that a diet high in salt and saturated fat can increase the risk of heart disease, while eating other foods, such as beans, can help to lower cholesterol and prevent heart disease? The message here is that what you absorb into your body plays a crucial role in your health and overall well-being. Eating more of the right foods, and reducing your intake of the potentially harmful ones, can contribute enormously to how well you feel and the state of your physical health.

So which are the right foods to eat and which are the wrong ones? It is not always easy to decide. For example, too much salt can lead to higher blood pressure and depleted adrenal glands, but to cut it out completely would be very unwise because we need a certain amount each day in order to stay healthy. Salt actually helps to keep our fluid levels in balance and our muscles healthy. The amount we need, however, is very low—less than 5 g/1 teaspoon per day. Since many foods we buy have salt added already—for example, cheese or ready-prepared foods such as

pizzas—we can usually get the amount we need without having to add extra salt to our meals. It is the habit of adding extra salt to our food that tends to push us over the healthy limit.

Basically, a balanced diet should consist of plenty of fruit, vegetables, whole grains and cereals, dairy products, and smaller quantities of protein foods from animal sources (such as meat, fish, eggs, or dairy products) as well as from nonanimal sources (such as beans, peas, nuts, and seeds). A vegetarian diet is also perfectly healthy, as long as it is balanced and contains all the essential nutrients.

Dos and don'ts for a healthy diet

Here are some tips to help keep your diet healthy and your body in peak physical condition:

DO eat regular meals—never skip them, especially breakfast. Skipping meals will only encourage your body to go into "starvation mode" and store up fat.

DO eat at least five portions of fruit and vegetables each day. They can be fresh, frozen or canned, but vary them as much as possible. Not all fruits and vegetables contain the same amount of health-giving nutrients, but when you are in any doubt, you can estimate that one portion is equal to about 3 oz/85 g. Any of the following foods also equal one portion:

• one 2/3 cup glass of fruit juice
• one orange, apple, nectarine, peach, or banana
• half a grapefruit
• two plums
• a quarter of a cucumber
• one bell pepper or tomato

• a 3 oz/85 g portion of cauliflower or broccoli
• three heaping tablespoons of any vegetable, for example peas, carrots, corn, beans, or pulses.

DO eat more whole grains, like oats, barley, rye, and corn. Choose whole wheat bread and pasta instead of white varieties, and whole grain brown rice instead of polished white rice.

DO eat oily fish regularly, at least three times a week if you can.

DO choose organic produce wherever possible; organic foods are free from artificial additives and pesticides, and are a much healthier choice.

DO drink eight glasses of water a day. One glass is equal to 1 cup, so this means at least 75/8 cups daily. You need a regular and adequate intake of water in order to flush toxins from the body and replace water lost through urine and sweat. If you do not drink enough water, you will become dehydrated. Dehydration causes symptoms such as headaches,

tiredness, and loss of concentration. Prolonged dehydration can lead to constipation and kidney stones.

DON'T eat too much saturated fat. Reduce your intake of greasy fried foods and fatty red meat.

DON'T eat too many sugary foods, such as candies, chocolate, puddings, desserts, and sodas.

DON'T buy processed foods. Processed foods are often full of artificial additives, such as preservatives, colors, and sweeteners—even packaged salad greens have undergone chemical processing before they reach the retailers' shelves. Instead choose foods that are fresh and in their natural state. The benefits in terms of better flavor and more health-giving nutrients far outweigh the convenience of ready-prepared, packaged foods.

DON'T drink too much caffeine. It is a powerful stimulant and can make you feel lively, but in excess it can lead to health problems. Too much caffeine

can lead to irritability, insomnia, and feverish symptoms. Very high doses can cause more serious problems. For example, medical research has reported that people who drink five or more cups of coffee a day have a 50 percent higher risk of a heart attack than people who do not drink coffee. The main sources of caffeine are coffee, tea, cola drinks, and cocoa, so avoid these drinks as much as possible. Switch to herbal teas and fruit juices instead. Some medicines also contain caffeine, so check the ingredients before you take them, and use an alternative if possible.

DON'T consume too much alcohol. Keep your consumption to less than one drink per day (for women), or two drinks per day (for men). In the US a drink is defined as 1 1/2 fl oz/ 45 ml of (80%-proof) distilled spirits, 5 fl oz/150 ml of wine, or 12 fl oz/ 350 ml of regular beer.

DON'T add salt to your food, or at least taste the food before you add salt, then keep added salt to a minimum.

HEALTH AND SAFETY

THE KITCHEN IS OFTEN THE FOCAL POINT OF THE HOME. HOWEVER, IT IS ALSO THE RISKIEST AREA: FIRES ARE MUCH MORE LIKELY TO BREAK OUT IN THE KITCHEN THAN IN ANY OTHER PART OF THE HOME, AND THERE IS A RISK OF INFESTATION BY PESTS OR POTENTIALLY HARMFUL BACTERIA. ADOPTING GOOD HYGIENE HABITS AND TAKING SENSIBLE PRECAUTIONS WILL PROTECT YOUR HOUSEHOLD FROM UNNECESSARY ACCIDENTS AND ILLNESSES.

Kitchen hygiene

Cleanliness is essential in the kitchen. Keep all kitchen surfaces scrupulously clean, and wash your hands thoroughly with soap and water when preparing food. Use a separate towel to dry your hands, not a dish towel. Whenever you go out of the kitchen or touch another surface, such as a door handle or a curtain, even if it is only for a few moments, remember that your hands will quickly pick up bacteria hanging around the home, even if you think your home is scrupulously clean, so always wash your hands again before resuming any food preparation.

Make sure you use different cutting boards and utensils for cooked and raw foods to prevent cross-contamination of bacteria, especially when you are preparing meat or poultry. If you can afford it and have the room to store them, it is a good idea to have several different colored cutting boards for different purposes. You can keep one for raw meat, one for cooked meat, one for a pet's food, and so on. Wash cutting boards and utensils well in hot, soapy water before and after each use.

Change and wash dish cloths and dish towels regularly. Use a covered garbage can and disinfect it on a regular basis.

Food preparation

Make sure that you thoroughly wash any foods that need cleaning, such as soil-covered vegetables, and pat dry with paper towels. You should also thaw thoroughly any frozen food that requires it, especially meat and poultry, and do not refreeze once it has thawed. The best place to defrost food is in the refrigerator. However, if you are short of time, you can thaw it in a cool room as long as it is well covered to prevent any potentially harmful bacteria from contaminating it.

Throw away any thawed juices from meat and poultry—do not use them in your dishes. And remember never to reuse a marinade, especially if it has been used for meat or poultry.

When reheating cooked meat dishes, remember that they may be reheated once only, to a temperature of at least 167°F/75°C.

Do not leave cooked rice uncovered at room temperature for any length of time. Potentially harmful bacteria can multiply quickly on cooked rice, so if you have to store it, cover it with plastic wrap as soon as possible, and keep it in the refrigerator until you are ready to use it. The same goes for any cooked meats or poultry.

Safe storage

Always buy food as fresh as possible, and from a reputable supplier. Check any "use by" or "best before" dates, because sometimes out-of-date items languish on retailers' shelves and are bought by the unwary. Cover all exposed foods with plastic wrap before refrigerating. If you buy a whole bird, remove any giblets from the cavity, cover with plastic wrap, and refrigerate separately from the bird. Store raw and cooked meat and poultry separately in different parts of your refrigerator.

Store your potatoes in a dark place, away from sunlight, or they will turn green—even fluorescent lighting can make them turn green. Green patches in potatoes contain a chemical called solanine. Solanine tastes bitter, and in large concentrations it can give you an upset stomach, so do not buy any potatoes with green patches. If, despite your best efforts, a potato you have

Storing potatoes
Potatoes should be stored away from the sunlight in a dark place to prevent green patches from forming. The green patches contain a substance called solanine, which can upset stomachs.

bought or grown has developed a small green patch, cut the patch out, then use the rest of the potato. If the green covers a large area, you may be better off discarding the whole potato.

Kitchen first aid

Every kitchen should have a basic first-aid kit. Your standard kit should include rubber gloves, antiseptic wipes, burn cream, eye pads, safety pins, different sized dressings, and triangular bandages. Catering establishments use blue adhesive bandages in order to make them easier to spot should they fall off. Although you don't have to use this type at home, their deep-blue coloring makes them ideal for home use too.

A fire blanket is also a good precaution in a kitchen. It can be a very useful item to have on hand in case a fire breaks out, and it can also be used to help to keep a shock victim comfortable until help arrives.

Fire safety

As an absolute minimum, fit a battery-operated smoke alarm outside your kitchen, and check the battery regularly. Do not position it in the kitchen itself or over a direct source of smoke or heat, as it may be set off accidentally. Even better, ask a qualified electrician to install smoke and heat detectors throughout your home—for reliability they should be wired up to your mains electricity supply. It is also

a good idea to keep a fire extinguisher in the kitchen. Here are some other tips for kitchen fire safety:
• Keep electrical leads, oven mitts, and dish towels away from the cooker.
• Keep your cooker clean, especially the broiler and oven. A buildup of fat can catch fire.
• Do not let your sleeves or other loose clothing hang over the stove while you are cooking.

• Never leave pans on the cooker unattended. If you have to leave them, even for a few seconds, perhaps to answer the telephone, remove them from the heat.
• When you've finished cooking, make sure the cooker or oven is turned off.
• If a pan catches fire and you can't put it out easily and quickly, don't take any risks with your safety. Leave the house at once (making sure that you

close all doors behind you as you go), and call the Fire Department at once. If the fire is small and you are confident you can handle it, put a fire blanket over it, or alternatively run a cloth under the tap, wring it out, and then cover the pan with it. Do not throw water into the pan because this action could exacerbate the problem. Turn off the heat as soon as you can get to it safely.

EQUIPMENT

A SELECTION OF CAREFULLY CHOSEN TOOLS IS ESSENTIAL IN THE KITCHEN. IF YOU ARE A BEGINNER, YOU CAN MAKE DO WITH A FEW MULTIPURPOSE UTENSILS, THEN ADD TO THEM AS YOUR CONFIDENCE GROWS. IF YOU ARE AN EXPERIENCED COOK, YOU MAY WANT TO ADD TO THE BASIC TOOLS WITH SOME MORE SOPHISTICATED ITEMS, SUCH AS A PASTA MACHINE.

Measuring equipment

The items listed here are useful for measuring liquids and solid foods. If you have cups and spoons in imperial, metric, and cups, it is sensible to stick to just one measuring method.

Liquid measuring cup

Cups (available in all different sizes from 1 cup to 8 cups) are useful for measuring liquid ingredients. Choose ones that show imperial, metric, and cup measurements. They are available in glass and plastic.

Measuring spoons

These spoons are ideal for measuring both liquid and dry ingredients accurately.

Dry measuring cups

These cups usually come in a nesting set of four different sizes: 1/4, 1/3, 1/2, and 1 cup, and are used for measuring the volume of dry ingredients. The rim is usually level with the top measurement specified. Dry measuring cups are usually available in plastic or metal.

Knives

Buy the best quality knives you can afford because they will last longer, and keep them sharp. The first three listed here are the essential knives; the rest can be added later.

Small paring knife

A paring knife is invaluable for cutting vegetables, fruit, meat, and cheese. It is 2½–3½ inches/ 6–9 cm long.

Cook's knife

This good, multipurpose knife is 6–12 inches/15–30 cm long, and is essential for slicing and chopping.

Bread knife

This long serrated knife is ideal for slicing bread.

Small serrated knife

This knife is most often used for cutting vegetables and fruit. It is usually about 5 inches/13 cm long.

Measuring cup

Measuring spoons

Bread knife

Carving knife

Baker's spatula

Cleaver

The flat, rectangular blade of this knife is ideal for cutting meat joints.

Filleting knife

This knife has a flexible blade of about 8 inches/20 cm in length, and is used for vegetables, fruit, and raw fish.

Carving knife

This knife has a blade about 12 inches/30 cm long, with a point for easy carving around the bones of joints. It usually comes with a carving fork, which has two long prongs and sometimes a guard to protect against accidents.

Mezzaluna

The mezzaluna has two handles and a curved blade, and is used for chopping herbs and vegetables.

Baker's spatula

This tool is used for spreading rather than cutting, and it has many uses in the kitchen. It is ideal for frosting cakes.

Knife sharpener

Although this has a handle like a knife, instead of a blade it has a long rod of roughened steel. When the edge of a knife is run along the rod at a 45° angle, it sharpens the blade.

Other cutting tools and equipment

In addition to a basic set of knives, you will need some other cutting tools. Some of these tools are very specific, such as the zester, while others are for more general use.

Can opener

This everyday tool comes in many varieties, from hand-operated to wall-mounted automatic devices.

Zester

A citrus zester has a rectangular metal head with holes along the top edge. The holes are there to help remove fine shavings of zest without picking up the white pith.

Vegetable peeler

You can buy a swivel-bladed version or one that has a slicing blade in the middle and a sharp tip for coring.

Grater

There are different graters for different purposes, but a good, multipurpose version to buy is a hollow box-shaped grater with a handle at the top and different cutting holes on each side.

Apple corer

This hollow, cylindrical tool is essential for removing cores from apples and pears quickly and easily.

Pastry cutters

These round circles are available in metal or plastic and are useful for cutting pastry circles. They are also ideal for shaping cookies.

Kitchen scissors

Choose stainless-steel all-purpose scissors and keep them especially for use in the kitchen.

Small paring knife

Cook's knife

Zester

Vegetable peeler

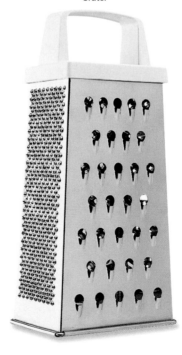

Grater

Pots and pans

When you are buying pots and pans, choose the best quality you can afford. If cared for properly, they will more than repay the extra cost because they will last for many years.

Pans

You will need a small, preferably nonstick, milk pan for making sauces and scrambled eggs, and at least three other different sized pans—small, medium, and large. Choose pans that have secure lids. A large casserole dish or Dutch oven with a lid is useful for casseroles, stews, and whole birds.

Skillets

You will need a small omelet pan, and a larger skillet for more substantial foods. Nonstick varieties are ideal for cooking lowfat meals,

but are not essential. A ridged stovetop grill pan imparts a lovely stripy effect to food and is ideal for chargrilling beef and tuna steaks.

Steamer

Steamers come in different varieties. For example, you can buy a folding metal steamer that adjusts to any size of pan. You can also buy metal and bamboo steamers that are placed on top of the pan—some have more than one tier so that you can steam more than one food at a time. In addition, there are electric steamers, which are useful if you want to save space on the stove.

Wok

A wok is a deep, rounded, bowl-shaped pan with a handle. It is ideal for cooking stir-fries.

Pan

Large pan with lid

Skillet

Ovenware and bakeware

Nonstick baking equipment is useful because it will help you to slide out your culinary creations with ease. Take care not to scour it, however, or you will scratch the nonstick coating.

Baking sheets

Some of these rectangular and square metal sheets are flat and others have a lip around the edges. They are essential for baking a variety of foods, from oven-roasted vegetables and pizzas to meringues and cookies.

Cake pans

These pans come in different sizes, but, to start with, a couple of 8-inch/20-cm diameter shallow pans will come in handy for making sponges, and a deeper 9-inch/23-cm diameter springform cake pan will be useful for making larger cakes.

Tart pans and dishes

These pans and dishes are usually round, and often have a fluted edge. They are ideal for baking quiches and tarts, and come in a variety of sizes. The best type to buy is the loose-bottom, stainless steel variety, because it conducts the heat better than ceramic ones and enables food to be lifted out easily.

Pie pans and dishes

These pans come in a variety of shapes and sizes, and are usually fairly deep with a protruding rim for pastry edging.

Roasting pans

These metal pans are deeper than baking sheets, and are ideal for roasting meat and poultry.

Muffin pans

These rectangular pans usually come with 12 large, round indentations, which are ideal for making savory or sweet muffins, individual fruit pies or Yorkshire puddings.

Loaf pans

These rectangular pans have deep sides and come in different sizes. They are useful for baking bread or savory nut roasts.

Ramekins

These small, round dishes have many uses in the kitchen. They are very handy for making individual soufflés and crème caramels. They also double up nicely as serving dishes for butter, olives, and nuts.

Ramekins

Straining equipment

The following items are useful in any kitchen. In particular, a strainer is essential for sifting dry ingredients like flour, while a colander makes light work of draining a variety of foods.

Strainers

These come in metal or plastic, and are useful for sifting flour and straining liquid ingredients.

Colander

A colander is a perforated bowl that is used for draining liquid from foods. Colanders are available in different sizes and different materials, usually metal or plastic. They may have one or two handles and a flat base so that they can sit steadily on a counter.

Egg separator

Although this small, round, slotted spoon is not essential, new cooks in particular will find it helpful for separating egg yolks from whites.

Dredger

This mesh-covered container is especially useful for sprinkling confectioners' sugar or cocoa onto cakes and desserts.

Bowls and basins

You can buy bowls and basins in a variety of different materials and sizes, but metal will react with acid ingredients such as lime juice, so do not use metal bowls for acid-based marinades.

Mixing bowls

Mixing bowls are available in a variety of materials, including ceramic, glass, plastic, and stainless steel. At least one large mixing bowl is essential, although several bowls of different sizes are even better. For example, you will need a smaller bowl to whip cream. You can also buy bowls that are sufficiently decorative to double up as serving bowls at the table.

Ovenproof bowls

These come in different sizes and materials, including metal, ceramic, plastic, and glass. A large ovenproof bowl is ideal for making a substantial summer pudding or Christmas pudding for a large household, while a set of smaller bowls is useful for making individual chilled or steamed puddings. It is often worth recycling bowls from store-bought desserts too.

Strainer

Colander

Large mixing bowl

Ovenproof bowl

Slotted spatula

Draining spoon

Serving/basting spoon

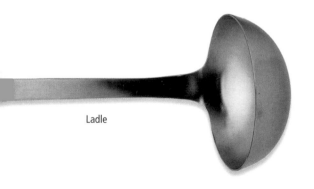

Ladle

Spoons and spatulas

Spoons and spatulas are very helpful for lifting, turning, shaping, draining, and serving a variety of foods. Here are some of the utensils you will find most useful.

Slotted spatula
This slotted lifting tool is essential when lifting floppy food, such as omelets, fried eggs, or fish fillets from skillets.

Draining spoon
This large, slotted spoon is ideal for lifting solid foods out of liquids so that the liquid drains away, and for skimming scum from the surface of simmering liquids, such as stock, and from jellies, jams, and marmalade.

Serving/basting spoon
This large spoon is useful for serving food onto plates. It has a groove on one side to direct the flow of juices and sauces.

Ladle
This is helpful for ladling soups into bowls or punch into glasses.

Tongs
A set of tongs is handy for turning hot food on a griddle or a barbecue.

Wooden spoon
This type of spoon is available in different sizes and is handy for mixing ingredients evenly, without scratching the delicate surfaces of pans and bowls.

Spatula
This utensil is available in wood or plastic, and is used for folding mixtures such as egg whites. The plastic type is also ideal for scraping down the sides of mixing bowls to get all the mixture out.

Spatula

Wooden spoons

Hot handles

Do not leave spoons and spatulas with metal handles to stand in the pan while cooking on a hot stove. Metal handles can get very hot, and are likely to cause burns.

Hand balloon whisks

Potato masher

Other useful utensils

You can add to your cooking utensils as and when you need them. Here are some of the items you are likely to find most useful and will want to buy sooner rather than later.

Lemon squeezer
These usually come in plastic or glass. They have a strainer to catch any pips, and a bowl underneath to catch the lemon juice.

Corkscrew and bottle opener
You can buy these individually or combined into one utensil. The lever-action corkscrew is the easiest kind to use.

Pastry brush
Brushes are useful for sealing pies with water and for glazing.

Garlic press
A garlic press is not essential but is handy for crushing garlic cloves cleanly and efficiently. Some have a detachable grille for easy cleaning.

Hand whisks
Whisks are available in a variety of shapes and sizes. The most common is the balloon whisk, which is useful for whisking egg whites and cream.

Rolling pin
This long, cylindrical utensil comes in wood, glass, or ceramic, and is essential for rolling out pie dough.

Potato masher
This utensil is essential for mashing potatoes and other vegetables such as rutabaga.

Mortar and pestle
These two utensils come as a pair in a variety of sizes and materials, such as marble and porcelain. They are used for crushing herbs and spices. It is a good idea to buy the largest and sturdiest you can afford.

Lemon squeezer

Garlic press

Pastry brushes

Cutting boards
If you can, buy several different colored boards so that you can keep one for raw meat and poultry, one for cooked meats, and so on.

Wire cooling racks
These metal racks can be round or rectangular, and are ideal for cooling cakes, cookies, and bread. It is often essential to have two racks to accommodate larger batches.

Skewers
Long stainless-steel skewers are a good choice, although other materials, such as wood, are also available. Skewers are essential for cooking kabobs. They are also useful for inserting into cakes and joints of meat to test if they are cooked all the way through.

Pie funnel
This little funnel is available in a variety of shapes and materials, and is used to hold up the pie dough in pies. It also prevents the pie dough from becoming soggy by allowing the steam to escape.

Ice-cream scoop
This tool is useful for scooping neat domes of ice cream or mashed potato onto plates.

Decorative molds
These molds are available in many shapes and sizes, and in plastic or metal. They can be used for shaping mousses, ice creams, jellies, and creamy desserts.

Pastry bags and tips
These come in various sizes and shapes and are useful for creating piped decorations in frosting or cream on cakes and desserts.

Thermometers
You can buy thermometers to test the temperature of your refrigerator and oven, and for meat, sugar, and deep-fat frying.

Kitchen timers
Timers are available in different designs and sizes, and are useful for monitoring the cooking times of dishes. Many ovens also come with a handy built-in timer.

Machines and electric utensils

There is a wide variety of machines and electrical devices for the kitchen, and these make quick and easy work of preparing food—especially useful when catering for families or parties.

Food processor

This multipurpose machine has metal blades that chop, shred, and grate foods. Usually, it also comes with a selection of other attachments that mix and knead ingredients, such as sponge mixes and pie dough.

Blender

A blender is useful for puréeing foods and mixing drinks, such as soups, batters, milk shakes, and smoothies. It is also known as a liquidizer.

Pasta machine

This machine is not essential because store-bought pasta is excellent these days. But if you prefer to make your own fresh pasta, you will find a machine indispensable for rolling and cutting pasta into noodles, ribbons, and various decorative shapes.

Grinder

This very useful machine is essential for grinding nuts and coffee beans. It is also ideal for making fresh bread crumbs, as are food processors and blenders.

Free-standing mixer

This machine, which is also called a food mixer, has a large bowl and a selection of mixing tools, such as a whisk and a dough kneader. It enables you to beat and whisk foods much faster than you can by hand.

Hand-held mixer

This tool, which you can hold over a bowl or pan, is more portable than a free-standing mixer. It is suitable for light mixtures, such as eggs and cream, but for more substantial mixtures you will find a free-standing mixer easier to use.

Hand-held blender

This portable version of the blender lets you purée food in a pan while it is cooking on the stove.

Deep-fryer

This heavy-based machine usually comes with a wire basket that can be hooked onto the side of the machine for easy draining of the cooking oil.

Pressure cooker

This deep, heavy electric pan is not essential, but it is useful for steaming food such as rice in about half the normal cooking time.

Slow cooker

This small appliance is very useful for cooking stews and casseroles slowly, and saves you having to use the oven. It also uses less electricity than an oven does. Simply add the food, cover, plug it in, and wait for the lovely aromas to emerge.

Free-standing mixer

Pasta machine

Conversion charts

Oven temperatures

Celsius	Fahrenheit	Oven heat
110°	225°	very cool
120°	250°	very cool
140°	275°	cool
150°	300°	cool
160°	325°	moderate
180°	350°	moderate
190°	375°	moderately hot
200°	400°	moderately hot
220°	425°	hot
230°	450°	very hot
240°	475°	very hot

Spoon measurements

1 teaspoon of liquid = 5 ml

1 tablespoon of liquid = 15 ml

Other measurements

Liquid volume

Metric	Imperial/cup
60 ml	2 fl oz/$\frac{1}{4}$ cup
100 ml	$3\frac{1}{2}$ fl oz
150 ml	5 fl oz/$\frac{2}{3}$ cup
200 ml	7 fl oz
300 ml	10 fl oz/$1\frac{1}{4}$ cups
450 ml	16 fl oz
500 ml	17 fl oz
600 ml	1 pint/$2\frac{1}{2}$ cups
700 ml	$1\frac{1}{4}$ pints
850 ml	$1\frac{1}{2}$ pints
1 litre	$1\frac{3}{4}$ pints/4 cups
1.5 litres	$2\frac{3}{4}$ pints
2.8 litres	5 pints
3 litres	$5\frac{1}{4}$ pints/12 cups

Weight

Imperial	Metric
$\frac{1}{8}$ oz	5 g
$\frac{1}{4}$ oz	10 g
1 oz	25 g
$1\frac{3}{4}$ oz	50 g
$2\frac{3}{4}$ oz	75 g
3 oz	85 g
$3\frac{1}{2}$ oz	100 g
$5\frac{1}{2}$ oz	150 g
8 oz	225 g
$10\frac{1}{2}$ oz	300 g
1 lb	450 g
1 lb 2 oz	500 g
2 lb 4 oz	1 kg
3 lb 5 oz	1.5 kg

Linear

Imperial	Metric
$\frac{1}{16}$ inch	2 mm
$\frac{1}{8}$ inch	3 mm
$\frac{1}{4}$ inch	5 mm
$\frac{3}{8}$ inch	8 mm
$\frac{1}{2}$ inch	1 cm
$\frac{3}{4}$ inch	2 cm
1 inch	2.5 cm
2 inches	5 cm
3 inches	7.5 cm
4 inches	10 cm
8 inches	20 cm
12 inches/1 foot	30 cm
18 inches/$1\frac{1}{2}$ feet	46 cm
20 inches/$1\frac{2}{3}$ feet	50 cm

PREPARATION TECHNIQUES

YOU WILL FIND THIS SECTION A VALUABLE SOURCE OF REFERENCE FOR ALL THE BASIC PREPARATION TECHNIQUES YOU ARE LIKELY TO NEED IN EVERYDAY COOKING. THERE ARE ALSO SOME ADVANCED TECHNIQUES FOR THE MORE EXPERIENCED COOK.

GRIND ①
To crush food, such as nuts or coffee beans, to a powder or into very small pieces. For this job, you can use a mortar and pestle for a coarser result, or a coffee grinder or food processor.

INFUSE
To steep flavorful ingredients, such as herbs or spices, in a liquid in order to flavor it.

BARD
This means to wrap pieces of fat, such as bacon, around lean cuts of meat and poultry to keep them moist and impart more flavor. For example, you can wrap chicken or turkey breasts with slices of bacon before baking. You can also wrap a meatloaf with bacon slices to keep it moist during baking.

CRUSH ②
This technique is useful for bringing out the flavor of garlic and herbs, and can be done by pressing the flat side of a knife blade down onto the garlic or herbs. You can also adapt this technique to make cookie crumbs for cheesecakes. Simply place the cookies in a plastic bag, tie the end, then use a rolling pin to crush the cookies inside the bag.

FOLD ③
This technique involves mixing a light mixture into a heavier one using a spoon or spatula in a figure-eight movement. This is done to keep the air within the mixture.

BASTE
When you spoon juices or fat over food during cooking, it is known as "basting." It helps to keep the food moist and seal in the flavor.

BEAT ④
This technique involves using a fork, spoon, or electric mixer in a vigorous

stirring motion to remove any lumps from sauces and incorporate air into omelets and cake batters.

RUB IN ⑤

This technique is mainly used when making pie dough. Using the fingertips, rub the fat into the flour, lifting it high over the bowl in order to trap air in the mixture, making it lighter and giving a better result.

MARINATE

This term means to soak food in a marinade for a few hours or days to tenderize it and give it more flavor. You can marinate meat, poultry, fish, and vegetables. Marinades usually consist of oil and perhaps alcohol or vinegar, and are flavored with different mixtures of herbs and spices.

DEGLAZE

This technique is used after sautéeing food (normally meat). After the food and excess fat have been removed from the pan, a small amount of liquid—such as stock or wine—is stirred in to loosen browned bits of food in the pan. This mixture often forms the base for a sauce to accompany the food.

KNOCK BACK

This entails knocking the air out of bread dough after it has risen.

CLARIFY

You can clarify butter or a liquid. To clarify butter, heat it slowly to separate the milk solids, which sink to the bottom of the pan, skimming any foam off the top. Clarified butter, such as Indian ghee, has a higher smoke point than ordinary

butter so you can cook with it at higher temperatures. To clarify a liquid, such as a stock, add egg whites and/or egg shells to it and simmer for 10 minutes then cool and strain it. The egg whites or shells draw out the impurities.

SHRED ⑥

This technique involves using a small, sharp knife or grater to cut food into very thin lengths.

LINE

To line a pan with something to prevent food from sticking during cooking. The most common method is to rub butter or oil over the surface of the pan, then cover with baking parchment before adding the food. You can also use bacon slices as a lining for savory nonvegetarian dishes.

MARBLE

This technique is used to combine two differently colored ingredients in order to create a marbled effect. For example, you can mix melted white chocolate into melted semisweet chocolate to create a marbled pattern.

SCORE

To make light incisions on the surface of a food, particularly meat, poultry, and fish, in order to facilitate cooking, allow fat to drain, and create a decorative effect.

BLEND

Blending involves combining two or more ingredients together by stirring with a spoon or puréeing with an electric blender. It is a useful technique for soups, milk shakes, and smoothies.

BUTTERFLY

To butterfly a leg of lamb, insert the knife into the cavity of the leg bone and cut to one side to open out the meat; then make a shallow surface cut down the center to keep the meat open flat. You can also butterfly other foods, such as chicken breasts or large shrimp.

KNEAD

This technique uses the heel of the hand to pull and stretch bread dough in order to develop the gluten in the flour so that the bread will keep its shape when it has risen. You can also knead dough in a food processor that has a dough hook.

SKIM

To remove scum or fat from the surface of a simmering liquid with a large slotted spoon or ladle.

WHISK

Whisking involves beating a light mixture, such as cream and eggs, vigorously with a whisk to incorporate more air. You can use a balloon whisk (but it takes a lot of effort), an electric hand mixer, a free-standing mixer, or a food processor with a whisk attachment.

ZEST

To remove the outer layer of citrus fruit. A zester shaves off the zest without picking up the bitter white pith underneath.

CHIFFONADE

A French term meaning "made of rags." It refers to the effect you get when you roll leafy vegetables together, then slice them crosswise into ribbons with a sharp knife.

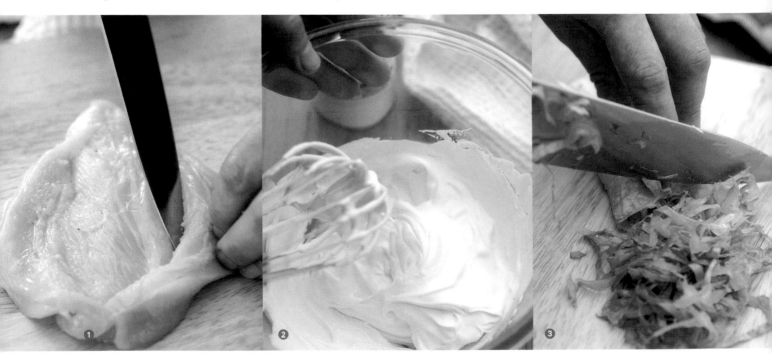

ENRICH

To add a rich ingredient to a dish in order to create a richer texture or flavor. For example, you can add butter to a dough, or cream to a sauce.

GLAZE

This involves brushing water, beaten egg, or sugar and water onto pie dough before baking to give it a glossy shine (and make it crunchy if sugar is added). To glaze a ham, remove the skin from the partly cooked meat then coat the outer surface with sugar and mustard and continue cooking. You can glaze sweet dishes with melted jelly or chocolate.

LARD

To lard means to insert strips of pork fat into a lean cut of meat to flavor it and keep it moist.

EMULSIFY ④

Emulsifying means adding one liquid to another in a slow, gradual stream while stirring or blending rapidly. This is how mayonnaise is made, by adding oil in a slow stream to a beaten egg mixture while whisking or blending vigorously.

TENDERIZE ⑤

This involves pounding meat, such as a beef steak, with a mallet in order to break down the tough fibers. You can also tenderize meat by marinating it.

CHOP

To cut food into small pieces using a sharp knife. For example, to chop a herb, hold the tip of the knife blade down with one hand, then use your other hand to raise the handle of the knife up and down as you chop the herb.

You can chop food coarsely or finely, depending on your requirements. Coarsely chopped means that the food will be left in larger pieces than when finely chopped.

MASH ⑥

To reduce food, usually cooked potatoes and other root vegetables, to a pulp using a potato masher or a free-standing mixer.

STEEP

Steeping means to soak an ingredient in hot liquid in order to release its flavor into the liquid.

JULIENNE

This technique involves cutting food, such as carrots and celery, into fine sticks or strips.

CUT

To use a sharp knife to make an incision or separate a food into smaller pieces.

DRESS

This can mean to add a dressing to a salad, to decorate a dish before serving, or to pluck and truss poultry.

GREASE OR OIL

To rub a little butter or oil over the surface of a pan to prevent food sticking to it during cooking.

TRUSS ①

To pull poultry or game into shape then secure with string or skewers before cooking. This technique is particularly useful for preventing dressing from falling out of a bird.

CREAM

Creaming is similar to beating, in that you use a fork, spoon, or electric mixer to beat ingredients together until they are smooth. This technique is usually associated with something rich and creamy, such as butter.

SPATCHCOCK

To remove the backbone from a bird and secure it so that it can be cooked flat and therefore more rapidly. To remove the backbone, first tuck under the wings and remove the wishbone. Then turn the bird over and cut along each side of the backbone to remove it. Use your hands to push down on the bird's breast and flatten it. Finally, push a metal skewer through the thighs and another through the wings and breast to secure the bird.

PURÉE ②

To reduce food to a smooth pulp. You can do this by pushing food through a strainer or using a blender.

MACERATE

To soak a food in a liquid, often alcohol, to soften it.

OPEN FREEZE

This technique means to freeze foods, uncovered, in a single layer. For example, you can cut fruit, such as mango, into small pieces, spread them out on a tray, and freeze them uncovered. Then transfer individually to a freezer bag and use as required.

CURE

To preserve a food by salting or smoking it.

DEGORGE

This is soaking meat, poultry, or fish in a solution of cold water and salt to remove impurities. It also means salting eggplants to remove their bitter juices.

GRIND

To grind food, such as meat, into small pieces using a knife or grinder.

DREDGE

To sprinkle flour onto a counter when rolling out pie dough, or confectioners' sugar or cocoa over desserts.

CRIMP ❸

This technique means to use the finger and thumb of one hand and the index finger of the other hand to "pinch" pie dough together around the edge of a pie or pasty. This gives it a decorative effect.

SIFT ❹

This technique involves shaking dry ingredients, such as flour, through a strainer to remove lumps and introduce more air into the mixture.

DICE

To cut food into small, regular-shaped cubes. You can use a sharp knife or a special dicing utensil.

GRATE

To shred food into small pieces. You can use a box grater or food processor.

PEEL

Peeling involves removing the outer skin or rind from foods such as oranges, avocados, or potatoes. Depending on the food, you can use your hands, a sharp knife, or a vegetable peeler.

SHUCK

This is how we remove the husks from corn, the shells from peas, and the shells from oysters.

CROSS-HATCH ❺

To score criss-cross patterns on the surface of foods to allow them to absorb marinades or be removed from their skins. You can cross-hatch the outer layer of fat on a pork joint before cooking to allow the fat to drain and create a decorative effect.

SNIP

To cut green leafy vegetables or herbs into very small pieces using kitchen scissors.

STRAIN ❻

This involves pushing food through a strainer in order to create a purée.

COOKING METHODS

IN THIS SECTION YOU WILL FIND ALL THE TRADITIONAL COOKING TECHNIQUES, FROM BOILING TO ROASTING, AS WELL AS THE INCREASINGLY POPULAR HEALTH-CONSCIOUS METHODS, SUCH AS STEAMING AND STIR-FRYING.

FRY ①

This method involves cooking food in hot fat, usually oil, in a skillet. Frying food gives it a delicious flavor. You can shallow-fry, or deep-fry food. Deep-frying needs a lot more oil and can be dangerous, so it is always better to shallow-fry food if possible. However, for some foods, such as tempura (a Japanese dish of batter-coated pieces of fish and vegetables) and Scotch eggs, deep-frying is unavoidable. You can also stir-fry food: this method needs only a little oil and is a very healthy way to cook.

DEEP-FRY ②

This technique involves immersing food completely in very hot oil and cooking it at a high temperature. It is important to choose the correct oil: peanut and soybean oil have the highest smoke points (the temperature at which the oil begins to emit smoke) and are therefore the most suitable for deep-frying. Canola and corn oil have the next highest, and are also suitable. Sunflower-seed oil has a lower smoke point and should not be used for deep-frying. Deep-frying food is dangerous because it is possible to spill the hot oil or the

pan can catch fire, so great care must be taken and the pan should never be left unattended. A thermostatically controlled deep-fryer is a safer and easier option, but still needs care and attention during use. The oil should be heated to a high temperature in order to allow rapid cooking; the high temperature will also help to seal the food and prevent it from absorbing too much oil. When the food is cooked, lift it out carefully using a spatula or slotted spoon, or the wire basket if using a deep-fryer. Let any excess oil drain away from the food on paper towels.

DRY-FRY ③

This method involves cooking food or spices in a skillet without using fat or oil. For example, you can cook Indian spices, flat breads, or Mexican tortillas in a dry skillet. You can also dry-fry pumpkin seeds (pepitas) or pine nuts until they are golden and lightly toasted.

PAN-FRY ④

This is another quick and healthy way of cooking food. It involves cooking food quickly in a skillet with either no fat at all (as in dry-frying) or with the absolute minimum amount of fat necessary. Some foods, such as bacon slices, have enough fat content of their own, and therefore do not need any added fat. In fact, the fat they emit during cooking can be enough to pan-fry other foods at the same time— in this way, the dish has a minimum amount of fat and maximum flavor.

SHALLOW-FRY ⑤

This method of cooking is suitable for foods that will not burn easily—for example, foods that are protected in some way, such as foods coated with flour, bread crumbs, or batter. You will need to add enough oil so that the food will not stick to the pan or burn. Take care to heat the oil to a high temperature because this will help to seal the food when it is added and prevent it from absorbing too much oil. (Food cooked in oil that has not reached the right temperature will be soggy and laden with oil.) Cook the food in the oil for the required time, then turn it over and cook on the other side. Use a slotted spatula to lift out the food, and let any excess oil drain away from the hot food on paper towels. Where this method differs from sautéing is that the food is not moved around the pan, and generally a little more oil is used.

STIR-FRY ⑥

This method comes from Asia and is another very healthy way to cook because of the small amount of oil needed. Foods such as meat, poultry, and vegetables are cut into small, similar sized pieces and cooked rapidly, while being tossed constantly, in a wok. You can also use a large skillet for stir-frying, but a wok is better because the food cooks more rapidly as it comes into contact with the hot sides of the wok.

Chinese cooking distinguishes between four or five different methods of stir-frying, but two are the most common. The first is a very rapid technique, where the food is fried in a little oil at the highest heat while being tossed constantly. Foods cooked in this way are often marinated first. The other technique is less vigorous and more moist: the food is cooked in a little liquid, such as a stock, and constantly turned and moved around the pan. Noodles and sauce are often added toward the end of the cooking time. It is important not to overfill the wok, or the food will steam instead of fry.

BOIL ①

To cook food in a liquid (usually water, milk, or stock) in a pan at boiling point (212°F/100°C). Not all foods are boiled continually: sometimes they are "brought to a boil," then the temperature is reduced and the food is left to simmer (bubble gently). You can cook many foods in this way, such as vegetables, rice, pasta, meat, and eggs. You can also boil a liquid rapidly for a period of time in order to evaporate excess moisture (see Reduce).

SIMMER ②

To cook food in liquid that is just below boiling point; there will be very gentle bubbles on the surface of the liquid. This method is often combined with the boiling technique, where a food is first brought to a boil, then the heat is reduced and the food is allowed to simmer for a period of time.

BLANCH

Blanching is a useful technique for loosening skins on foods such as tomatoes, preserving the color of vegetables, reducing any bitterness in ingredients, and preparing foods for freezing. Blanching also helps to reduce the salt content in cured meats. To blanch a food, simply immerse it in boiling water for a few seconds, then plunge it into cold water to prevent further cooking.

REDUCE ③

Although this is not a complete cooking method in its own right, it is a useful technique, especially for sauces. To reduce a liquid, simply boil it down rapidly in an uncovered pan. This evaporates the liquid and makes the sauce thicker.

STEAM ④

Steaming is a very healthy way to cook, because the food does not come into direct contact with the liquid and therefore more of the nutrients are preserved. Steaming is suitable for a wide range of foods, from poultry and fish to vegetables and puddings. If you use a folding metal steamer, simply bring a small amount of water to a boil in the bottom of the pan, place the steamer inside, add the food, cover the pan, and steam until cooked to your taste. Bamboo steamers are used in a similar way. You can also steam puddings: bring enough water to a boil to come halfway up the side of the ovenproof bowl, then place the bowl inside the pan and steam the pudding for the recommended time (taking care to top up with boiling water if necessary during cooking).

SAUTÉ ⑤

This is similar to frying, but involves moving the food around the skillet to prevent it browning too rapidly. Usually a small amount of oil or butter is used to oil or grease the pan and prevent the food burning.

CARAMELIZE ⑥

This term most often refers to the method of caramelizing sugar or onions. To caramelize sugar, heat it until it melts into a syrup. The color varies from light golden to dark brown, depending on the cooking time. A sugar thermometer is useful here, to get the sugar to the required temperature. When the sugar is removed from the heat, it quickly sets and becomes brittle, but retains its caramelized appearance. You can also sprinkle sugar over a food

and caramelize it under a preheated hot broiler or by heating its surface with a kitchen blow torch. To caramelize onions, cook them gently in butter for 30 minutes, or until they turn a rich golden brown.

SEAR 1

To sear means to brown meat, poultry, and fish rapidly over high heat. This process helps to seal in the juices and keeps the center of the food moist.

POACH 2

To poach means to cook food in a liquid at just below boiling point and it is a very gentle method of cooking. The liquids commonly used for poaching are water and alcohol. You can poach poultry, fish, eggs (as long as they are very fresh), and fruit.

SWEAT 3

To cook food (often vegetables such as onions) gently in water or fat until they are softened but not brown.

FLAMBÉ 4

Strictly speaking, to flambé is more food presentation than cooking method, but since it involves warming an ingredient it is included here. Flambé is a French word meaning "flamed." It involves sprinkling liqueur over a food,

---

Poaching fruit

Pour enough wine or sugar syrup into a pan to cover the fruit. Bring to a simmer, add the pitted fruit, and let simmer for 15 minutes, or until tender. Lift out the fruit, reduce the liquid by boiling it down, then pour it over the fruit.

---

such as a Christmas pudding, then setting the alcohol alight just before serving. It makes a dramatic spectacle at the table, and also burns off the alcohol content.

TOAST

This process uses dry heat to cook foods. For example, you can toast nuts by baking them dry in the oven or cooking them under a hot broiler. You can also toast bread under the broiler, or you can spear marshmallows on forks and toast them over a fire.

BAKE

To bake means to cook food in an oven using dry heat at the correct temperature. For example, you can bake potatoes, cakes, cookies, breads, and custards.

BAKE BLIND 5

To bake a pastry shell without a filling. To bake blind, first line a pie pan or tart dish with rolled-out pie dough, prick it with a fork, place a layer of baking parchment over the pie dough, and weight it down with ceramic or metal baking beans. Then bake it. If you haven't got any baking beans, you can use dried beans or pulses instead. Baking blind helps to ensure that the pie dough stays crisp after the filling is added, and is especially necessary if the filling does not need to be cooked, or needs only a very short time to cook.

ROAST 6

Roasting is similar to baking, in that food is cooked in the oven using dry heat. In this case, however, the process is often used for meat, poultry, and vegetables. It is usually necessary to add a little fat when roasting foods to keep them moist. Roasting can really bring out the flavor of a food: for example, bell peppers that have been roasted are extra sweet and flavorful. You can also roast a wide variety of other vegetables, not just potatoes and parsnips, but also garlic, onions, carrots, fennel, sweet potatoes, eggplants, and rutabaga.

BRAISE

This is a long, slow way to cook food. It is especially useful for tough cuts of meat, and for poultry and vegetables. To braise foods, first brown them in oil, then cook them very slowly in a small amount of flavored liquid, such as stock or wine, in a dish with a tight-fitting lid. You can cook them on a stove or in an oven.

4

5

6

CASEROLE

This method is similar to braising; you can use a large, heavy-bottom casserole dish or a Dutch oven with a tight-fitting lid. First brown the food in oil, add a small amount of flavored liquid, cover with a lid, then cook very slowly in the oven. Sometimes a casserole can be likened to a stew, where the food is cut into smaller pieces and more cooking liquid is added. After cooking, you can serve the food directly from the casserole dish.

STEW ❶

Stewing is a very slow method of cooking. It is similar to braising, except that the food is cut into smaller pieces and more liquid is used. This technique is suitable for meat (especially tough cuts because the long cooking process helps to tenderize the meat), poultry, fish, vegetables, grains such as barley, and certain fruits such as apples, pears, peaches, and nectarines.

POT-ROAST ❷

This technique is very similar to braising in that it involves cooking food (usually meat, especially beef) very slowly in a covered pot in the oven. Only a very little liquid is used.

Chargrilled vegetables

To ring the changes to chargrilled vegetables, mix 1 tablespoon olive oil, 1 teaspoon lemon juice, 1 teaspoon each chopped fresh rosemary and thyme, and season to taste with salt and pepper. Brush the mixture over the vegetables, and chargrill as required.

GRIDDLE ❸

Traditionally, a griddle is a flat, usually rimless, pan, which is used to cook crêpes and drop scones with the minimum of oil. Griddles usually have a long handle and are often made of a heavy metal that conducts heat well, such as cast iron. Nowadays, the term "griddle" is often confused with chargrill.

CHARGRILL ❹

Chargrilling enables you to cook food in the minimum amount of fat; it also gives the food attractive charred stripes. You can cook meat, poultry, fish, and vegetables in this way. Simply heat a ridged stovetop grill pan on the stove, brush the food with a little oil (never brush the oil onto the pan directly), then place the food on the heated pan.

Cook according to the recipe, turning the food over once to cook on the other side. You can also chargrill food on a metal grid set over hot coals.

BARBECUE ⑤

With this method the food is usually cooked on a mesh over hot coals. The barbecue apparatus can range from a simple portable tray consisting of a mesh with flammable, slow-burning paper underneath, to an elaborate electric barbecue. Foods are often marinated first, in order to give them more flavor and to aid the cooking process. Always barbecue your food outdoors in the open air in order to waft away any carbon monoxide fumes given off by the lit charcoal. Also, in order to prevent burns, use long-handled utensils to lift and turn the food.

BROIL ⑥

Broiling is a quick and healthy way to cook food. Modern cookers usually have an integral broiler; they also come with a broiler pan with a wire mesh to allow excess fat to drain away. A broiler should always be preheated before use. Broiling is a very versatile method of cooking: you can cook meat, poultry, fish, and vegetables under a broiler, and toast other foods such as bread and cheese. Broiling food involves cooking it directly under the heat source, which ensures that the outside of the food is browned quickly, while the inside stays moist.

BLOW TORCH

One of the cook's best-kept secrets is blow torching food. This method of cooking is simple, quick and effective. You can buy a kitchen blow torch from any reputable kitchen equipment store, and you will find it inexpensive and convenient. It has a variety of uses. For example, to make a crunchy, caramelized topping for crème brûlées, simply sprinkle them generously with white sugar until the surfaces are completely covered. Now ignite your blow torch and adjust the air for a blue flame. Apply the flame to the sugar until it caramelizes and turns golden brown. You can also peel a bell pepper by blow torching instead of roasting it. This method is especially suitable if you are short of time or have only one or two bell peppers to peel. Spear the bell pepper with a fork, then turn it over the flame of the blow torch until the skin is charred and black. Transfer the pepper to a plastic bag, leave for 15 minutes, then peel off the skin in the usual way.

PANTRIES

A GOOD STORE OF NONPERISHABLE FOOD STUFFS IS AN ESSENTIAL PART OF EVERY COOK'S KITCHEN. WELL-STOCKED KITCHEN CUPBOARDS, AND PERHAPS A PANTRY, ENSURE THAT YOU ALWAYS HAVE A GOOD SELECTION OF STAPLE ITEMS ON HAND FOR EVERY OCCASION. MAKE SURE YOU CHECK THE "USE-BY" DATES OF YOUR STORED ITEMS REGULARLY, AND DISCARD ANY THAT HAVE BECOME OUT OF DATE.

Oils

There are many different varieties of oil available these days, but it is not necessary to buy them all. You simply need oil that is suitable for drizzling and for cooking at high temperatures.

Olive oil

This mildly fruity oil is ideal for drizzling over salads. It can range from a champagne color to bright green. The best oils are cold-pressed—this is a chemical-free process that uses only pressure and produces a low level of acidity. You can also flavor it with different ingredients—for example, try adding some herbs, such as basil leaves, or some garlic to it—after a day or two the oil will become infused with their flavor. Its smoke point (the temperature at which it begins to smoke) is 410°F/210°C.

Extra virgin olive oil

Produced from the first cold-pressing of the olives, this oil has a very low acid level. It is the most expensive type of olive oil, and has a peppery, fruity flavor. You can use it for drizzling over salads and hot dishes such as pizzas. Its smoke point is 410°F/210°C.

Sunflower-seed oil

This is a good multipurpose oil that can be used for most cooking purposes. However, it is not recommended for deep-frying because this method needs an oil with a higher smoke point. The smoke point of sunflower-seed oil is 390°F/199°C. Sunflower-seed oil has a very light flavor and is therefore ideal in dressings.

Sesame-seed oil

This oil comes in two varieties: one has a light color and a nutty flavor, the other is darker and has a stronger flavor. The darker one is most often used in Asian dishes. This oil is excellent for frying and stir-frying. Its smoke point is 410°F/210°C.

Vegetable oil

A blend of various oils, mainly canola, soybean, coconut, and palm. It is best used for frying rather than in salads because it is quite greasy.

Peanut oil

A combination of a very mild flavor and a high smoke point of 450°F/232°C makes peanut oil extremely versatile. It is therefore suitable for dressings and mayonnaise, and for drizzling over dishes, as well as for all forms of cooking, including deep-frying.

Corn oil

This oil is economical to buy, and therefore is a good choice for cooking. However, it has a strong, distinctive flavor that makes it unsuitable for dressings and drizzling over dishes. Its smoke point is 410°F/210°C.

Olive oil

Extra virgin olive oil

Sunflower-seed oil

Canola oil

This oil is gaining in popularity because it contains less saturated fat than other oils. It also contains the omega-3 essential fatty acid, which is now widely believed to help reduce cholesterol levels. It has a mild flavor and so is suitable for salad dressings as well as for cooking. Its smoke point is 444°F/229°C.

Soybean oil

This economical oil is extracted from soybeans and has a light yellow color. Like canola oil, its popularity is growing because it is low in saturated fat. Its smoke point is 450°F/232°C, which makes it ideal for all types of cooking, including deep-frying. However, it has a strong taste and is therefore not suitable for dressings or for drizzling over finished dishes.

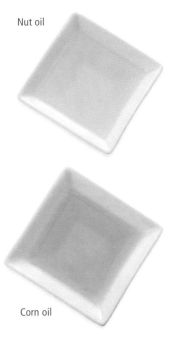

Nut oil

Corn oil

Vinegars

Vinegar adds a pungent kick to dressings, marinades, sauces, and a wide range of dishes. It is available in different varieties, and here are some of the most popular types.

Malt vinegar

This is made from malted barley and is available in two varieties: a colorless form, which is very strong and is used for pickling, and a dark brown variety, which is used in chutneys and on traditional British fish and french fries. This vinegar is not suitable for dressings.

Cider vinegar

This vinegar is made from apples and has a strong, sharp taste. It is best used with meats and in pickles and chutneys.

Wine vinegars

These are available in different varieties, mainly red, white, and sherry. They can be used in dressings, marinades and sauces, and can be sprinkled over food.

Balsamic vinegar

This delicious vinegar is thick, dark and slightly sweet. It is made from grape juice that is aged in barrels over a period of years.

Speciality vinegars

These vinegars can be made with fruits such as berries, nuts, or a wide variety of herbs. Other popular favorites are rice vinegar (used in Asian cooking) and cane vinegar, which has a rich, slightly sweet taste.

Vegetable oil

Basil-flavored olive oil

Malt vinegar

Red wine vinegar

Balsamic vinegar

Flour

Keep your flour fresh by storing it in an airtight container with a tight-fitting lid in a cool, dry place. You can store white flours for 6–8 months, and whole wheat flours for up to 2 months.

Cornstarch

This powdery flour is made from corn kernels and is used for thickening sauces, soups, and desserts. It is usually mixed with a small quantity of cold liquid to make a smooth paste before being added to hot dishes.

All-purpose flour

This flour is used for thickening sauces as well as for making batters and pie dough.

Self-rising flour

All-purpose flour that has had baking powder and salt added is known as self-rising flour. It is used for making cakes and cookies.

Whole wheat flour

This flour has a stronger flavor than white flour and contains wheat germ, which means it has a higher fiber, fat, and nutrient content. However, since it has a higher fat content, it should be stored in the refrigerator to stop it going rancid.

White bread flour

This flour is used for making bread. It contains a high level of gluten, which helps to give the bread dough its elasticity. If you are using a whole wheat variety, keep it in an airtight container in the refrigerator.

Rice flour

This powdery flour is made from white rice, and is used mainly in baked foods and to make Asian rice-flour noodles.

1 Whole wheat flour
2 Cornstarch
3 All-purpose flour
4 Malted brown flour
5 White bread flour
6 Self-rising flour

Pasta, noodles, and grains

All these different dried pasta shapes, noodles, and grains keep well in the pantry. They are ideal for cooking quick, satisfying meals at short notice.

Long-shaped pasta

There are different varieties of dried long-shaped pastas, including spaghetti, fettuccine (narrow ribbons), tagliatelle (slightly wider ribbons), and vermicelli (very fine, hair-like lengths). These pastas are usually made with durum wheat or whole wheat flour, and may be colored using ingredients such as spinach (green), beet juice (red), tomatoes (orange-red), or even squid ink (black).

Short-shaped pasta

Dried short shapes of pasta include conchiglie (shells), fusilli (spirals), farfalle (bows), and tubular varieties such as penne and macaroni. These shapes are particularly good for holding chunky sauces.

Other shapes of dried pasta

Other favorite shapes to keep in your pantry include lasagna (rectangular sheets) and cannelloni (large tubes).

Dried noodles

Most noodles are associated with Asian cooking. The main difference between noodles and long-shaped pasta is that noodles usually have egg added, such as Chinese egg noodles. Alternatively, sometimes they are made from rice flour. Noodles are very popular in stir-fries and soups. Many varieties need no cooking—you simply soak them in hot water for a few minutes before adding to the dish of your choice.

Long-grain rice

You can buy white and brown varieties of long-grain rice. When cooked, the grains stay dry and separate and do not clump together. This rice is used in savory dishes.

Medium-grain rice

These grains are a little shorter than long-grain rice, and more moist. They tend to clump together when cooked. This rice is used in savory dishes such as Spanish paella and Japanese sushi.

Short-grain rice

This rice has short, fat grains that are more starchy and moist than medium- and long-grain rice. There are different varieties, including pearl rice (used in Asian cooking) and risotto rice.

Easy-cook rice

The grains in easy-cook rice are polished and partly boiled so that they are quick and easy to cook and stay fluffy and separate. Easy-cook rice is a convenient alternative to white or brown rice, but does not have as much flavor.

Wild rice

Despite its name, wild rice is not actually a rice—it is a marsh grass that is cultivated in the United States and Canada. The grains are long and black and have a nutty flavor. Wild rice is expensive, so for economic reasons it is often mixed with less-expensive brown long-grain rice.

Bulgur wheat

This comprises wheat kernels that have had the bran removed. They are then steamed, dried, and ground into different degrees of coarseness. The result is a golden-brown grain that has a nutty flavor. It can be cooked like rice and is also excellent in salads.

Couscous

This is not a true grain, but pieces of semolina dough that have been rolled, dampened, and coated with a fine wheat flour. It makes a fine accompaniment to savory dishes.

Cornmeal

This yellow grain is made from cornmeal and is very popular in Italian cooking. It can be eaten hot or cold. It can also be cooked in a slab then cut into squares and broiled or fried.

Spaghetti

Noodles

Long-grain brown rice

Assorted dried pasta shapes

Pulses

Beans, lentils, and peas are known as pulses, and they are good sources of protein. All pulses except lentils and split peas need soaking for at least 8 hours, then boiling rapidly for 10 minutes before cooking for around 45 minutes. The exception is soybeans, which need even longer. It is a good idea to keep some ready-to-use canned pulses to hand for impromptu meals.

Cannellini beans
A type of haricot bean, these long, creamy white beans are excellent in soups and salads.

Red kidney beans
These red, kidney-shaped beans can be added to soups, salads, stews, and other savory dishes such as chili con carne.

Aduki beans
These beans are small and red and are popular in Japanese cooking,

especially coated with sugar. They are also good in savory dishes such as soups and salads.

Lima beans
These white, kidney-shaped beans are excellent in soups and salads.

Black-eye peas
These beans are small and beige and have a circular black "eye." They are commonly found in Chinese cooking, and are particularly popular in sauces, stir-fries, and soups.

Cranberry beans
These oval-shaped beans have pale pink to maroon streaked skin. They are creamy when cooked and are excellent in soups, dips, and other savory dishes.

Soybeans
Although most soybeans are yellow, they can also be black, brown, or green. They are much richer in nutrients than the other pulses, and are particularly full of protein, as well as iron and calcium. Soybeans are used to make cooking oils and margarine, flour, soymilk, and cheeses, soy sauce, tofu, miso, and textured vegetable protein. They are good in soups and other savory dishes, particularly curries. They should be soaked for at least 12 hours, drained, and rinsed, then covered with fresh water and brought to a boil. Boil them for the

first hour of cooking, then simmer them for the remaining 2–3 hours that it takes to cook them.

Chickpeas
These round, beige pulses have a nutty flavor and are excellent in soups, stews, and salads, as well as ground up in dips such as hummus. Like soybeans, they need a longer soaking and cooking time than many pulses, so it is good to keep some canned chickpeas on hand for when you are short of time.

Lentils
These tiny, disk-shaped pulses are available in different varieties and colors. Red and orange lentils become mushy when cooked, and are therefore ideal puréed and used in soups and sauces. The green and continental brown varieties (Puy lentils) keep their shape when cooked and are ideal in warm winter salads, sauces, stews, and other savory dishes.

Split peas
These small peas are disk-shaped and split along a natural seam. They can be yellow or green, and are excellent cooked and puréed. They are also good in soups, bakes, and other savory dishes.

Red kidney beans

Red lentils

Aduki beans

Chickpeas

Cannellini beans

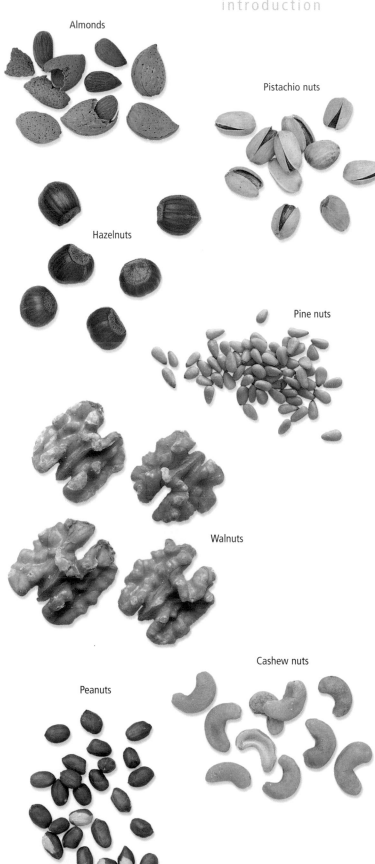

Almonds

Pistachio nuts

Hazelnuts

Pine nuts

Walnuts

Cashew nuts

Peanuts

Nuts and seeds

Nuts and seeds have a high oil content, and can quickly go rancid. If they have shells, store them in a cool, dry place. If they do not have shells, refrigerate them in airtight containers.

Almonds

These lozenge-shaped nuts have a thin brown covering and a cream center. They come in two types, sweet and bitter, but it is the sweet variety that is normally used. Available whole, blanched, chopped, and crystallized, they are excellent in both savory and sweet dishes, from salads and savory bakes to cakes, cookies, and marzipan.

Hazelnuts

These small, round nuts have a brown covering and a cream interior, and a rich, sweet flavor. They are especially popular in granola and cereals, savory dishes, and bakes, such as nut loaf, as well as sweet dishes, including cakes and cookies.

Walnuts

These nuts have a large, round, wrinkled shell and two double lobes inside. The nuts have a delicious creamy taste and are good in salads and savory bakes, as well as sweet dishes and cakes. They also make a very flavorful oil.

Pecan nuts

These nuts are golden brown with a beige interior. They have a very high-fat content. They are used in a variety of savory dishes, and desserts such as pecan pie.

Cashew nuts

These creamy, butter-flavored kidney-shaped nuts have a high-fat content and are delicious roasted and added to stir-fries and bakes.

Pistachio nuts

These pale green nuts have a delicate flavor. They are often used in dressings and also to decorate desserts.

Pine nuts

These small, oval nuts are creamy in color and in flavor. They are excellent toasted or dry-fried, and are used in salads and rice dishes, sauces such as pesto, and also savory and sweet dishes.

Peanuts

Despite their name, peanuts are not nuts, but legumes and are very versatile. They are used to make oil and also peanut butter, which in turn makes a delicious satay sauce. They are also good in salads, side dishes, and stir-fries.

Seeds

A selection of seeds can be very useful in your pantry. Sunflower seeds, for example, are rich in essential fatty acids and are delicious sprinkled into granola and salads. Pumpkin seeds (pepitas) are also nutritious and make a good snack. Sesame seeds are popular in Asian cooking and are delicious toasted and in stir-fries. Dill seeds have an anise flavor and are good with fish and vegetables. Caraway seeds have a pungent flavor and are used in soups, stews, vegetable dishes, and in bread. Poppy seeds are slightly sweet and make an attractive decoration sprinkled over salads and bread rolls.

Dried herbs

It is always worthwhile having a collection of dried herbs. They are especially useful for dishes that require a long cooking time, such as casseroles. Use half the recommended fresh quantity.

Oregano
This herb has a strong flavor and is perfect sprinkled on pizzas and in pasta sauces.

Basil
This popular herb is delicious in sauces and is particularly good with tomatoes.

Sage
This herb is good in egg, cheese, poultry, and meat dishes.

Dill
This is an excellent herb with vegetables and fish.

Rosemary
A pungent herb that goes well with poultry and meat, and also root vegetables, especially potatoes.

Mixed herbs
This combination usually consists of oregano, rosemary, and thyme, plus one or two other herbs. Mixed herbs can be used in a variety of savory dishes, including sauces and Italian dishes such as pizza and pasta.

Spices and seasonings

A selection of spices in your pantry is extremely useful for enhancing the flavor of dishes. Some spices, such as ginger and turmeric, are also said to aid digestion.

Ginger
This hot, pungent spice has a lemony flavor when fresh, but a sweeter flavor when dried. It is particularly used in Indian cooking, as well as in chutneys, desserts, and baked goods such as cakes, notably gingerbread, and cookies.

Turmeric
A peppery spice with a distinctive yellow color. Turmeric is often used instead of the more expensive saffron. It is especially good in curries and rice dishes such as paella.

Saffron
This yellow spice has a slightly bitter flavor and a pungent aroma. It is sold in strands and is used in dishes to color and flavor them.

Coriander
This spice has an aromatic flavor and is excellent with meat, poultry, and vegetables.

Cumin
This spice has a strong, slightly bitter flavor, and is particularly good with poultry and vegetables.

Cloves
A sweet spice with a strong flavor. Use whole cloves to stud hams and fruits, and ground cloves to add flavor to desserts.

Nutmeg
This spice has a sweet flavor and is used in savory and sweet dishes.

Mace
This spice has a sweet flavor and is excellent in soups and sauces.

Paprika

Basil

Cumin

Sage

Oregano

Rosemary

Cloves

Cinnamon
A very popular spice, cinnamon is sweet and fragrant and is used in desserts and baked foods such as cakes, sweet pies, and cookies.

Curry powder
This is a blend of spices, and the flavor varies from mild to hot. It adds a distinctive flavor to sauces and savory dishes.

Allspice
A mixture of sweet spices, such as cinnamon, cloves, mace, and nutmeg, plus one or two others. It gives a delicious flavor to desserts, cakes, cookies, and drinks.

Chili powder
This is a blend of dried chilies. It adds a kick to sauces and savory dishes.

Turmeric

Ground ginger

Five-spice powder
This blend of five spices usually contains cinnamon, cloves, fennel seed, Szechuan peppercorns, and star anise. It is very popular in Chinese cooking, and gives a wonderful flavor to stir-fries.

Paprika
This has a hot flavor and an attractive red color. It is ideal as a garnish.

Peppercorns
These come in different varieties. Ground black or white peppercorns are an extremely popular seasoning for a wide variety of savory foods and also some sweet dishes such as balsamic strawberries. You can also buy green peppercorns.

Salt
This is a great favorite as a seasoning, but care must be taken not to overuse it or it will overpower the food, and be bad for health.

Peppercorn

Sugars and syrups

Store your sugar in a dry place at room temperature. Syrups should be kept in tightly sealed containers at room temperature or in the refrigerator.

Granulated sugar
This basic, cheap sugar is essential in your pantry. Use it to sweeten drinks and cereals and to sprinkle on desserts.

Superfine sugar
This sugar is finer than granulated sugar and dissolves quickly, so it is ideal for meringues and cakes.

Confectioners' sugar
This very fine sugar is ideal for making frosting and for dusting cakes and desserts.

Brown sugar
This stronger-flavored sugar comes in various shades, from pale gold to chocolate brown.

Raw brown sugar
This crunchy brown sugar is delicious sprinkled over desserts and cakes before being broiled or baked.

Honey
This comes in a variety of flavors and colors, as either clear, liquid honey or opaque, set honey. It has many uses, from glazing ham and flavoring vegetables to sweetening desserts and drinks.

Corn syrup
This clear, corn syrup is made from evaporated sugar cane juice. It is used in a variety of dishes, and to top crêpes and ice cream.

Maple syrup
This syrup has a delicious sweet flavor and can be used in a wide variety of savory and sweet dishes. It is very popular on crêpes.

1 Confectioners' sugar
2 Brown sugar
3 Superfine sugar
4 Raw brown sugar
5 Granulated sugar

45

Sauces, pastes, and condiments

A good selection of sauces and condiments is invaluable in the kitchen, and will ensure you always have the right ingredient on hand to add exciting and interesting flavors to your dishes.

Tomato ketchup

This sauce is popular in British cooking and is added to cooked foods such as french fries and hamburgers. It is also good as an ingredient in dressings and relishes.

Brown sauce

This strongly flavored sauce is a traditional British accompaniment to a fried breakfast.

Soy sauce

This popular sauce is essential for stir-fries and other Asian dishes. You can buy the Chinese version, which is salty, or the Japanese type, which is slightly sweeter.

Worcestershire sauce

This strongly flavored sauce is made with onions, molasses, and anchovies, and is used to season meats, gravies, and soups, and occasionally cocktails.

Pesto sauce

Pesto is made from basil, garlic, pine nuts, Parmesan cheese, and olive oil. It is ideal for quick pasta meals.

Tabasco sauce

This very hot chili sauce is used in dishes to give them a kick, such as Mexican salsas. It is also used to season certain cocktails.

Hoisin sauce

This sweet soy-based sauce with a sticky texture is very popular in Chinese cooking. It is known by various names, such as Peking sauce.

Thai fish sauce (nam pla)

This salty sauce is made from fermented fish and has a very strong taste and smell. It is used to flavor Thai dishes and as a table condiment.

Horseradish sauce

Horseradish is a root with a very hot flavor. It makes an excellent creamy white sauce, which is very good with meat, poultry, fish, and egg dishes.

Plum sauce

This fruity sauce is popular in Chinese cooking and is traditionally served with egg rolls and also Peking duck.

Harissa

This North African condiment is made from oil, garlic, herbs, and spices, and is served with soups and couscous.

Sesame-seed paste

A thick paste made from finely ground sesame seeds. It is used to flavor Middle Eastern dishes.

Thai curry paste

This is available in different varieties: green is the hottest, yellow is the mildest, and red varies in the amount of heat. It is a popular ingredient in Thai dishes.

Miso

A paste made from fermented soybeans. It is used in Japanese cooking to thicken and flavor soups and other dishes.

Tomato paste

This is a concentrate that is useful in sauces and soups because of its intense flavor.

Strained canned tomatoes

The juice strained from canned tomatoes is ideal for soups and sauces, and for spreading over pizzas.

Mustards

You can buy different types of mustard. Dijon mustard has a strong flavor and is used in dips and dressings. English mustard is very hot and is useful in dips and dressings. Coarse-grain mustard is usually milder, and is good with a variety of savory dishes, especially meats.

1 Soy sauce
2 Coarse-grain mustard
3 Tabasco sauce
4 Thai fish sauce
5 Pesto sauce
6 Horseradish sauce

Canned and bottled foods

Keep a selection of cannned and bottled foods on hand, such as pulses, fish, vegetables, and pickled items, and you will never be short of ingredients for delicious meals at short notice.

Canned pulses

You can buy a wide variety of canned beans, such as red kidney beans and chickpeas, which will save you time because you do not have to soak them or cook them. Cans of baked beans in tomato sauce are indispensable for quick meals.

Canned fish

Canned fish, such as tuna, salmon, crab, anchovies, sardines, and pilchards, are versatile items to have in the pantry. They are particularly useful when added to pastas and salads.

Canned tomatoes

Canned tomatoes can be used in a wide variety of dishes, from sauces and soups to stews and casseroles.

Coconut milk

Canned coconut milk is very useful for cooking Thai dishes, particularly creamy curries and desserts.

Corn

Canned corn is deliciously sweet and ideal in salads, soups, bakes, and casseroles.

Canned sardines

Water chestnuts

These are popular in Chinese cooking, and are particularly good in stir-fries.

Olives

It is always useful to keep a can or bottle of olives on hand. They make ideal tapas for unexpected guests and are delicious in salads and pastas and on pizzas.

Sun-dried tomatoes

These are very good in Italian recipes, particularly salads, pastas, and bread.

Pickled foods

Onions, gherkins, and capers make perfect accompaniments and garnishes for meat and vegetable dishes.

Dried fruits and berries

A selection of dried fruits and berries is very useful to keep on hand. They make ideal snacks and can be used in a wide variety of savory and sweet dishes, from granola, vegetable curries, and meat dishes to desserts and sweet pies. Dried fruits and berries include currants, raisins, apricots, prunes, figs, dates, mangoes, pears, apples, bananas, cranberries, and blueberries.

Other items

Here is a selection of other items you will find useful to keep in your pantry.

Bouillon cubes

These are very convenient for soups, casseroles, and other dishes, particularly if you have do not have enough time to make fresh stock.

Gelatin

You need gelatin to set mousses and jellies. You can also buy a vegetarian equivalent, such as agar agar.

Chocolate and cocoa

These are useful for desserts and baked goods, and also for some savory dishes.

Vanilla

You can buy vanilla in bean or liquid form (extract) as a flavoring. Vanilla is particularly delicious in desserts.

Alcohol

White wine, red wine, and sherry are handy for a variety of savory and sweet dishes. Although not essential, flavored liqueurs are also useful, such as orange, coffee, and almond.

Vanilla beans

Refrigerator and freezer essentials

Your chilled essentials should include eggs, milk, and yogurt. You should also keep some butter, including an unsalted variety for baking and desserts. Bread is another essential, not just as an accompaniment, but for making bread crumbs and recipes such as crostini. Cheeses should include an all-purpose firm variety, such as Cheddar, and also Parmesan, as well as cream cheese. You may find bacon slices useful. Tofu is full of protein: it is good in stir-fries and is useful for vegetarian meals. In the freezer, you might like to keep frozen shrimp and fish fillets, vegetables, and ice cream.

PART TWO

MAIN COMMODITIES AND RECIPES

1

EGGS AND DAIRY

EGGS AND DAIRY PRODUCTS, SUCH AS MILK, BUTTER,
AND CHEESE, ARE EXCELLENT SOURCES OF PROTEIN.
THEY ARE ALSO VERY VERSATILE FOODS AND CAN
BE USED TO ENRICH A WIDE RANGE OF SWEET AND
SAVORY DISHES. IN THIS SECTION YOU WILL FIND A
MOUTHWATERING ARRAY OF EGG AND DAIRY RECIPES
TO DELIGHT EVERY MEMBER OF YOUR HOUSEHOLD.

INTRODUCTION

NOWADAYS WE CAN BUY A WIDE RANGE OF DELICIOUS EGGS, FROM FACTORY PRODUCED WHITE AND BROWN TO FREE-RANGE AND ORGANIC. LIKEWISE, MORE DAIRY PRODUCTS ARE AVAILABLE THAN BEFORE, AND WE CAN CHOOSE FROM AN EVER-INCREASING ARRAY OF MILK, YOGURT, CREAM, BUTTER, AND CHEESE, WHICH ARE FULL OF PROTEIN AND VERY EASY TO PREPARE AND COOK.

Buying and storing eggs

Always buy your eggs from a reputable supplier, and do not buy any with cracked shells. Ensure the eggs are as fresh as possible by checking the "best before" date on the carton. In many cases the "best before" date is also printed on the eggshells themselves. You can also check an egg's freshness by floating it in water: if it sinks to the bottom of the bowl horizontally, it is very fresh; if it stays vertical with its tip on the bottom, it is less fresh; if it floats to the top it is stale and should be discarded.

Store your eggs, pointed ends down, in their carton in the door of your refrigerator or in a cool place in your kitchen. Separated egg whites will keep in the refrigerator in a lidded container for a week, and in the freezer for three months. Egg yolks or whole beaten eggs will keep in the refrigerator for up to 2 days, or in the freezer for up to 3 months (add a little salt to them before freezing). When freezing eggs, or indeed any food, always label the container with the date of freezing and what it contains.

Eggs are best cooked at room temperature, so get them out of the refrigerator 2–3 hours before they are needed, if possible.

Whisking egg whites

Eggs that are 3–5 days old are best for whisking. Make sure that everything is clean and that your bowl is free of grease. Place the egg whites the bowl. If you are whisking by hand, use a large balloon whisk in an upward, circular movement. Alternatively, use a hand-held electric whisk or free-standing food mixer. If the recipe calls for a "soft peaks" consistency, the mixture should form peaks that are soft and will flop over. If you need "firm peaks," the peaks should stand rigid.

Scrambling eggs

Allow 2 eggs and 1 tablespoon of milk per person. Whisk together the eggs and milk in a bowl, then season with salt and pepper. Melt 1 tablespoon of butter in a nonstick pan, then pour in the egg mixture. Stir constantly over low heat for 5–7 minutes until almost set, then remove from the heat. Stir for 1 more minute, then serve.

Boiling eggs

To boil eggs, bring a small pan of water to a boil. Reduce the heat to a simmer, add a pinch of salt, then carefully add the eggs (if they have been

---

Safety

Eggs can carry harmful bacteria and may cause food poisoning if not thoroughly cooked, so do not give dishes with raw or lightly cooked eggs to people who may be particularly vulnerable, such as pregnant or breastfeeding women, babies and toddlers, the elderly, people who are ill, or convalescents.

Free-range hen egg

Medium duck egg

Large duck egg

refrigerated, bring them out about an hour beforehand to allow them to come to room temperature). Simmer gently for 4–5 minutes for soft-cooked, and 9–10 minutes for hard-cooked (no longer, or a dark ring will appear around the yolk). Remove with a slotted spoon and plunge into cold water to prevent further cooking. Serve as required.

Frying eggs

Heat 1–2 tablespoons of oil in a skillet until hot (but not smoking). Break the eggs carefully into the skillet so that the yolks remain intact. Cook over medium heat, occasionally basting with the hot oil to help the yolk set, for 3–4 minutes. Use a slotted spatula to lift out the eggs and allow the oil to drain away. Serve immediately.

Poaching eggs

Eggs need to be very fresh for poaching or they will break up in the water. You can use a nonstick egg poacher for this, or alternatively use the following method. Take a small skillet and fill it with enough water to cover an egg.

Bring the water to a boil, then reduce the heat to a simmer. Add a pinch of salt. Break the egg carefully into a cup, then pour it gently into the boiling water so that the yolk does not break. Cook for 3–4 minutes, depending on how you like your eggs; you may find it helpful to baste the egg with a little of the cooking liquid to ensure it is cooked. Lift it out with a slotted spoon and serve.

Separating eggs

There are some clever devices available for separating yolks from egg whites—for example, you can buy a spoon-shaped implement that has holes in to allow the egg white to pass through, leaving the egg yolk intact. If you don't have a separating gadget, you can use the shell method (using cold eggs makes this method easier). ❶ Crack the egg shell gently on the edge of a bowl. ❷ Open the shell slowly, allowing the white to drip into the bowl. ❸ Taking care not to break the yolk, pass it from one shell half to the other. ❹ Repeat until the yolk and white are fully separated. Alternatively, open the egg into your hand and let the white drip through your fingers to separate.

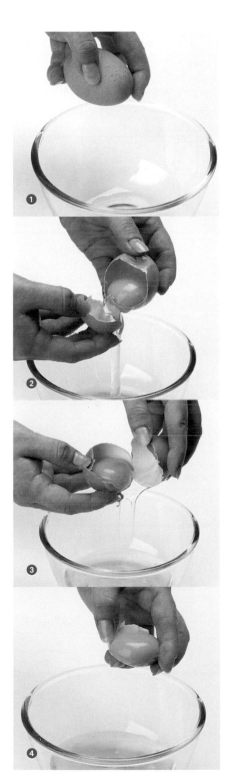

Small duck egg

Goose egg

Quail egg

Buying and storing milk

Milk is a good source of protein and calcium. The most commonly available is fresh cow's milk, which comes in whole ($3\frac{1}{2}$% fat), lowfat (less than 2% fat), and skim (less than $\frac{1}{2}$% fat). Other varieties include homogenized, which has the fat spread throughout the milk so that there is no creamy layer on top, and ultrapasteurized milk, which has been heated quickly to around 300°F/149°C, then cooled and vacuum-packed to ensure a shelf-life without refrigeration of around six months. You can also buy sweetened condensed milk, which is very thick and sweet; evaporated milk, which is sterilized in cans and often used to replace whole milk; buttermilk, which tastes like yogurt or thickened lowfat milk; and dry milk, which you can reconstitute with water and use in place of fresh milk. If you are sensitive to cow's milk, you can buy goat milk or sheep's milk, or milk made from soy or rice instead.

These days most fresh milk is pasteurized (heated then quickly cooled) in order to kill off any harmful bacteria, although some unpasteurized milk is available, often straight from the farm (see Safety box, opposite).

Always check the "best before" date on milk before you buy it, and store fresh milk in the refrigerator. Keep it covered to prevent contamination.

Buying and storing yogurt

Yogurt is made by fermenting milk with healthy bacteria. It has a slightly tangy taste and is a healthy choice because it is thick and creamy yet low in fat. Strained plain yogurt is the thickest and has the creamiest consistency. You can also freeze yogurt for a healthy lowfat alternative to ice cream. Check the "best before" date before buying, and store it in the refrigerator. Keep it covered when not in use.

Buying and storing butter

Butter is made by churning cream until it separates into semisolids. It comprises at least 80% fat and the other 20% is made up of milk solids and water. Sometimes it is colored with annatto (a natural color made from the paste of seeds). Butter is available in salted and unsalted varieties: unsalted is essential for sweet dishes. You can also buy "spreadable" butter: this has been blended with oil so that it will stay soft and can be spread more easily. Make sure your butter is always tightly

Fresh milk

Clotted cream

Butter

Yogurt

wrapped to prevent it from absorbing odours. Check the "best before" date on the packaging. Butter also freezes well, for up to 6 months in the freezer.

Buying and storing cream

Cream is made from the fattiest part of milk. It therefore has a higher fat content than milk, and a milder flavor. Half-fat and light cream have the lowest fat contents: the former is useful for pouring into drinks such as coffee, and the latter is ideal for sauces and soups. Sour cream (around 18–20% fat) has a slightly tangy taste and is ideal in savory dishes, as is the higher fat crème fraîche (up to 50% fat). Whipping cream has a high fat content (30–35%) and, as its name suggests, is ideal for whipping and piping into decorative shapes.

Heavy cream has a very high fat content (over 40%) and should therefore be used sparingly. It is a delicious luxury for special occasions, perhaps to enrich a sauce or accompany a dessert. Clotted cream has the highest fat content of all (around 60%) and is very thick. It is ideal on biscuits or as an accompaniment for special desserts.

All cream should be kept covered and stored in the refrigerator. Use it by the "best before" date on the carton.

Buying and storing cheese

Cheese is made from milk that is allowed to thicken and then separate into curds (semisolids) and whey (a liquid). Fresh cheeses are rindless and vary in consistency. Typical cheeses in this category are cream cheese and cottage cheese. Soft and semihard cheeses are firmer, and range from creamy soft cheeses with rinds, such as Brie, to firmer cheeses such as Port Salut. Generally, the harder the cheese, the higher the fat content, and hard cheeses have the highest fat of all. They are often easy to grate, and range from Cheddar cheese to Parmesan. Blue cheeses are also available: these have blue veins running through them and a strong flavor and aroma (the veins are made by a friendly bacteria). Blue cheese varieties include Gorgonzola and Stilton. You can also buy cheese made from goat milk and sheep's milk.

Keep your cheese tightly wrapped. Store fresh cheese in the coldest part of the refrigerator, and the other cheeses in the warmest part. Hard cheeses can be grated ready for use and kept in the refrigerator for up to one week. Use cheeses by the "best before" date. You can also freeze hard cheeses, but they will have a crumblier texture when they are defrosted. Grated cheese also freezes well but is only suitable for cooking, not for adding to salads.

Cheddar

Parmesan

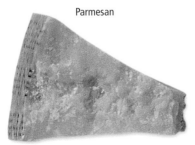

Stilton

Curd cheese

Safety

Unpasteurized milk is available from specialist suppliers, but there is still a risk of disease and therefore this milk should not be given to vulnerable people, especially pregnant or breastfeeding women, babies and toddlers, the elderly, people who are ill, or convalescents.

EGGS BENEDICT WITH QUICK HOLLANDAISE SAUCE

THIS DELICIOUS RECIPE IS QUICK AND EASY TO PREPARE. IT MAKES AN EXCELLENT BREAKFAST, LUNCH, OR SUPPER, OR A TASTY SNACK AT ANY TIME OF DAY. YOU CAN ALSO SUBSTITUTE BACON FOR THE HAM, OR USE SPINACH IF YOU ARE CATERING FOR VEGETARIANS.

serves
4

preparation
30 minutes

cooking
12–15 minutes

ingredients
- 1 tbsp white wine vinegar
- 4 eggs
- 4 English muffins
- 4 slices good-quality ham

QUICK HOLLANDAISE SAUCE
- 3 egg yolks
- 7/8 cup butter
- 1 tbsp lemon juice
- pepper

1 Fill a wide skillet three-quarters full with water and bring to a boil over low heat. Reduce the heat to a simmer and add the vinegar. When the water is barely simmering, carefully break the eggs into the skillet. Leave for 1 minute, then, using a large spoon, gently loosen the eggs from the bottom of the skillet. Let cook for an additional 3 minutes, or until the white is cooked but the yolk is still soft, basting the top of the egg with the water from time to time.

2 Meanwhile, to make the hollandaise sauce, place the egg yolks in a blender or food processor. Melt the butter in a small pan until bubbling. With the motor still running, gradually add the hot butter in a steady stream until the sauce is thick and creamy. Add the lemon juice, and a little warm water if the sauce is too thick, then season to taste with pepper. Remove from the blender or food processor and keep warm.

3 Split the muffins and toast them on both sides. To serve, top each muffin with a slice of ham, a poached egg, and a generous spoonful of hollandaise sauce.

cook's tip

For best results when poaching eggs, break them into a cup first, then slide into the hot water. If you prefer firmer yolks, poach for a little longer than the suggested three minutes.

EGGS FLORENTINE

THIS TASTY DISH IS RICH IN PROTEIN AND MINERALS, INCLUDING IRON, CALCIUM, AND ZINC. IT ALSO WORKS VERY WELL FOR VEGETARIANS, AS LONG AS YOU USE A CHEDDAR THAT IS MADE FROM NON-ANIMAL RENNET. IF NECESSARY, YOU CAN REPLACE THE WHOLE WHEAT FLOUR WITH WHITE FLOUR.

serves
2–4
(2 as a light
snack or 4 as
part of a brunch)
preparation
50 minutes
cooking
45–55 minutes

ingredients
- 1 lb/450 g fresh spinach leaves, thoroughly washed
- 4 tbsp unsalted butter
- 2 oz/55 g white mushrooms, sliced
- 3/8 cup pine nuts, toasted
- 6 scallions, chopped
- 4 eggs
- scant 1/4 cup whole wheat flour
- 1 1/4 cups milk, warmed
- 1 tsp English mustard
- 3 oz/85 g sharp Cheddar cheese, grated
- salt and pepper

1 Preheat the oven to 375°F/190°C. Shake off any excess water from the spinach, place in a large pan with the water clinging to the leaves and sprinkle with a little salt. Cover and cook over medium heat for 2–3 minutes, or until wilted. Drain, pressing out any excess liquid, then chop.

2 Heat 1 tablespoon of the butter in a small pan over medium heat. Add the mushrooms and cook for 2 minutes, stirring frequently. Add the pine nuts and scallions and cook for an additional 2 minutes. Remove, season to taste with salt and pepper, and sprinkle over the spinach. Set aside until required.

3 Meanwhile, fill a skillet with cold water and bring to a boil, then reduce the heat to a gentle simmer. Carefully break an egg into a cup and slip into the water. Add

the remaining eggs and cook for 4–5 minutes, or until set. Carefully remove the eggs with a slotted spoon and arrange on top of the spinach mixture.

4 Melt the remaining butter in a pan and stir in the flour. Cook for 2 minutes, then remove from the heat and gradually stir in the milk. Return to the heat and cook, stirring constantly, until the mixture comes to a boil and has thickened. Stir in the mustard, then 1/2 cup of the cheese. Continue stirring until the cheese has melted. Add salt and pepper to taste, then pour over the eggs, completely covering them. Sprinkle with the remaining cheese.

5 Cook in the preheated oven for 20–25 minutes, or until piping hot and the top is golden brown and bubbling. Serve at immediately.

SWEET SOUFFLÉ OMELET

THE MOUTHWATERING FILLING OF SWEET CHERRY TOMATOES, MUSHROOMS, AND BABY SPINACH
LEAVES IS A WONDERFUL CONTRAST TO THE LIGHT FLUFFY OMELETS, WHICH HAVE TO BE COOKED
ONE BY ONE. MAKE SURE THE OIL IS REALLY HOT BEFORE YOU COOK THE OMELETS.

serves
4

preparation
50 minutes

cooking
20–25 minutes

ingredients
- 6 oz/175 g cherry tomatoes
- 8 oz/225 g mixed mushrooms (such as white, cremini, shiitake, oyster, and wild mushrooms)
- 4 tbsp fresh vegetable stock
- small bunch fresh thyme
- 8 eggs, separated (for 4 egg yolks and 8 egg whites)
- 8 tbsp water
- 4 tsp olive oil
- ⅝ cup baby spinach leaves, rinsed
- salt and pepper
- fresh thyme sprigs, to garnish

1 Halve the tomatoes and place them in a pan. Wipe the mushrooms with paper towels, trim if necessary and slice if large. Place in the pan.

2 Add the stock and thyme to the pan. Bring to a boil, cover, and let simmer for 5–6 minutes until tender. Drain, remove the thyme and discard, and keep the mixture warm.

3 Meanwhile, whisk the egg yolks with the water until frothy. Whisk the 8 egg whites in a clean, grease-free bowl until stiff and dry.

4 Spoon the egg yolk mixture into the egg whites and, using a metal spoon, fold the whites and yolks into each other until well mixed. Take care not to knock out too much of the air.

5 For each omelet, brush a small omelet pan with 1 teaspoon oil and heat until hot. Pour in a quarter of the egg mixture and cook for 4–5 minutes, or until the mixture has set.

6 Preheat the broiler to medium. Slide the omelet pan under the broiler and finish cooking the omelet for 2–3 minutes until set.

7 Transfer the omelet to a warmed serving plate. Fill the omelet with a few baby spinach leaves and a quarter of the mushroom and tomato mixture. Flip over the top of the omelet, garnish with thyme sprigs, and serve immediately.

SPANISH TORTILLA

THERE IS HARDLY A TAPAS BAR IN SPAIN THAT DOESN'T SERVE THIS SIMPLE BUT DELICIOUS, THICK OMELET. IT'S SO WELL LOVED IN SPAIN THAT, GENERATIONS AGO, IT WAS SAID THAT COUNTRY GIRLS COULD IMPROVE THEIR CHANCES OF MARRYING EARLY BY MAKING AN EXCELLENT TORTILLA.

makes
8–10 slices

preparation
30 minutes, plus
15 minutes'
resting

cooking
35–40 minutes

ingredients
- ½ cup olive oil
- 1 lb 5 oz/600 g potatoes, peeled and thinly sliced
- 1 large onion, thinly sliced
- 6 large eggs
- salt and pepper
- fresh flat-leaf parsley sprigs, to garnish

1 Heat a 10-inch/25-cm skillet, preferably nonstick, over high heat. Add the oil and heat. Reduce the heat, then add the potatoes and onion and cook for 15–20 minutes until the potatoes are tender.

2 Beat the eggs in a large bowl and season generously with salt and pepper. Drain the potatoes and onion through a strainer over a heatproof bowl to reserve the oil. Very gently stir the vegetables into the eggs; let stand for 10 minutes.

3 Use a wooden spoon or spatula to remove any crusty bits stuck to the bottom of the skillet. Reheat the skillet over medium–high heat with 4 tablespoons of the reserved oil. Add the egg mixture and smooth the surface, pressing the potatoes and onions into an even layer.

4 Cook for about 5 minutes, shaking the skillet occasionally, until the bottom is set. Use a spatula to loosen the side of the tortilla. Place a large plate over the top and carefully invert the skillet and plate together so the tortilla drops onto the plate.

5 Add 1 tablespoon of the remaining reserved oil to the skillet and swirl around. Carefully slide the tortilla back into the skillet, cooked side up. Run the spatula around the tortilla, to tuck in the edge.

6 Continue cooking for 3 minutes, or until the eggs are set and the bottom is golden brown. Remove the skillet from the heat and slide the tortilla onto a plate. Let stand for at least 5 minutes before cutting. Garnish with parsley sprigs and serve warm or at room temperature.

cook's tip
If you are worried about inverting the tortilla, finish cooking it in the skillet under a medium–high broiler, about 4 inches/10 cm from the heat source, until the runny egg mixture on top is set. The tortilla will not, however, have its characteristic "rounded" edge.

QUICHE LORRAINE

THIS ELEGANT VERSION OF THE CLASSIC FRENCH TART IS DELICIOUS AS IT IS, OR IT CAN FORM THE BASIS OF AN EVEN MORE ELABORATE QUICHE. YOU CAN, FOR EXAMPLE, ARRANGE COOKED OR CANNED ASPARAGUS SPEARS ON THE TOP, OR SMOTHER IT WITH A LAYER OF SAUTÉED MUSHROOMS.

makes
1 x 9-inch/
23-cm quiche
preparation
30 minutes, plus
45 minutes'
chilling and
cooling
cooking
40–50 minutes

ingredients
PIE DOUGH
- scant 1¼ cups all-purpose flour, plus extra for dusting
- pinch of salt
- ½ cup butter, diced
- 1 oz/25 g romano cheese, grated
- 4–6 tbsp ice water

FILLING
- 4 oz/115 g Gruyère cheese, thinly sliced
- 2 oz/55 g Roquefort cheese, crumbled
- 6 oz/175 g rindless lean bacon, broiled until crisp
- 3 eggs
- ⅔ cup heavy cream
- salt and pepper

1 To make the pie dough, sift the flour with the salt into a bowl. Add the butter and rub it in with your fingertips until the mixture resembles bread crumbs. Stir in the grated cheese, then stir in enough of the water to bind. Shape the dough into a ball, wrap in foil, and chill in the refrigerator for 15 minutes.

2 Preheat the oven to 375°F/190°C. Unwrap and roll out the dough on a lightly floured counter. Use to line a 9-inch/23-cm quiche pan. Place the pan on a baking sheet. Prick the bottom of the pastry shell all over with a fork, line with foil or waxed paper, and fill with baking beans. Bake in the preheated oven for 15 minutes until the edges are set and dry. Remove the beans and lining and bake the pastry shell for an additional 5–7 minutes, or until golden. Let cool slightly.

3 For the filling, arrange the cheese over the bottom of the pastry shell, then crumble the bacon evenly on top. Place the eggs and cream in a bowl and beat together until thoroughly combined. Add salt and pepper to taste. Pour the mixture into the pastry shell and return to the oven for 20 minutes, or until the filling is golden and set.

4 Remove from the oven and cool the quiche in the pan for 10 minutes. Transfer to a wire rack to cool completely. Cover and store in the refrigerator, but return to room temperature before serving.

CHEESE FONDUE (BLUE CHEESE)

IT'S GOOD TO SEE THE CLASSIC SWISS FONDUE RETURNING TO POPULARITY—IT'S EASY, INEXPENSIVE, AND DELICIOUS. AS A TRADITIONAL FORFEIT, YOU HAVE TO DRINK A GLASS OF WINE EVERY TIME YOUR DIPPER FALLS OFF THE FORK, SO THE EVENING SHOULD GO WITH A SWING.

serves

4

preparation

10 minutes

cooking

20 minutes

ingredients

- 1 garlic clove, peeled and halved
- scant 2 cups dry white wine
- 5 tbsp brandy
- 12 oz/350 g Gruyère cheese, grated
- 12 oz/350 g Gorgonzola cheese, crumbled
- 1 tbsp cornstarch
- 2 tbsp light cream
- salt and pepper

DIPPERS

- fresh crusty bread, cut into bite-size pieces
- bite-size pieces of lightly cooked vegetables wrapped in cooked ham or strips of lightly cooked bacon

1 Rub the inside of an ovenproof fondue pot with the garlic. Discard the garlic. Pour in the wine and 3 tablespoons of the brandy, then transfer to the stove and bring to a gentle simmer over low heat. Add a small handful of the cheeses and stir constantly until melted. Continue to add the cheese gradually, stirring constantly after each addition, until all the cheese has been added. Continue to stir until thoroughly melted and bubbling gently.

2 Mix the cornstarch with the remaining brandy in a small bowl. Stir the cornstarch mixture into the fondue and continue to stir for 3–4 minutes until thickened and bubbling. Stir in the cream and season to taste with salt and pepper.

3 Using protective gloves, transfer the fondue pot to a lit tabletop burner. To serve, allow your guests to spear pieces of bread and ham-wrapped vegetables onto fondue forks and dip them into the fondue.

cook's tip

It is important to add the cheese gradually and stir constantly until it has completely melted before adding any more. Otherwise, the mixture will "split"—that is, the fat will separate. Keep the heat very low and, ideally, use an earthenware fondue pot rather than a metal one.

EGGPLANT GRATIN

THIS DISH IS FULL OF MEDITERRANEAN FLAVORS, AND IS RICH IN VITAMINS, INCLUDING VITAMIN C, AS WELL AS MINERALS AND PROTEIN. IT MAKES AN EXCELLENT APPETIZER, OR A SATISFYING LUNCH OR SUPPER IF ACCOMPANIED BY SOME FRESH CRUSTY BREAD.

serves
4 as a starter
preparation
15 minutes
cooking
40 minutes

ingredients
- 4 tbsp olive oil
- 2 onions, finely chopped
- 2 garlic cloves, very finely chopped
- 2 eggplants, thickly sliced
- 3 tbsp chopped fresh flat-leaf parsley
- ½ tsp dried thyme
- 14 oz/400 g canned chopped tomatoes
- 6 oz/175 g mozzarella cheese, coarsely grated
- 6 tbsp freshly grated Parmesan cheese
- salt and pepper

1 Heat the oil in a skillet over medium heat. Add the onion and cook for 5 minutes, or until softened. Add the garlic and cook for a few seconds, or until just beginning to color. Using a slotted spoon, transfer the onion mixture to a plate. Cook the eggplant slices in batches in the same skillet until they are just lightly browned.

2 Preheat the oven to 400°F/200°C. Arrange a layer of eggplant slices in the bottom of a shallow ovenproof dish. Sprinkle with some of the parsley, thyme, salt and pepper. Add a layer of onion, tomatoes, and mozzarella, sprinkling parsley, thyme, salt and pepper over each layer.

3 Continue layering, finishing with a layer of eggplant slices. Sprinkle with the Parmesan cheese. Bake, uncovered, in the preheated oven for 20–30 minutes, or until the top is golden and the eggplants are tender. Serve hot.

cook's tip

It is a good idea to salt the eggplant slices first in order to draw out some of their bitterness. Simply sprinkle them with salt and leave them in a colander for an hour. Then rinse well, carefully squeeze out the moisture, and pat dry with paper towels.

CRÊPES

IN BRITAIN CRÊPES ARE ASSOCIATED WITH SHROVE TUESDAY, OR "PANCAKE DAY," WHEN PEOPLE ARE MEANT TO USE UP ANY RICH FOODS—PARTICULARLY EGGS—WHICH SHOULD NOT BE EATEN DURING LENT. IN OTHER COUNTRIES THE DAY IS KNOWN AS "MARDI GRAS" OR "FAT TUESDAY."

makes
10

preparation
10 minutes,
plus 30 minutes'
resting

cooking
15 minutes

ingredients
- ¾ cup all-purpose flour
- pinch of salt
- 1 egg, beaten
- 1¼ cups milk
- 10 tsp butter (for sweet crêpes) or oil (for savory ones)

TO SERVE
- lemon wedges
- superfine sugar
- warmed honey or jelly

1 Place the flour and salt in a mixing bowl. Make a well in the center and add the egg and half the milk. Using a whisk, beat the egg and milk together and gradually incorporate the flour. Continue beating until the mixture is smooth and there are no lumps. Gradually beat in the remaining milk. Pour the batter mixture into a pitcher and let stand for 30 minutes.

2 Heat a 7-inch/18-cm heavy-bottom skillet over medium heat. Add 1 teaspoon of the butter or oil, depending on what you are going to eat with the crêpes.

3 Pour in enough batter to just cover the bottom and swirl the batter around the skillet while tilting it so that you have a thin, even layer.

Cook for about 30 seconds and then lift up the edge of the crêpe and see if it is brown. Loosen the crêpe and flip it over with a spatula. Alternatively, have a go at tossing the crêpe by flipping the skillet quickly with a deft flick of the wrist and catching it carefully.

4 Cook on the other side until golden brown, then turn out onto a warmed plate, cover with foil, and keep warm while you cook the crêpes in the remaining butter or oil. Layer the crêpes with waxed paper so you can separate them at the end.

5 Serve the crêpes with lemon and sugar, warmed honey, or jelly, or a filling of your choice.

MERINGUES

THESE ARE JUST AS MERINGUES SHOULD BE—AS LIGHT AS AIR AND AT THE SAME TIME CRISP, WITH
A MELT-IN-THE-MOUTH QUALITY. MAKE SURE THAT THE BOWL YOU USE TO THE WHISK EGG WHITES
IS COMPLETELY CLEAN AND GREASE-FREE, OR YOUR MERINGUE MIXTURE WILL COLLAPSE.

makes
13

preparation
15 minutes, plus
8 hours' cooling

cooking
1½ hours

ingredients
- 4 egg whites
- salt
- scant ⅔ cup granulated sugar
- scant ⅔ cup superfine sugar
- 1¼ cups heavy cream, lightly whipped, to serve

1 Preheat the oven to 250°F/120°C. Line 3 baking sheets with sheets of baking parchment.

2 Place the egg whites and a pinch of salt in a large clean bowl and, using an electric hand-held whisk or balloon whisk, whisk until stiff. (You should be able to turn the bowl upside down without any movement from the whisked egg whites.)

3 Whisk in the granulated sugar, a little at a time; the meringue should begin to look glossy at this stage.

4 Sprinkle in the superfine sugar, a little at a time, and continue whisking until all the sugar has been incorporated and the meringue is thick, white, and forms peaks.

5 Transfer the meringue mixture to a pastry bag fitted with a ¾-inch/ 2-cm star tip. Pipe about 26 small whirls of the mixture onto the prepared baking sheets.

6 Bake in the preheated oven for 1½ hours, or until the meringues are pale golden in color and can be easily lifted off the paper. Let them cool overnight in the turned-off oven.

7 Just before serving, sandwich the meringues together in pairs with the cream and arrange on a serving plate.

variation
For a finer texture, replace the granulated sugar with superfine sugar.

LEMON MERINGUE PIE

A SWEET, TANGY FILLING AND A LOVELY LIGHT TOPPING CONTRAST SUPERBLY WITH A CRISP PASTRY SHELL. THIS POPULAR DESSERT LOOKS EVERY BIT AS LOVELY AS IT TASTES. IT'S USUALLY SERVED HOT AND THERE'S RARELY ANY LEFT OVER, BUT, IF THERE IS, IT'S ALSO DELICIOUS COLD.

serves

4

preparation

25 minutes, plus 30 minutes' resting

cooking

1 hour

ingredients

PIE DOUGH

- generous 1³⁄₈ cups all-purpose flour, plus extra for dusting
- scant ³⁄₄ cup butter, diced, plus extra for greasing
- scant ³⁄₈ cup confectioners' sugar, sifted
- finely grated rind of 1 lemon
- 1 egg yolk, beaten
- 3 tbsp milk

FILLING

- 3 tbsp cornstarch
- 1¹⁄₄ cups cold water
- juice and grated rind of 2 lemons
- ³⁄₄ cup superfine sugar
- 2 eggs, separated

1 To make the pie dough, sift the flour into a large bowl. Add the butter and rub it in until the mixture resembles bread crumbs. Mix in the remaining ingredients. Knead briefly on a lightly floured counter. Let rest for 30 minutes.

2 Preheat the oven to 350°F/180°C. Grease an 8-inch/20-cm ovenproof tart dish with butter.

3 Roll out the dough to a thickness of ¹⁄₄ inch/5 mm and line the dish

with it. Prick with a fork, then line with waxed paper and fill with baking beans. Bake for 15 minutes. Remove from the oven, then reduce the oven temperature to 300°F/150°C.

4 To make the filling, mix the cornstarch with a little water to form a paste. Pour the remaining water into a pan. Stir in the lemon juice and rind and cornstarch paste. Bring to a boil, while stirring, and cook for 2 minutes. Cool slightly,

then stir in 5 tablespoons of the sugar and the egg yolks and pour into the pastry shell. Whisk the egg whites in a separate bowl until stiff. Gradually whisk in the remaining sugar and spread over the pie. Bake in the oven for 40 minutes, or until the meringue is light brown. Remove and serve.

cook's tip

To produce a perfectly smooth meringue, whisk in the sugar a tablespoon at a time.

CRÈME BRÛLÉE TARTS

CARAMELIZED SUGAR MAKES A CONTRASTING AND DECORATIVE TOPPING ON THE CREAMY
FILLING IN THESE TARTS. IT IS STRANGE THAT WE ALL THINK CRÈME BRÛLÉE IS FRENCH BECAUSE IT
WAS ACTUALLY INVENTED IN THE ENGLISH UNIVERSITY TOWN OF CAMBRIDGE.

serves
6

preparation
25 minutes, plus
2½ hours' cooling
and chilling
overnight

cooking
30 minutes

ingredients

PIE DOUGH
- generous 1 cup all-purpose flour, plus extra for dusting
- ⅛ cup superfine sugar
- generous ½ cup butter, cut into small pieces
- 1 tbsp water
- raw brown sugar, for sprinkling
- fresh red currants, to decorate

FILLING
- 4 egg yolks
- ¼ cup superfine sugar
- 1¾ cups heavy cream
- 1 tsp vanilla extract

1 To make the pie dough, place the flour and sugar in a large bowl. Add the butter and rub it in with your fingertips until it resembles bread crumbs. Add the water and mix to a soft dough. Wrap the dough in plastic wrap and let chill for 30 minutes.

2 Roll out the dough on a lightly floured counter and use to line 6 x 4-inch/10-cm tart pans. Prick the bottom of the dough with a fork and let chill for 20 minutes.

3 Preheat the oven to 375°F/190°C. Line the pastry shells with foil and baking beans and bake in the oven for 15 minutes. Remove the foil and beans and cook for an additional 10 minutes until crisp and golden. Let cool.

4 Meanwhile, make the filling. Place the egg yolks and superfine sugar in a bowl and beat together until thick and pale. Heat the cream and vanilla extract in a pan until just below boiling point, then pour it onto the egg mixture, whisking constantly.

5 Return the mixture to a clean pan and bring to just below boiling point, stirring, until thick. Do not boil or it will curdle.

6 Let the mixture cool slightly, then pour it into the tart pans. Let cool then let chill overnight.

7 Preheat the broiler to medium. Sprinkle the tarts with the raw brown sugar. Place under the hot broiler for a few minutes until browned on top. Cool, then let chill for 2 hours before serving with fresh red currants.

cook's tip

The secret of crisp, light pie dough is to handle it as little as possible. When you're rubbing in the butter, use only the tips of your fingers, as the palms of your hands will warm up and partially melt the butter. If it's a hot day—or the kitchen is well heated —rinse your hands under cold running water, then dry before you start. Place the water for mixing the dough in the refrigerator to chill before using.

CRÈME CARAMEL

THIS CREAMY DESSERT WITH ITS CARAMELIZED TOPPING IS A FAVORITE THROUGHOUT EUROPE—CALLED CRÈME CARAMEL IN FRANCE, FLAN IN SPAIN, AND BAKED CUSTARD IN BRITAIN. THE CONTRASTING TEXTURES AND FLAVORS MAKE IT A TOP CHOICE FOR ADULTS AND KIDS ALIKE.

serves
4–6
preparation
15 minutes, plus
24 hours' chilling
cooking
1 1/2–1 3/4 hours

ingredients
- butter, for greasing
- generous 3/4 cup plus 2 tbsp superfine sugar
- 4 tbsp water
- 1/2 lemon
- generous 2 cups milk
- 1 vanilla bean
- 2 large eggs
- 2 large egg yolks

TO DECORATE
- sugared fruit
- fresh mint sprigs

1 Preheat the oven to 325°F/160°C. Lightly grease the side of a soufflé dish. To make the caramel, place generous 1/3 cup sugar with the water in a pan over medium high heat and cook, stirring, until the sugar dissolves. Boil until the syrup turns a deep golden brown.

2 Immediately remove from the heat and add in a few drops of lemon juice. Pour into the soufflé dish and swirl around. Set aside.

3 Pour the milk into a pan. Slit the vanilla bean lengthwise and add it to the milk. Bring to a boil, remove the pan from the heat and stir in the remaining sugar, stirring until it dissolves. Set aside.

4 Beat the eggs and egg yolks together in a bowl. Pour the milk mixture over them, whisking. Remove the vanilla bean. Strain the egg mixture into a bowl, then transfer to the soufflé dish.

5 Place the dish in a roasting pan with enough boiling water to come two-thirds up the side.

6 Bake in the preheated oven for 75–90 minutes, or until a knife inserted in the center comes out clean. Let cool completely. Cover with plastic wrap and let chill for at least 24 hours.

7 Run a round-bladed knife around the edge. Place an up-turned serving plate on top of the soufflé dish, then invert the plate and dish, giving a sharp shake halfway over. Lift off the soufflé dish and serve, decorated with sugared fruit and mint sprigs.

RICH VANILLA ICE CREAM

THIS RICH ICE CREAM PROVIDES A DELICIOUS FINISH TO A MEAL. YOU CAN SERVE IT EITHER AS IT IS, OR WITH A TOPPING OF YOUR CHOICE, SUCH AS A CHOCOLATE OR FRUIT SAUCE. IT ALSO MAKES AN EXCELLENT ACCOMPANIMENT TO FRUIT DESSERTS AND SWEET PIES.

serves
4–6

preparation
20 minutes, plus
30 minutes'
infusing and 4–6
hours' cooling
and freezing

cooking
15–20 minutes

ingredients
- 1¼ cups light cream
- 1¼ cups heavy cream or 2½ cups whipping cream
- 1 vanilla bean
- 4 large egg yolks
- generous ½ cup superfine sugar

1 Pour the light and heavy cream into a large heavy-bottom pan. Split open the vanilla bean and scrape out the seeds into the cream, then add the whole vanilla bean. Bring almost to a boil, then remove the pan from the heat and let infuse for 30 minutes.

2 Place the egg yolks and sugar in a large bowl and whisk together until pale and the mixture leaves a trail when the whisk is lifted. Remove the vanilla bean from the cream, then slowly add the cream to the egg mixture, stirring constantly with a wooden spoon. Strain the mixture into the rinsed-out pan or a double boiler and cook over low heat for

10–15 minutes, stirring constantly, until the mixture thickens enough to coat the back of the spoon. Do not allow the mixture to boil or it will curdle. Remove the custard from the heat and let cool for at least 1 hour, stirring occasionally to prevent a skin from forming.

3 If using an ice-cream machine, churn the cold custard in the machine following the manufacturer's instructions. Alternatively, freeze the custard in a freezerproof container, uncovered, for 1–2 hours, or until it begins to set around the edges. Turn the custard into a bowl and stir with a fork or beat in a food processor until smooth. Return to the freezer and freeze for an additional 2–3 hours until firm, or until required. Cover the container with a lid for storing.

CHOCOLATE CHIP ICE CREAM WITH HOT CHOCOLATE FUDGE SAUCE

THE ADDITION OF CHOCOLATE PIECES AND THE CHOCOLATE FUDGE SAUCE IN THIS RECIPE PROVIDES A PERFECT COUNTERPOINT TO THE CREAMINESS OF THE ICE CREAM. THIS IS A POPULAR DESSERT WITH CHILDREN AND ADULTS ALIKE.

serves
4–6

preparation
20 minutes, plus 30 minutes' infusing and 4–6 hours' cooling and freezing

cooking
15–20 minutes

ingredients
- 1¼ cups milk
- 1 vanilla bean
- 4 oz/115 g milk chocolate
- generous ⅜ cup superfine sugar
- 3 egg yolks
- 1¼ cups whipping cream

CHOCOLATE FUDGE SAUCE
- 1¾ oz/50 g milk chocolate, broken into pieces
- 2 tbsp butter
- 4 tbsp milk
- 1⅛ cups packed brown sugar
- 2 tbsp corn syrup

1 Pour the milk into a heavy-bottom pan. Add the vanilla bean and bring almost to a boil. Remove from the heat and let infuse for 30 minutes. Meanwhile, chop the chocolate into small pieces.

2 Place the sugar and egg yolks in a large bowl and whisk together until pale and the mixture leaves a trail when the whisk is lifted. Remove the vanilla bean from the milk, then slowly add the milk to the sugar mixture, stirring constantly with a wooden spoon. Strain the mixture into the rinsed-out pan or a double boiler and cook over low heat for 10–15 minutes, stirring constantly, until the mixture thickens enough to coat the back of the spoon. Do not boil or it will curdle.

3 Remove the custard from the heat and let cool for at least 1 hour, stirring occasionally to prevent a skin from forming. Meanwhile, whip the cream until it holds its shape. Chill in the refrigerator until required.

4 If using an ice-cream machine, fold the cold custard into the whipped cream, then churn in the machine following the manufacturer's instructions. Just before the ice cream freezes, add the chocolate pieces. Alternatively, freeze the custard in a freezerproof container, uncovered, for 1–2 hours, or until it begins to set around the edges. Turn the custard into a bowl and stir with a fork or beat in a food processor until smooth. Fold in the whipped cream and chocolate pieces. Return to the freezer and freeze for an additional 2–3 hours, or until firm or required. Cover with a lid for storing.

5 Make the sauce just before serving the ice cream. Place the chocolate, butter, and milk in a heatproof bowl set over a pan of simmering water and heat gently, stirring occasionally, until the chocolate has melted and the sauce is smooth. Transfer the mixture to a heavy-bottom pan and stir in the sugar and corn syrup. Heat gently until the sugar has dissolved, then bring to a boil and boil, without stirring, for 5 minutes. Serve the hot sauce poured over the ice cream.

TIRAMISÙ

LITERALLY MEANING "PICK ME UP," THIS SOPHISTICATED DESSERT HAS A REPUTATION FOR DOING EXACTLY THAT. IT'S NOT A TRADITIONAL DISH, BUT SINCE ITS INVENTION ABOUT THIRTY YEARS AGO IT HAS BECOME A FIRM FAVORITE ACROSS THE GLOBE.

serves
4
preparation
20 minutes, plus
2 hours' chilling
cooking
none

ingredients
- scant 1 cup strong black coffee, cooled to room temperature
- 4 tbsp orange liqueur, such as Cointreau
- 3 tbsp orange juice
- 16 Italian ladyfingers
- 1⅛ cups mascarpone cheese
- 1¼ cups heavy cream, lightly whipped
- 3 tbsp confectioners' sugar
- grated rind of 1 orange
- 2¼ oz/60 g semisweet chocolate, grated

TO DECORATE
- chopped toasted almonds
- crystallized orange peel
- chocolate shavings

1 Pour the cooled coffee into a pitcher and stir in the orange liqueur and orange juice. Place 8 of the ladyfingers in the bottom of a serving dish, then pour over half of the coffee mixture.

2 Place the mascarpone in a separate bowl together with the cream, confectioners' sugar, and orange rind and mix well. Spread half of the mascarpone mixture over the coffee-soaked ladyfingers, then arrange the remaining ladyfingers on top. Pour over the remaining coffee mixture then spread over the remaining mascarpone mixture. Sprinkle over the grated chocolate and let chill in the refrigerator for at least 2 hours. Serve decorated with chopped toasted almonds, crystallized orange peel, and chocolate shavings.

cook's tip

You can decorate this dessert with chopped mixed nuts instead of chopped toasted almonds. Alternatively, try replacing the orange liqueur with the same quantity of almond-flavored liqueur, such as Amaretto.

CHOCOLATE MILK SHAKE

A CHOCOLATE MILK SHAKE IS A SPECIAL TREAT AT ANY TIME OF DAY, AND THIS ONE IS THE ULTIMATE INDULGENCE. IT HAS A RICH, DEEP MOCHA FLAVOR, AND THE CHOCOLATE ICE CREAM MAKES IT THICK ENOUGH TO EAT WITH A SPOON. UNSURPRISINGLY, IT IS VERY POPULAR WITH CHILDREN.

serves
4

preparation
10 minutes

cooking
none

ingredients
- 1¼ cups milk
- 2 tbsp chocolate syrup
- 2 tbsp coffee syrup
- 1 lb 12 oz/800 g chocolate ice cream

TO DECORATE
- ⅔ cup heavy cream, whipped
- cocoa, for sprinkling

1 Pour the milk, chocolate syrup, and coffee syrup into a food processor or blender and gently process until blended. Add the ice cream and process to a smooth consistency.

2 Pour the mixture into tall glasses.

3 To decorate, spoon the cream into a pastry bag fitted with a large, star-shaped tip. Pipe generous amounts of cream on top of the milk shakes. Sprinkle over the cocoa and serve with straws.

NECTARINE MELT

MANGO AND NECTARINE IS AN INSPIRED COMBINATION, MADE ALL THE MORE SPECIAL WITH THE CLEVER ADDITION OF LEMON SHERBET. NOT ONLY DOES THIS MAKE A DELICIOUS DRINK THAT CAN BE SERVED AS A DESSERT, IT IS ALSO A NUTRITIOUS AND HEALTHY CHOICE.

serves
2

preparation
10 minutes

cooking
none

ingredients
- generous 1 cup milk
- 12 oz/350 g lemon sherbet
- 1 ripe mango, seeded and diced
- 2 ripe nectarines, pitted and diced

1 Pour the milk into a food processor, add half of the lemon sherbet, and process gently until combined. Add the remaining sherbet and process until smooth.

2 When the mixture is thoroughly blended, gradually add the diced mango and nectarines and process until smooth.

3 Pour the mixture into tall glasses, add straws, and serve.

2

FISH AND SHELLFISH

WHO CAN RESIST THE AROMA AND FLAVOR OF FRESH
FISH AND SHELLFISH, LOVINGLY PREPARED? YOU CAN
COOK AND SERVE SEAFOOD IN A MULTITUDE OF WAYS,
FROM STIR-FRIES AND CHARGRILLS TO BAKES AND
BARBECUES. THIS SECTION PRESENTS A STUNNING
COLLECTION OF DISHES THAT YOU WILL WANT TO
MAKE AGAIN AND AGAIN.

INTRODUCTION

FISH AND SHELLFISH ARE VERY GOOD FOR YOU: THEY ARE FULL OF PROTEIN, IODINE, AND MAGNESIUM, WHICH ARE ESSENTIAL FOR BUILDING TISSUE, REGULATING THE METABOLISM, AND KEEPING THE BOWEL HEALTHY. OILY FISH IN PARTICULAR ARE RICH IN ESSENTIAL FATTY ACIDS, WHICH HELP TO LOWER CHOLESTEROL AND SUPPORT THE IMMUNE SYSTEM.

Buying and storing fresh fish

Nowadays there is a wide variety of fish available. You can buy fresh flatfish, such as flounder, sole, or halibut, or roundfish, such as cod, haddock, salmon, or trout. You can also buy preserved fish, which have been smoked, dried, or salted. When buying fresh whole fish, choose those that smell fresh or that smell of the sea. Avoid any that smell of ammonia. They should have moist, full eyes and shiny, firm bodies. You can ask your fish supplier to skin, gut, and fillet whole larger fish for you. Refrigerate the fish as soon as you get home. Fresh fish is best eaten on the day of purchase, but it will keep for a day or two if necessary. Frozen fish will keep for up to six months in the freezer, but will need thawing in the refrigerator for at least 8 hours before use. Oily fish, such as mackerel, should be wrapped well in clean damp cloths and stored in the refrigerator. Lower-fat white fish, such as cod and haddock, can be covered with plastic wrap. Use it by the "best before" date on the packaging.

Smoked fish

You can buy a wide variety of smoked fish. Smoked salmon is very popular and is usually served cold with slices of lemon. Smoked trout has a mild flavor and is best partnered with horseradish or slices of lemon. Smoked mackerel has a rich flavor and needs a sharp sauce, such as dill or mustard. Smoked haddock is delicious served with a creamy sauce or in kedgerees, while smoked cod is popular in pies. Kippered herrings are best broiled or poached. Fresh smoked fish should be wrapped well in plastic wrap and stored in the refrigerator. Smoked fish is often bought vacuum-packed. Store it in the refrigerator and use by the "best before" date.

Brown trout

Sole

White fish

There is a wide range of white fish available these days. Some are low in fat, such as cod and haddock, while others are rich in healthy essential fatty acids, such as sardines.

Cod
This roundfish has firm, white, flaky flesh and a mild flavor. It can be baked, broiled, poached, pan-fried, or deep-fried in batter or bread crumbs.

Haddock
Like cod, this roundfish has firm, white flesh and a mild flavor. It can be baked, broiled, poached, pan-fried, or deep-fried, and in many recipes is interchangeable with cod.

Hake
Milder-flavored than cod, this round-fish can be fried, baked, or steamed and is also useful in soups.

Trout
Like salmon, this roundfish is available farmed or wild, but the wild variety is rare. It can be pan-fried, broiled, poached, steamed, barbecued, or baked. This is an oily fish, which means that it is rich in essential fatty acids.

Halibut
This is a large flatfish that has firm flesh and an excellent flavor and are interchangeable in many recipes. You can fry, poach, steam, broil, or bake both these fish.

Sole
in the US, sole usually refers to the flatfish found in the Pacific Ocean, from California to Alaska. It has less flavor than the true sole found in European waters and needs a little added flavoring to bring out its best qualities. It can be pan fried, baked, steamed, or broiled.

Herrings, sardines, sprats, and whitebait
These small fish have lots of bones, so it is best to ask your fish supplier to remove the innards and as many bones as possible. They can be barbecued, deep-fried, baked, or broiled. They are also oily fish, and therefore rich in essential fatty acids.

Mackerel
This is a roundfish with a delicious flavor. It is at its best when simply broiled, but can also be fried or barbecued. It is another oily fish so is good for your health.

Flounder
This flatfish needs extra flavoring but is very good when pan-fried or deep-fried, baked, broiled, poached, or steamed.

Salmon
This roundfish is available farmed or wild. A popular fish, it can be pan-fried, broiled, poached, steamed, barbecued, or baked. Salmon en croûte or en papillote (salmon baked in pie dough or in parchment) are particularly popular dishes. Salmon is another oily fish.

Tuna
This is a round oily fish with firm, "meaty" flesh that makes wonderful steaks with only a very mild fish flavor. The steaks are excellent chargrilled for 2–3 minutes each side (do not overcook). You can also bake, barbecue, broil, braise, or stew fresh tuna.

Herring

Mackerel

Buying and storing shellfish

Shellfish can cause food poisoning, so always buy them as fresh as possible from a reputable supplier. Shellfish should smell fresh or sweet—avoid any that smell of chlorine or sulfur. If you are buying mussels, clams, or oysters, the shells should be tightly closed and not cracked or damaged.

Refrigerate shellfish in a covered container as soon as you get home and use on the day of purchase. If you buy live lobster or crabs, place something heavy on top of the container to stop them escaping. Handle shellfish as little as possible and prepare with thoroughly clean equipment and hands.

Preparation and cooking techniques

Preparation techniques vary enormously depending on the type of shellfish you are using. If you are in any doubt, your local fish supplier will be able to give you advice. Shellfish does not need to cook for long periods of time so stick to the recommended cooking times. Do not overcook it or you could impair the texture and/or taste. Squid, for example, becomes unpleasantly rubbery if cooked for too long.

Crab

Fresh and frozen shellfish

You can buy fresh shellfish from fish suppliers and many stores and supermarkets. In some cases, shrimp for example, you can also buy them ready prepared, cooked, and frozen.

Crab and lobster

You can buy crabs and lobsters live or cooked. If you buy them live, make sure the claws are tied with string to keep them still. Put them in the freezer for 1 hour before cooking to desensitize. To cook, take a large pan and pour in enough water or stock to cover the crab or lobster. Bring it to a boil, add the crab or lobster, cover the pan, and boil until it turns red. Allow 5 minutes of cooking for every 1 lb/ 450 g of crab. For a lobster, allow 5 minutes for the first 1 lb/450 g, plus an extra 3 minutes for each further 1 lb/450 g. To remove the cooked meat from the crab, crack the claws and remove and set aside the white meat. Snap off the tail, then use your hands to break the shell. Lift out the body, cut it in half lengthwise, and scoop out the meat. Then lift out the brown meat from the shell. The edible parts of a lobster are the meat in the tail and claws, the liver, and the roe if the lobster is female. Cooking a lobster and removing the meat can be fiddly, however, so it is usually best to ask your fish supplier to do this for you.

Mussels

Mussels

Use mussels on the day of purchase and keep them in lightly salted water before use. To clean and debeard them, use a small knife to scrape off any barnacles from the shells, then pull out and discard any clumps of hair (these are called "beards"). Use a stiff brush to scrub the shells under cold running water, then tap them all with the handle of the knife and discard any that do not close tightly. To steam them, heat a little liquid (water, stock, or wine) in a large pan, add the cleaned mussels, cover the pan, and steam them, shaking the pan occasionally, for 5–6 minutes. Remove from the heat and discard any mussels that remain closed. You can also broil or bake them half-shelled, or stew them shelled.

Oysters

These shellfish are usually eaten raw. Use a stiff brush to scrub the shells under cold running water, and discard any that are open. To open an oyster, insert a knife blade between the two shell halves and twist it to prise them open. Use a spoon to lift out the oyster inside (you will need to cut it from the muscle underneath). Serve it on a half-shell. You can also bake or broil oysters in their half-shells, or stew them shelled.

Shrimp

These come in different sizes and you can buy them shelled or unshelled, cooked or raw. Cooked, shelled shrimp are also available frozen. To shell and devein a raw shrimp, carefully peel off the shell (you can remove the tail or leave it on for decorative effect). Using a small knife, make a shallow cut along the dark vein to reveal it, then remove it with the knife's tip. Discard the vein, then rinse the shrimp under cold running water and pat dry with paper towels. Shrimp require very little cooking—for example, you need to stir-fry them for only 2–3 minutes until they turn pink. You can pan-fry, stir-fry, broil, bake, barbecue, or steam them.

Scallops

These have a delicate flavor and are becoming increasingly popular. They should be creamy-white with pink corals. They need a minimal amount of cooking, usually 1–2 minutes on each side if you are pan-frying them shelled. You can also broil or bake them in their half-shells.

Squid

You can buy squid whole or already prepared. The edible parts are the tentacles, fins, pouch, and the ink. Sauté the squid for 2–3 minutes only—do not overcook it or it will be rubbery. You can also deep-fry, bake, poach, and stew it.

Clams

Use a stiff brush to scrub the shells under cold running water, and discard any that open. To open a clam, insert a knife blade between the two shell halves and twist it to prise them open. Use a spoon to lift out the soft flesh inside. You can eat clams raw, or you can steam them in their shells for 4 minutes or until they have opened. You can also bake or broil them in their half-shells, or stew them shelled.

Shrimp

Lobster

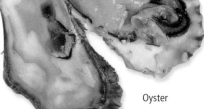

Oyster

Squid

SALMON COULIBIAC

THIS DELICIOUS FISH PIE IS IDEAL FOR ENTERTAINING. THE RECIPE ORIGINATED IN RUSSIA AND TRADITIONALLY CONTAINED BUCKWHEAT INSTEAD OF RICE. THE ORIGINAL VERSION WAS ALSO MUCH LARGER AND NEEDED MORE THAN ONE PERSON TO CARRY IT TO THE TABLE.

serves
4

preparation
40 minutes

cooking
50–60 minutes

ingredients
- ¼ cup long-grain rice
- pinch of salt
- 3 eggs
- 2 tbsp vegetable oil
- 1 onion, finely chopped
- 1 garlic clove, crushed
- 1 tsp finely grated lemon rind
- 2 tbsp chopped fresh parsley
- 1 tbsp chopped fresh dill
- 1 lb/450 g salmon fillet, skinned and cubed
- 1 lb 2 oz/500 g puff pastry
- butter, for greasing
- beaten egg, to glaze

QUICK HOLLANDAISE SAUCE
- ¾ cup butter
- 1 tbsp wine vinegar
- 2 tbsp lemon juice
- 3 egg yolks
- salt and pepper

1 Preheat the oven to 400°F/200°C. Cook the rice with the pinch of salt in plenty of boiling water for 7–8 minutes until tender. Drain well and set aside. Bring a small pan of water to a boil and add the eggs. Cook for 8 minutes from when the water returns to a boil. Drain and refresh under cold water. When cool enough to handle, shell and slice thinly.

2 Heat the oil in a skillet. Add the onion and cook gently for 5 minutes, or until softened. Add the garlic and cook for an additional 30 seconds. Add to the rice with the lemon rind, parsley, dill, and salmon.

3 Roll out the puff pastry to a rectangle measuring 16 x 12 inches/ 40 x 30 cm. Lift the pastry onto a lightly greased baking sheet. Spoon half the filling onto one half of the pastry, leaving a border of about ¾ inch/2 cm. Top with the sliced eggs, then the remaining filling.

4 Dampen the outside edges of the pastry with a little beaten egg then fold over the remaining pastry. Crimp the edges to seal well. Mark the pastry using a small sharp knife, taking care not to cut through the pastry. Decorate with pastry trimmings and brush with beaten egg.

5 Bake in the preheated oven for 30–35 minutes, or until the pastry is risen and golden.

6 To make the sauce, place the butter in a small pan and melt slowly. Place the wine vinegar and lemon juice in another pan and bring to a boil. Meanwhile, place the egg yolks and a pinch of salt in a food processor or blender and blend together. With the motor still running, gradually add the hot vinegar and lemon juice. When the butter begins to boil, start to pour this into the machine in a steady stream until all the butter has been added and the sauce has thickened. Season to taste with salt and pepper.

7 Keep warm by placing in a bowl over hot water. Serve the pie with the hollandaise sauce on the side.

FISH CAKES

THESE MOUTHWATERING FISH CAKES ARE FULL OF EXCITING ASIAN FLAVORS TO TEMPT THE TASTE
BUDS. THEY ARE IDEAL FOR ENTERTAINING BECAUSE YOU CAN MAKE BOTH THE FISH CAKES AND
DIPPING SAUCE IN ADVANCE, THEN FRY THE FISH CAKES AND REHEAT THE SAUCE WHEN NEEDED.

serves
4

preparation
25 minutes,
plus 30 minutes'
cooling

cooking
20 minutes

ingredients
- 1 lb/450 g white fish fillets,
  skinned and cut into cubes
- 1 egg white
- 2 kaffir lime leaves,
  coarsely torn
- 1 tbsp green curry paste
- 2 oz/55 g green beans,
  finely chopped
- 1 fresh red chili, seeded and
  finely chopped
- bunch of fresh
  cilantro, chopped
- 2 tbsp vegetable or peanut
  oil, for pan-frying
- 1 fresh green chili, seeded
  and sliced, to serve

DIPPING SAUCE
- generous ½ cup
  superfine sugar
- 1½ tbsp water
- ¼ cup white wine vinegar
- 1 small carrot, cut into
  thin sticks
- 2-inch/5-cm piece
  cucumber, peeled, seeded,
  and cut into thin sticks

1 Place the fish in a food processor
with the egg white, lime leaves,
and curry paste and process until
smooth. Transfer the mixture to
a bowl and stir in the green beans,
red chili, and cilantro.

2 With dampened hands, shape the
mixture into small patties, about
2 inches/5 cm across. Place them
on a large plate in a single layer and
let chill for 30 minutes.

3 Meanwhile, make the dipping
sauce. Place the sugar in a pan with

the water and vinegar and heat
gently, stirring until the sugar has
dissolved. Add the carrot and
cucumber, then remove from the
heat and let cool.

4 Heat the oil in a skillet and
pan-fry the fish cakes, in batches,
until golden brown on both sides.
Drain on paper towels and keep
warm while you cook the remaining
batches. If you like, reheat the
dipping sauce. Top the fish cakes with
chili slices and serve immediately
with the sauce.

BROILED TROUT FILLETS

THESE LIGHTLY BROILED TROUT FILLETS HAVE A DELICIOUS CRISPY COATING OF TOASTED NUTS AND MELTED CHEESE. THEY ARE RICH IN PROTEIN, AND ARE DELICIOUS SERVED WITH RICE AND TWISTS OF LEMON, OR FRESHLY BAKED WEDGES OF POTATO AND OTHER ROOT VEGETABLES.

serves
4

preparation
20 minutes

cooking
5 minutes

ingredients
- 2 tbsp chopped toasted hazelnuts
- 2 tbsp ground almonds
- 4 oz/115 g Cheddar cheese, grated
- 4 tbsp fresh bread crumbs, white or whole wheat
- 1 egg
- 1 tbsp milk
- 4 brown trout fillets, about 6 oz/175 g each
- 2 tbsp all-purpose flour
- salt and pepper
- fresh flat-leaf parsley sprigs, to garnish
- freshly cooked rice, to serve

1 Preheat the broiler to medium. Place the hazelnuts and almonds in a large bowl. Add the cheese and bread crumbs and mix together. Place the egg and milk in a separate bowl and beat together. Season to taste with salt and pepper.

2 Rinse the fish fillets and pat dry with paper towels. Coat the fillets in the flour, then dip them into the egg mixture. Transfer them to the bowl containing the nuts and cheese, and turn the fillets in the mixture until thoroughly coated.

3 Cook the fish under the hot broiler for 5 minutes, turning once during the cooking time, or until golden and cooked through. Remove from the broiler and transfer to warmed plates. Garnish with parsley sprigs and serve immediately with freshly cooked rice.

BROILED SARDINES

ALL ALONG EUROPE'S MEDITERRANEAN COAST, SMALL HARBORSIDE RESTAURANTS ARE GRILLING THE DAY'S CATCH OF SARDINES. THIS RECIPE MAKES FULL USE OF THE WONDERFUL FLAVORS OF THE MEDITERRANEAN, WITH A HINT OF CHILI SPICE IN THE DRESSING.

serves
4–6

preparation
30 minutes plus
2½ hours' cooling
and chilling

cooking
3–5 minutes

ingredients
- 12 sardines
- olive oil
- fresh flat-leaf parsley sprigs, to garnish
- lemon wedges, to serve

DRESSING
- ⅔ cup extra virgin olive oil
- finely grated rind of 1 large lemon
- 4 tbsp lemon juice, or to taste
- 4 shallots, thinly sliced
- 1 small fresh red chili, seeded and finely chopped
- 1 large garlic clove, finely chopped
- salt and pepper

1 Preheat the broiler to medium. To make the dressing, place all the ingredients in a screw-top jar, season with salt and pepper, then shake until blended. Pour into a nonmetallic baking dish that is large enough to hold the sardines in a single layer. Set aside until required.

2 To prepare the sardines, chop off the heads and make a slit all along the length of each belly. Pull out the insides, rinse the fish inside and out with cold water, and pat dry with paper towels.

3 Line the broiler pan with foil, shiny side up. Brush the foil with a little olive oil to prevent the sardines sticking. Arrange the sardines on the foil in a single layer and brush with a little of the dressing. Broil for 90 seconds.

4 Turn the fish over, brush with a little more dressing and continue broiling for 90 seconds, or until they are cooked through and flake easily.

5 Transfer the fish to the dish with the dressing. Spoon the dressing over the fish and let cool completely. Cover and let chill for at least 2 hours to allow the flavors to blend.

6 Transfer the sardines to a serving platter and garnish with parsley. Serve with lemon wedges for squeezing over.

GRILLED SEA BASS WITH STEWED ARTICHOKES

IN THIS IDEAL DISH FOR A LUNCH OR LIGHT SUPPER, BABY GLOBE ARTICHOKES ARE SLOWLY
COOKED WITH OLIVE OIL, GARLIC, THYME, AND LEMON TO CREATE A SOFT BLEND OF FLAVORS THAT
HARMONIZE VERY WELL WITH THE FISH, WITHOUT BEING OVERPOWERING.

serves
6
preparation
30 minutes
cooking
35–45 minutes

ingredients
- 4 lb/1.8 kg baby
  globe artichokes
- 2 1/2 tbsp fresh lemon
  juice, plus the cut halves
  of the lemon
- 2/3 cup olive oil
- 10 garlic cloves,
  finely sliced
- 1 tbsp chopped fresh
  thyme, plus extra to garnish
- 6 x 4 oz/115 g sea bass
  fillets
- 1 tbsp olive oil
- salt and pepper
- crusty bread, to serve

1 Peel away the tough outer leaves of each artichoke until the yellow-green heart is revealed. Slice off the pointed top at about halfway between the point and the top of the stem. Cut off the stem and pare off what is left of the dark green leaves around the bottom of the artichoke.

2 Submerge the prepared artichokes in water containing the cut halves of the lemon to prevent them browning. When all the artichokes have been prepared, turn them choke side down and slice thickly.

3 Heat the oil in a large pan. Add the artichoke pieces, garlic, thyme,

lemon juice, and seasoning, cover, and cook the artichokes over low heat for 20–30 minutes, without coloring, until tender.

4 Meanwhile, preheat a ridged stovetop broiler pan or light a barbecue. Brush the sea bass fillets with the 1 tablespoon olive oil and season well. Cook on the broiler pan or over hot coals for 3–4 minutes on each side until just tender.

5 Divide the stewed artichokes between plates and top each with a fish fillet. Garnish with chopped thyme and serve with crusty bread.

variation
Artichokes cooked this way also
suit cod, halibut, or salmon.

SOLE À LA MEUNIÈRE

USE FLOUNDER OR DOVER SOLE, WHICH IS IMPORTED FROZEN INTO THE UNITED STATES
FROM NORTHERN EUROPEAN COUNTRIES. IT IS DELICATELY FLAVORED, SO THE COMBINATION OF
CHOPPED FRESH PARSLEY, LEMON, AND MELTED BUTTER COMPLEMENTS THE FISH PERFECTLY.

serves

4

preparation

20 minutes

cooking

15 minutes

ingredients

- 4 tbsp all-purpose flour
- 1 tsp salt
- 4 x 14 oz/400 g Dover sole, cleaned and skinned
- generous ⅔ cup butter
- 3 tbsp lemon juice
- 1 tbsp chopped fresh parsley
- ¼ of a preserved lemon, finely chopped (optional)
- fresh parsley sprigs, to garnish
- lemon wedges, to serve

1 Preheat the broiler to medium. Mix the flour with the salt and place on a large plate or tray. Drop the fish into the flour, one at a time, and shake well to remove any excess. Melt 3 tablespoons of the butter in a small pan and use to brush the fish liberally all over.

2 Place the fish under the hot broiler and cook for 5 minutes on each side.

3 Meanwhile, melt the remaining butter in a pan. Pour cold water into a bowl that is large enough to take the bottom of the pan. Keep nearby.

4 Heat the butter until it turns a golden brown and begins to smell nutty. Remove at once from the heat and immerse the bottom of the pan in the cold water, to stop cooking.

5 Place the fillets on individual plates, drizzle with the lemon juice, and sprinkle with the parsley and preserved lemon, if using. Pour over the browned butter, garnish with parsley sprigs, and serve immediately with lemon wedges for squeezing over.

cook's tip

If you have a large enough skillet (or two) you can pan-fry the floured fish in butter, if you prefer.

PAELLA

PAELLA IS A RUSTIC SPANISH DISH OF SHELLFISH, SAUSAGE (CHORIZO), POULTRY, VEGETABLES, AND RICE, SEASONED WITH GOLDEN SAFFRON. IT IS BEST TO USE STARCHY RICE, SUCH AS RISOTTO, TO ENSURE YOU RECREATE THE TRADITIONAL CREAMINESS THAT IS THE HALLMARK OF THIS DISH.

serves
4
preparation
15 minutes
cooking
30 minutes

ingredients
- 3 tbsp olive oil
- 2 tbsp butter
- 2 garlic cloves, chopped
- 1 onion, chopped
- 2 large tomatoes, seeded and diced
- ¾ cup frozen peas
- 1 red bell pepper, seeded and chopped
- 1 cup risotto rice
- 2 tsp dried mixed herbs
- 1 tsp saffron powder
- scant 2 cups chicken stock
- 4 skinless, boneless chicken breasts
- 5½ oz/150 g lean chorizo, skinned
- 7 oz/200 g cooked lobster meat
- 7 oz/200 g shrimp, shelled and deveined
- 1 tbsp chopped fresh flat-leaf parsley
- salt and pepper

TO GARNISH
- pinch of cayenne pepper
- red bell pepper strips

1 Heat the oil and butter in a large skillet over medium heat. Add the garlic and onion and cook, stirring, for 3 minutes, or until slightly softened.

2 Add the tomatoes, peas, red bell pepper, rice, mixed herbs, and saffron and cook, stirring, for 2 minutes. Pour in the stock and bring to a boil. Reduce the heat to low and cook, stirring, for 10 minutes.

3 Chop the chicken into bite-size pieces and add to the skillet. Cook, stirring occasionally, for

5 minutes. Chop up the chorizo, add to the skillet and cook for 3 minutes. Chop up the lobster meat and add to the skillet with the shrimp and parsley. Season with salt and pepper and cook, stirring, for an additional 2 minutes.

4 Remove the skillet from the heat, transfer the paella to a large serving platter or individual plates, garnish with cayenne and red bell pepper strips, and serve.

TRADITIONAL GREEK BAKED FISH

THE TRADITIONAL GREEK WAY OF BAKING FISH IS TO COOK IT WHOLE WITH TOMATOES AND LEMONS (WHICH ARE EATEN WITH THE RIND ON), ALTHOUGH BOTH THE GREEKS AND THE TURKS CLAIM TO HAVE ORIGINATED THE METHOD. A VARIETY OF FISH CAN BE COOKED THIS WAY SO TAKE YOUR PICK.

serves
4–6

preparation
30 minutes

cooking
1 hour 20 minutes–1 hour 40 minutes

ingredients
- 5 tbsp olive oil
- 2 onions, thinly sliced
- 2 garlic cloves, finely chopped
- 2 carrots, thinly sliced
- 2 celery stalks, thinly sliced
- 2/3 cup dry white wine
- 14 oz/400 g canned chopped tomatoes
- pinch of sugar
- 1 large lemon, thinly sliced
- 2 tbsp chopped fresh flat-leaf parsley
- 1 tsp chopped fresh marjoram
- 2–3 lb/1–1.3 kg round whole fish, such as sea bream, sea bass, porgy, or red snapper, scaled and cleaned
- butter, for greasing
- salt and pepper

1 Preheat the oven to 350°F/180°C. Heat 4 tablespoons of the oil in a large pan. Add the onions and garlic and cook for 5 minutes until softened. Add the carrots and celery and fry for 5–10 minutes until slightly softened.

2 Pour the wine into the pan and bring to a boil. Add the tomatoes and their juice, the sugar, half the lemon slices, salt and pepper, and let simmer for 20 minutes. Add the parsley and marjoram.

3 Place the fish in a greased, shallow ovenproof dish. Pour the vegetables around the fish, arranging some of the lemon slices on top. Sprinkle with the remaining oil and season to taste with salt and pepper.

4 Bake the fish, uncovered, in the preheated oven for 45 minutes– 1 hour depending on the thickness of the fish, until tender. Serve immediately, straight from the oven.

SEAFOOD GRATIN

A DISH THAT IS COOKED "AU GRATIN" IS TRADITIONALLY TOPPED WITH BREAD CRUMBS AND/OR
CHEESE, AND THEN BAKED UNTIL GOLDEN BROWN. USUALLY IT IS THEN SERVED IN THE BAKING DISH.
THIS SEAFOOD GRATIN IS MADE WITH A WONDERFUL COMBINATION OF FRESH FISH AND SHELLFISH.

serves
4
preparation
15 minutes
cooking
1 hour

ingredients
- 1 lb/450 g cod fillets
- 8 oz/225 g shrimp, shelled and deveined
- 8 oz/225 g scallops
- 3 tbsp extra virgin olive oil
- 1 garlic clove, chopped
- 4 scallions, chopped
- 1 zucchini, sliced
- 15 oz/425 g canned plum tomatoes
- 2 tbsp chopped fresh basil
- scant 1 cup fresh bread crumbs
- 2¾ oz/75 g Cheddar cheese, grated
- salt and pepper
- freshly cooked broccoli and cauliflower, to serve

1 Preheat the oven to 375°F/190°C. Bring a large pan of water to a boil, then reduce the heat to medium. Rinse the cod, pat dry with paper towels and add to the pan. Cook for 5 minutes. Add the shrimp and cook for 3 minutes, then add the scallops and cook for 2 minutes. Drain, refresh under cold running water, and drain again.

2 Heat 2 tablespoons of the oil in a skillet over low heat. Add the garlic and scallions and cook, stirring, for 3 minutes. Add the zucchini and cook for 3 minutes, then add the tomatoes with their juice, and the basil. Season to taste with salt and pepper and let simmer for 10 minutes.

3 Brush a shallow baking dish with the remaining oil and arrange the seafood in it. Remove the pan from the heat and pour the sauce over the fish. Sprinkle over the bread crumbs and top with cheese. Bake in the oven for 30 minutes until golden. Serve with freshly cooked broccoli and cauliflower.

SHRIMP & PINEAPPLE CURRY

THIS DELICIOUS CURRY EXUDES EXCITING THAI AROMAS AND FLAVORS. IT LOOKS VERY IMPRESSIVE, YET IT TAKES ONLY A FEW MINUTES TO PREPARE AND COOK. IT HAS THE PERFECT PARTNER IN JASMINE RICE, BUT YOU COULD ALSO SERVE IT WITH COCONUT RICE.

serves
4
preparation
10 minutes
cooking
10–15 minutes

ingredients
- 2 cups coconut cream
- ½ fresh pineapple, peeled and chopped
- 2 tbsp Thai red curry paste
- 2 tbsp Thai fish sauce
- 2 tsp sugar
- 12 oz/350 g raw jumbo shrimp
- 2 tbsp chopped fresh cilantro
- edible flower, to garnish
- steamed jasmine rice, to serve

1 Place the coconut cream, pineapple, curry paste, fish sauce, and sugar in a large skillet. Heat gently over medium heat until almost boiling. Shell and devein the shrimp. Add the shrimp and chopped cilantro and let simmer gently for 3 minutes, or until the shrimp are cooked.

2 Garnish with a fresh flower and serve with steamed jasmine rice.

SQUID & RED ONION STIR-FRY

SQUID REALLY IS WONDERFUL IF QUICKLY COOKED AS IN THIS RECIPE—IT IS ONLY TOUGH AND RUBBERY IF IT IS OVERCOOKED. THE ADDITION OF THE GREEN PEPPER AND SLICED RED ONION IN THIS DISH PROVIDES AN IDEAL CONTRAST TO THE SQUID IN TERMS OF TEXTURE AND FLAVOR.

serves
4
preparation
10 minutes
cooking
12–15 minutes

ingredients
- 1 lb/450 g squid rings
- 2 tbsp all-purpose flour
- ½ tsp salt
- 1 green bell pepper
- 2 tbsp peanut oil
- 1 red onion, sliced
- 5 ¾ oz/160 g jar black bean sauce

1 Rinse the squid rings under cold running water and pat dry with paper towels.

2 Place the all-purpose flour and salt in a bowl and mix together. Add the squid rings and toss until they are finely coated.

3 Using a sharp knife, seed the bell pepper. Slice the bell pepper into thin strips.

4 Heat the peanut oil in a large preheated wok.

5 Add the bell pepper and red onion to the wok and stir-fry for 2 minutes, or until the vegetables are just beginning to soften.

6 Add the squid rings to the wok and cook for an additional 5 minutes, or until the squid is cooked through.

7 Add the black bean sauce to the wok and heat through until the juices are bubbling. Transfer to warmed bowls and serve immediately.

cook's tip

Serve this dish with fried rice or noodles tossed in soy sauce for a complete meal.

TEMPURA WHITEBAIT

TEMPURA IS A CLASSIC JAPANESE BATTER MADE WITH EGG, FLOUR, AND WATER. THE BATTER IS VERY COLD AND LUMPY, WHICH GIVES THE FINISHED DISH ITS CHARACTERISTIC APPEARANCE. IDEALLY, IT SHOULD BE EATEN STRAIGHT AWAY WHILE STILL HOT.

serves
4

preparation
15 minutes

cooking
10 minutes

ingredients
- 1 lb/450 g whitebait, thawed if frozen
- ¾ cup all-purpose flour
- 1¾ cups cornstarch
- ½ tsp salt
- scant 1 cup cold water
- 1 egg
- a few ice cubes
- vegetable oil, for deep-frying
- lemon wedges, to serve

CHILI AND LIME MAYONNAISE
- 1 egg yolk
- 1 tbsp lime juice
- 1 fresh red chili, seeded and finely chopped
- 2 tbsp chopped fresh cilantro
- scant 1 cup light olive oil
- salt and pepper

1 To make the mayonnaise, place the egg yolk, lime juice, chili, cilantro, and seasoning in a food processor and process until foaming. With the machine still running, gradually add the olive oil, drop by drop, until the mixture begins to thicken. Continue adding the oil in a steady stream until all the oil has been incorporated. Taste and adjust the seasoning and add a little hot water if the mixture is too thick. Set aside.

2 Rinse the whitebait and pat dry. Set aside on paper towels. Sift together the all-purpose flour, cornstarch, and salt into a large bowl. Whisk together the water, egg, and ice then pour onto the flour mix. Whisk briefly until the mixture is runny, but still lumpy with dry bits of flour still apparent.

3 Meanwhile, fill a deep pan about a third full with vegetable oil and heat to 375°F/190°C, or until a cube of bread browns in 30 seconds.

4 Dip the whitebait, a few at a time, into the batter and carefully drop into the hot oil. Deep-fry for 1 minute until the batter is crisp but not browned. Drain on paper towels and keep warm while you cook the remaining fish. Serve hot with the mayonnaise and lemon wedges.

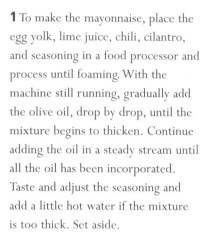
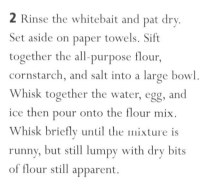

COD & FRENCH FRIES

THIS IS THE GENUINE ARTICLE—A CRUNCHY, DEEP GOLDEN BATTER SURROUNDING PERFECTLY COOKED FISH, SERVED WITH GOLDEN CRISPY FRENCH FRIES. IF YOU'VE NEVER HAD FRIES WITH MAYONNAISE, TRY THEM WITH THIS LOVELY MUSTARDY VERSION AND YOU'LL BE CONVERTED.

serves
4

preparation
30 minutes, plus
1 hour resting

cooking
40–50 minutes

ingredients
- 2 lb/900 g potatoes
- 4 x 6 oz/175 g thick pieces cod fillet, preferably from the head end
- vegetable oil, for deep-frying
- salt and pepper
- fresh parsley sprigs, to garnish
- lemon wedges, to serve

BATTER
- 1/2 oz/15 g fresh yeast
- 1 1/4 cups beer
- scant 1 2/3 cups all-purpose flour
- 2 tsp salt

MAYONNAISE
- 1 egg yolk
- 1 tsp whole grain mustard
- 1 tbsp lemon juice
- scant 1 cup light olive oil
- salt and pepper

1 To make the batter, cream the yeast with a little of the beer to a smooth paste. Gradually stir in the rest of the beer. Sift the all-purpose flour and salt into a bowl, make a well in the center, and add the yeast mixture. Gradually whisk to a smooth batter. Cover and let stand at room temperature for 1 hour.

2 To make the mayonnaise, place the egg yolk, mustard, lemon juice, and seasoning in a food processor. Process for 30 seconds until frothy. With the machine still running, gradually add the olive oil, drop by drop, until the mixture begins to thicken. Continue adding the oil in a steady stream until all the oil has

been incorporated. Taste and adjust the seasoning if necessary. Thin with a little hot water if the mayonnaise is too thick. Let chill until required.

3 Cut the potatoes into fries about 1/2 inch/1.5 cm thick. Heat a large pan half-filled with vegetable oil to 275°F/140°C, or until a cube of bread browns in 1 minute. Cook the fries in 2 batches for 5 minutes, or until they are cooked through but not browned. Place the fries to drain on paper towels and set aside.

4 Increase the heat to 325°F/160°C, or until a cube of bread browns in 45 seconds. Season the fish then dip into the batter. Deep-fry 2 pieces at

a time for 7–8 minutes until deep golden brown and cooked through. Drain on paper towels and keep warm while you cook the remaining fish. Keep all the fish warm while you finish cooking the fries.

5 Increase the heat to 375°F/190°C, or until a cube of bread browns in 30 seconds. Deep-fry the fries again, in 2 batches, for 2–3 minutes until crisp and golden. Drain on paper towels and sprinkle with salt.

6 Serve the fish with the fries, mayonnaise, and lemon wedges, and garnished with parsley sprigs.

CRISPY BAKED FLOUNDER

THIS CRISPY GOLDEN FISH DISH IS VERY EASY AND QUICK TO PREPARE, AND BAKES BEAUTIFULLY. ONCE IT IS IN THE OVEN YOU CAN LEAVE IT AND GET ON WITH OTHER THINGS, SO IT IS IDEAL FOR COOKS WHO ARE ON A TIGHT SCHEDULE OR WHO HAVE A BUSY LIFESTYLE.

serves
2

preparation
10 minutes

cooking
25 minutes

ingredients
- 4 oz/115 g flounder fillet
- 4 tbsp butter, diced
- 1 tbsp lemon juice
- salt and pepper

TOPPING
- 4 tbsp fresh white bread crumbs
- 1 tsp dried herbs, such as parsley, oregano, or thyme
- 1 tsp mustard powder (optional)
- 1 tbsp Cheddar cheese, grated

1 Preheat the oven to 350°F/180°C.

2 Arrange the fish in a single layer in a shallow ovenproof dish.

3 Dot 2 tablespoons of butter over the fish. Sprinkle with lemon juice and season with salt and pepper.

4 To make the topping, combine the bread crumbs with the herbs, mustard (if using), and grated cheese in a large bowl. Spoon the topping over the fish and dot with the remaining butter.

5 Bake in the oven for 20 minutes. If necessary, flash the dish under a hot broiler for an extra 3–4 minutes to brown the topping before serving.

cook's tip

To vary the ingredients and flavors, try using the same quantity of fresh cod or haddock fillet instead of the flounder. You can also vary the herbs—for example, try using 1 teaspoon dried dill instead of the parsley, oregano, or thyme.

SMOKED FISH PIE

THIS IS A CLASSIC VERSION OF A FISH PIE WITH BEAUTIFULLY FLAVORED SMOKED FISH, AND SHRIMP AND VEGETABLES. IT IS VERY EASY TO PREPARE AND COOK, AND THE TANTALIZING AROMAS AND FLAVORS WILL HAVE EVERY MEMBER OF YOUR HOUSEHOLD CLAMORING FOR MORE.

serves
6
preparation
10 minutes
cooking
1½ hours

ingredients
- 2 tbsp olive oil
- 1 onion, finely chopped
- 1 leek, thinly sliced
- 1 carrot, diced
- 1 celery stalk, diced
- 4 oz/115 g white mushrooms, halved
- grated rind 1 lemon
- 12 oz/350 g skinless, boneless smoked cod or haddock fillet, cubed
- 12 oz/350 g skinless, boneless white fish, cubed
- 8 oz/225 g cooked shelled shrimp
- 2 tbsp chopped fresh parsley
- 1 tbsp chopped fresh dill, plus sprigs to garnish
- cooked vegetables, to serve

SAUCE
- 4 tbsp butter
- 4 tbsp all-purpose flour
- 1 tsp mustard powder
- 2½ cups milk
- 3 oz/85 g Gruyère cheese, grated

TOPPING
- 1 lb 8 oz/675 g potatoes, unpeeled
- 4 tbsp butter, melted
- 1 oz/25 g Gruyère cheese, grated
- salt and pepper

1 For the sauce, heat the butter in a large pan and when melted add the flour and mustard powder. Stir until smooth and cook over very low heat for 2 minutes without coloring. Slowly beat in the milk until smooth. Simmer gently for 2 minutes then stir in the cheese until smooth. Remove from the heat and place some plastic wrap over the surface of the sauce to prevent a skin from forming. Set aside.

2 Meanwhile, to make the topping, boil the whole potatoes in plenty of salted water for 15 minutes. Drain the potatoes well and leave them until they are cool enough to handle.

3 Preheat the oven to 400°F/200°C. Heat the oil in a clean pan. Add the onion and cook for 5 minutes until softened. Add the leek, carrot, celery, and mushrooms and cook for an additional 10 minutes, or until the vegetables have softened. Stir in the lemon rind and cook briefly.

4 Add the softened vegetables with the fish, shrimp, parsley, and dill to the sauce. Season to taste with salt and pepper and transfer to a greased 7¼-cup casserole dish.

5 Peel the cooled potatoes and grate them coarsely. Mix with the melted butter. Cover the filling with the grated potato and sprinkle with the grated Gruyère cheese.

6 Cover loosely with foil and bake in the preheated oven for 30 minutes. Remove the foil and bake for an additional 30 minutes, or until the topping is tender and golden and the filling is bubbling. Garnish with dill sprigs and serve with a selection of your favorite vegetables.

cook's tip
White fish such as haddock, angler fish, or hake would be suitable to use in this dish.

CHARGRILLED TUNA WITH CHILI SALSA

A FIRM FISH SUCH AS TUNA IS AN EXCELLENT CHOICE FOR BARBECUES, BECAUSE IT IS QUITE MEATY AND DOES NOT BREAK UP DURING COOKING. HERE IT IS SERVED WITH A COLORFUL AND SPICY CHILI SALSA. IT MAKES AN EXCELLENT CHOICE FOR PEOPLE ON A LOWFAT DIET.

serves
4

preparation
15 minutes, plus
1 hour marinating

cooking
20 minutes

ingredients
- 4 tuna steaks, about
  6 oz/175 g each
- grated rind and juice
  of 1 lime
- 2 tbsp olive oil
- salt and pepper
- fresh cilantro sprigs,
  to garnish

CHILI SALSA
- 2 orange bell peppers
- 1 tbsp olive oil
- juice of 1 lime
- juice of 1 orange
- 2–3 fresh red chilies,
  seeded and chopped
- pinch of cayenne pepper

1 Rinse the tuna thoroughly under cold running water and pat dry with paper towels, then place in a large shallow nonmetallic dish. Sprinkle the lime rind and juice and the oil over the fish. Season to taste with salt and pepper, cover with plastic wrap, and let marinate in the refrigerator for up to 1 hour.

2 Preheat the barbecue. To make the salsa, brush the bell peppers with the olive oil and cook over hot coals, turning frequently, for 10 minutes, or until the skin is blackened and charred. Remove from the barbecue and let cool slightly, then peel off the skins and discard the seeds. Place the bell peppers in a food processor with the remaining salsa ingredients and process to a purée. Transfer to a bowl and season to taste with salt and pepper.

3 Cook the tuna over hot coals for 4–5 minutes on each side until golden. Transfer to plates, garnish with cilantro sprigs, and serve immediately with the salsa.

cook's tip

You can make the chili salsa in advance. Halve the orange bell peppers and cook, skin-side upward, under a preheated hot broiler. Cook until blackened and charred, then continue as in Step 2.

3

MEAT

RED MEAT IS VERY NUTRITIOUS AND CAN PLAY A
VALUABLE PART IN A HEALTHY DIET, ESPECIALLY IF YOU
CHOOSE LEAN CUTS TO KEEP THE SATURATED FAT
LEVELS TO A MINIMUM. IT IS FULL OF VITAMINS AND
MINERALS, ESPECIALLY IRON AND PROTEIN. ON THE
FOLLOWING PAGES YOU WILL FIND SOME DELICIOUS
RECIPES TO MAKE THE MOST OF ANY CUT OF MEAT.

INTRODUCTION

MEAT IS RICH IN PROTEIN AND EASY TO COOK. IT MAKES AN EXCELLENT CENTERPIECE TO ANY MEAL, AND YOU CAN CHOOSE FROM A WIDE RANGE OF JOINTS AND CUTS, FROM THE ECONOMICAL TO THE INDULGENT, TO SUIT ANY OCCASION.

Buying and storing meat

Always buy your fresh meat from a reputable supplier. For lamb, choose firm, pinkish, marbled meat; avoid any that looks dark and soggy. The fat should be cream-colored, not yellow. For pork, choose moist, pinkish meat with white fat. Avoid any meat that looks oily or that has yellow fat. For beef, look for meat that is deep burgundy red, not bright red; the fat should be cream-colored, not yellow. Choose beef that has a marbling of fat through it—this will ensure that the meat stays moist during cooking. For veal, the flesh should be a very pale pink and the fat white. If it is turning red, it means that the meat is older than it should be.

If you are buying a joint of meat, allow 6–12 oz/175–350 g per person, depending on whether the meat is on or off the bone.

As soon as you get the meat home, unwrap it and transfer it to a clean dish (the dish should have a lip deep enough to catch any juices). Cover it with plastic wrap and store in the refrigerator away from any cooked meats in order to prevent cross-contamination. Leave any prepackaged meat in its wrapping in the refrigerator and use by the "best before" date. Unpackaged ground lamb, beef and pork is best used within 1–2 days of purchase. Fresh cuts of beef and pork will keep in the refrigerator for 2–3 days, and cooked beef and pork can be refrigerated for 4–5 days. Fresh lamb cuts will keep for up to 4 days in the refrigerator. Before cooking, bring out the meat (keep it covered) and allow it to come back to room temperature for about 30 minutes before cooking. You can freeze small cuts of beef or pork for up to 6 months, and lamb for up to 3 months. Make sure you thaw the meat thoroughly in a refrigerator or cool room before cooking: allow 6 hours per 1 lb/450 g.

Preparation techniques

There is a range of techniques you can use to prepare and/or improve your chosen cuts of meat before cooking. Some of them are done purely for presentation, while other techniques help to tenderize the meat or facilitate thorough cooking.

LAMB CHOPS

Use a sharp knife to remove the excess fat around the edge.

PORK CHOPS AND ROUND STEAKS

Use a sharp knife to make incisions in the fat at intervals of 1 inch/2.5 cm around the edge.

TOP ROUND STEAK

Use a sharp knife to remove any excess fat. Slice the meat across the grain, then cut across the slices to form smaller pieces or cubes of meat.

TENDERIZE THIN CUTS OF MEAT

Put them between sheets of waxed paper and pound with either a meat mallet or the bottom of a pan.

STUFF AND TIE A BONELESS JOINT

Put it skin-side down and arrange the dressing evenly over the surface. Roll up the joint from the thick end, tie a piece of clean string lengthwise around the joint, then knot it and trim off the ends. Now tie further pieces of string cross-wise around the joint at intervals of about 1 inch/2.5 cm. Knot each one in turn and trim the ends.

BUTTERFLY A LEG OF LAMB

Push a chef's knife into the cavity of the bone, then cut sidewise to part the meat. Open it out and make a light incision down the center of the meat so that it stays open and flat.

PREPARE A RACK OF LAMB

Remove the skin and excess fat, leaving a layer of fat about ¾-inch/1.5-cm thick. Cut off the bone at the back, then remove the fat from the ends of the bones (to a length of about 2 inches/5 cm). Use a knife to scrape out the meat from between the bones.

Choosing cuts of meat

There are many different cuts of meat available. Choosing the right cut will help to ensure the perfect result for your chosen recipe. When in doubt, ask your local butcher for advice.

Beef

For roasting, choose sirloin, beef round, tenderloin, and rib. Tenderloin and steaks are excellent for broiling, pan-frying, or barbecuing. For stewing, use chuck or beef round.

Pork

For roasting, choose the belly, leg, loin, shoulder, tenderloin, chops, or steaks. For broiling, use the belly, scallops, loin, shoulder, tenderloin, chops, or steaks. The belly, loin, tenderloin, chops, or steaks are good for barbecues. For frying, use the loin, tenderloin, chops, steaks, and bacon. To stew, use the leg or loin.

Veal

The breast, loin, and shoulder are best for roasting, while the loin, round, and chops are ideal for broiling and barbecuing. For pan-frying, choose the loin or round, and for stewing or braising use the knuckle, shoulder, or breast.

Lamb

The leg is the most popular choice for roasting, but you can also roast the shoulder, saddle, and breast. For broiling, try chops, noisettes, and leg. The leg or chops are ideal for barbecues, and for pan-frying use noisettes. Finally, for stewing, braising, or casseroles, use the shoulder or shank.

Beef

Pork

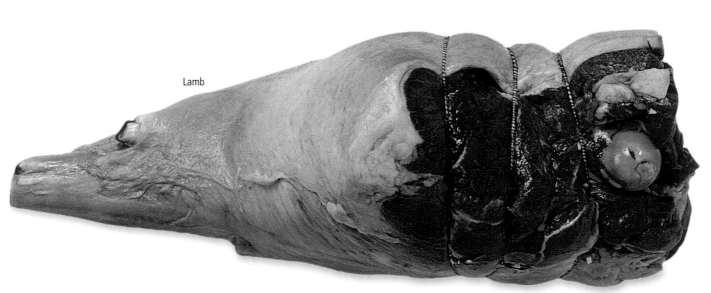

Lamb

Cooking and carving techniques

Techniques for cooking and carving joints of meat are not difficult, but they do have to be performed properly in order to get the best out of the meat. Follow the instructions given here for perfect results every time.

ROASTING AND CARVING A BONED JOINT

This technique is suitable for boned joints of lamb, pork, and beef. Rub the surface with a little oil, followed by some salt and some crushed peppercorns (use a mortar and pestle for this). Place on a rack in a roasting pan, then roast in the oven, basting once or twice during cooking. Remove from the oven and cut off the strings. Wrap the meat in foil and let stand for 15–20 minutes. To carve, steady the meat with a fork, then carve slices downward from one end.

ROASTING AND CARVING A LEG OF LAMB

Using a sharp knife, score a criss-cross pattern in the fat, then rub all over the surface with a little oil, followed by some salt and freshly ground black pepper. Place the meat on a rack in a roasting pan and roast in the oven, basting once or twice during cooking.

To test if the meat is cooked all the way through, pierce a skewer or knife into the thickest part. The juices that run out will be clear if the meat is cooked. If not, return it to the oven and cook until it is done. Remove from the oven and wrap the meat in foil. Let stand for 15–20 minutes. To carve, turn the leg meat-side up, then steady the meat with a fork. Start carving from the knuckle end. When you have finished, turn over the leg and carve horizontal slices.

Using a meat thermometer

A meat thermometer is a useful device for testing whether a joint of meat is cooked thoroughly. Thorough cooking is particularly important in the case of pork, which can carry harmful bacteria and cause food poisoning if not cooked all the way through. Simply insert the thermometer into the thickest part of the meat at the start of cooking. Take care to ensure that it does not come into contact with any bone, because this could give a false reading. When the thermometer reaches the required temperature, the meat is cooked. The recommended temperatures for different meats are shown below.

Cooking temperatures

Lamb	Medium rare	167°F/75°C
	Well done	176°F/80°C
Pork	Well done	194°F/90°C
Beef	Rare	149°F/65°C
	Medium rare	158°F/70°C
	Well done	167°F/75°C

Oven temperatures and roasting times

Please note that individual oven temperatures and cooking times vary, so the following cooking times are approximate only. Remember to preheat the oven before cooking in order to ensure the best results.

Meat	Joint	Weight	Temperature	Cooking time
Lamb	Whole leg	5 lb 8 oz/2.5 kg	350°F/180°C	2$\frac{1}{4}$ hours (medium rare) or 2$\frac{1}{2}$ hours (well done)
Lamb	Whole shoulder	5 lb 8 oz/2.5 kg	350°F/180°C	2$\frac{1}{4}$ hours (medium rare) or 2$\frac{1}{2}$ hours (well done)
Pork	Loin (boned)	5 lb 8 oz/2.5 kg	350°F/180°C 425°F/220°C	3 hours at lower temperature, then 20 minutes at higher temperature (well done)
Pork	Shoulder (boned)	5 lb 8 oz/2.5 kg	350°F/180°C 425°F/220°C	3 hours at lower temperature, then 20 minutes at higher temperature (well done)
Beef	Sirloin	5 lb 8 oz/2.5 kg	400°F/200°C	1$\frac{3}{4}$ hours (rare), 2$\frac{1}{4}$ hours (medium rare), or 2$\frac{1}{2}$ hours (well done)
Beef	Round	4 lb 8 oz/2 kg	350°F/180°C	1$\frac{1}{2}$ hours (rare), 2 hours (medium rare), or 2$\frac{1}{2}$ hours (well done)

Oven temperatures and heat descriptions

You may come across recipes that do not give a specific temperature: instead they will simply recommend cooking in a "moderate" or "hot" oven. Here is a list of these heat descriptions and their correct corresponding temperatures.

Oven heat description	Fahrenheit	Centigrade
Very cool	225–250°	110–120°
Cool	275–300°	140–150°
Moderate	325–350°	160–180°
Moderately hot	375–400°	190–200°
Hot	425°	220°
Very hot	450°	230°

ROAST BEEF WITH YORKSHIRE PUDDINGS

ROAST BEEF IS PROBABLY THE MEAL FOR WHICH THE BRITISH ARE KNOWN BEST AROUND THE WORLD. OLD PAINTINGS SHOW THE FEASTS OF TUDOR TIMES, FEATURING HUGE RIBS OF BEEF SERVED AT COURT—A MAGNIFICENT HISTORICAL REMINDER OF JUST HOW BEEF OUGHT TO BE SERVED.

serves
8

preparation
15 minutes, plus
10–15 minutes'
resting time

cooking
1 hour 55
minutes–2½ hours

ingredients
- 6 lb/2.7 kg prime rib of beef
- 2 tsp English mustard powder
- 3 tbsp all-purpose flour
- 1¼ cups red wine
- 1¼ cups beef stock
- 2 tsp Worcestershire sauce (optional)
- salt and pepper

YORKSHIRE PUDDINGS
- scant 1⅔ cups all-purpose flour
- 1 tsp salt
- 2 eggs, beaten
- 2½ cups milk
- 4 tbsp roast beef drippings or olive oil

cook's tip

Roast beef is the most difficult roast to get right, because, unlike other meats, you need to cook it so that it is still pink in the center; careful timing is all. The best roast beef is a rib cooked on the bone, but this must be a good size.

1 Preheat the oven to 450°F/230°C.

2 Season the meat with salt and pepper and rub in the mustard and 1 tablespoon of the flour.

3 Place the meat in a roasting pan large enough to hold it comfortably and roast for 15 minutes. Reduce the heat to 375°F/190°C and cook for 15 minutes per 1 lb/450 g, plus 15 minutes (1 hour 45 minutes for this joint) for rare beef or 20 minutes per 1 lb/450 g, plus 20 minutes (2 hours 20 minutes) for medium beef. Baste the meat occasionally to keep it moist and if the pan becomes too dry, add a little stock or red wine.

4 Remove the meat from the oven and place on a hot serving plate, cover with foil, and let stand in a warm place for 10–15 minutes.

5 To make the gravy, pour off most of the fat from the pan (reserve it for the Yorkshire puddings), leaving behind the meat juices and the sediment. Place the pan on the top of the stove over medium heat and scrape all the sediments from the bottom of the pan. Sprinkle in the remaining flour and quickly mix it into the juices with a small whisk. When you have a smooth paste,

gradually add the wine and most of the stock, whisking constantly. Bring to a boil, then turn down the heat to a gentle simmer and cook for 2–3 minutes. Season with salt and pepper and add the remaining stock, if needed, and a little Worcestershire sauce, if liked.

6 To make the Yorkshire puddings preheat the oven to 425°F/220°C. Place the flour in a bowl with the salt. Make a well in the center of the flour and add the eggs. Using a wooden spoon, gradually stir in the eggs and milk and beat until smooth. Let stand for 30 minutes. Heat the drippings or oil in 24 individual Yorkshire pudding pans for several minutes in the top of the oven. Remove the pans from the oven, pour in the batter, and bake for 10–15 minutes until the puddings are puffed up and golden brown.

8 When ready to serve, carve the meat into slices and serve on hot plates. Pour the gravy into a warmed pitcher and take direct to the table to serve with the Yorkshire puddings.

BEEF BOURGUIGNON

BEEF BOURGUIGNON USES A TRADITIONAL METHOD OF PREPARATION FROM THE BURGUNDY REGION OF FRANCE. IT CONTAINS SUCCULENT BEEF BRAISED IN RED WINE, COMPLEMENTED BY BACON, ONIONS, AND MUSHROOMS. SERVE IT WITH FRESH CRUSTY BREAD TO SOAK UP THE JUICES.

serves
6

preparation
40 minutes

cooking
3¼ hours

ingredients
- 2 tbsp olive oil
- 6 oz/175 g piece unsmoked bacon, sliced into thin strips
- 3 lb/1.3 kg stewing beef, cut into 2 inch/5 cm pieces
- 2 carrots, sliced
- 2 onions, chopped
- 2 garlic cloves, very finely chopped
- 3 tbsp all-purpose flour
- 3 cups red wine
- 1½–2 cups beef stock
- 1 bouquet garni sachet
- 1 tsp salt
- ¼ tsp pepper
- 3 tbsp butter
- 12 oz/350 g pearl onions
- 12 oz/350 g white mushrooms
- 2 tbsp chopped fresh parsley, to garnish

1 Heat the oil in a large, ovenproof casserole over medium heat. Add the bacon and brown for 2–3 minutes. Remove with a slotted spoon. Add the beef in batches to the casserole and cook until browned. Drain and keep with the bacon. Add the carrots and chopped onions to the casserole and cook for 5 minutes. Add the garlic and fry until just colored. Return the meat and bacon to the casserole. Sprinkle on the flour and cook for 1 minute, stirring. Add the wine, enough stock to cover, the bouquet garni, salt and pepper. Bring to a boil, cover, and let simmer gently for 3 hours.

2 Heat half the butter in a skillet. Add the pearl onions, cover and cook until softened. Remove with a slotted spoon and keep warm. Heat the remaining butter in the skillet. Add the mushrooms and cook briefly. Remove and keep warm.

3 Strain the casserole liquid into a clean pan. Wipe the casserole with paper towels and tip in the meat, bacon, mushrooms, and onions. Remove the surface fat from the cooking liquid, simmer for 1–2 minutes to reduce, then pour over the meat and vegetables. Serve sprinkled with chopped parsley.

BEEF STROGANOFF

BEEF STROGANOFF GETS ITS NAME FROM THE 19TH CENTURY RUSSIAN DIPLOMAT COUNT PAUL STROGANOV. THIS DELICIOUS DISH OF BEEF, ONIONS, AND MUSHROOMS HAS A RICH, CREAMY SAUCE, AND THE COMBINATION OF RED WINE AND GARLIC GIVES IT AN UNFORGETTABLE FLAVOR.

serves
4

preparation
5 minutes

cooking
12–15 minutes

ingredients
- scant ⅓ cup all-purpose flour
- 1 tsp paprika
- 1 lb 9 oz/700 g round steak, very thinly sliced into strips
- 4 tbsp butter
- 1 onion, finely chopped
- 1 garlic clove, finely chopped
- 8 oz/225 g white mushrooms
- 1 tbsp lemon juice
- 2 tbsp dry red wine
- 2 tbsp tomato paste
- 1½ cups sour cream
- salt and pepper
- 2 tbsp snipped fresh chives, to garnish

1 Place the flour and paprika in a plastic bag and season with salt and pepper. Shake to mix, then add a few steak strips at a time and shake to coat.

2 Melt the butter in a large, heavy-bottom skillet over low heat. Add the onion and garlic and cook, stirring occasionally, for 5 minutes, or until softened. Increase the heat to high, add the steak strips, and cook, stirring constantly, until browned all over. Stir in the mushrooms, lemon juice, and wine, reduce the heat, and let simmer for 5 minutes.

3 Stir in the tomato paste and sour cream and adjust the seasoning, if necessary. Garnish with the chives and serve immediately.

cook's tip

Beef stroganoff is traditionally served over noodles, but you can also serve it on a bed of freshly cooked rice. Use a light, fluffy long-grain rice to partner this dish.

HUNGARIAN BEEF GOULASH

THIS AUTHENTIC HUNGARIAN STEW IS MADE WITH THE TRADITIONAL INGREDIENTS OF BEEF, VEGETABLES, AND PAPRIKA, AND HAS A RICH, PUNGENT FLAVOR. IT IS CUSTOMARY TO SERVE IT ON A PLATE OF HOT, BUTTERED NOODLES, WITH GENEROUS AMOUNTS OF SOUR CREAM.

serves
4
preparation
30 minutes
cooking
3 hours

ingredients
- 2 tbsp vegetable oil
- 1 lb 8 oz/675 g stewing beef, cubed
- 3 onions, finely chopped
- 1 green bell pepper, seeded and diced
- 2 garlic cloves, very finely chopped
- 2 tbsp tomato paste
- 2 tbsp all-purpose flour
- 14 oz/400 g canned chopped tomatoes
- generous 1 cup beef stock
- 1 bay leaf
- 3 tbsp chopped fresh parsley
- 1 tbsp paprika
- 1 tsp salt
- 1/4 tsp pepper

TO SERVE
- buttered noodles
- sour cream

1 Heat the oil in an ovenproof casserole over medium–high heat. Add the meat and cook until evenly browned. Remove with a slotted spoon, transfer to a bowl, and set aside until required.

2 Add the onions and bell pepper. Cook for 5 minutes, stirring occasionally, until softened. Add the garlic and cook until just colored. Stir in the tomato paste and flour. Cook for 1 minute, stirring.

3 Return the meat to the casserole. Add the remaining ingredients and bring to a boil. Cover and let simmer over low heat for 2 1/2 hours, stirring occasionally. Add water or more stock if necessary.

4 Remove the lid and let simmer for 15 minutes, stirring to prevent sticking, until the sauce has thickened and the meat is very tender. Serve with buttered noodles and a bowl of sour cream.

CLASSIC BEEF FAJITAS

THIS RECIPE CONTAINS SIZZLING MARINATED STRIPS OF MEAT ROLLED UP IN SOFT FLOUR TORTILLAS WITH A TANGY SALSA. IT IS A REAL MEXICAN TREAT, AND PERFECT FOR RELAXED ENTERTAINING. SIMPLY PASS ROUND THE INGREDIENTS AND LET YOUR GUESTS ROLL THEIR OWN FAJITAS.

serves
4–6
preparation
30 minutes,
plus 3–8 hours'
marinating
cooking
10–15 minutes

ingredients
- 1 lb 9 oz/700 g beef skirt steak, cut into strips
- 6 garlic cloves, chopped
- juice of 1 lime
- large pinch of mild chili powder
- large pinch of paprika
- large pinch of ground cumin
- 1–2 tbsp extra virgin olive oil
- 12 flour tortillas
- butter, for greasing
- vegetable oil, for cooking
- 1–2 avocados, pitted, sliced, and tossed with lime juice
- ½ cup sour cream
- salt and pepper

PICO DE GALLO SALSA
- 8 ripe tomatoes, diced
- 3 scallions, sliced
- 1–2 fresh green chilies, such as jalapeño or serrano, seeded and chopped
- 3–4 tbsp chopped fresh cilantro
- 5–8 radishes, diced
- ground cumin

1 Combine the beef with half the garlic, half the lime juice, the chili powder, paprika, cumin, and olive oil. Add salt and pepper, mix well and let marinate for at least 30 minutes at room temperature, or up to overnight in the refrigerator.

2 To make the salsa, place the tomatoes in a bowl with the scallions, green chili, cilantro, and radishes. Season to taste with cumin, and salt and pepper. Set aside.

3 Heat the tortillas one by one in a lightly greased nonstick skillet, wrapping each in foil as you work, to keep warm.

4 Heat a little oil in a large, heavy-bottom skillet over high heat. Add the meat and stir-fry until browned and just cooked through.

5 Serve the sizzling hot meat with the warm tortillas, the salsa, avocado, and sour cream for each person to make his or her own rolled-up fajitas.

cook's tip
A lettuce and orange salad makes a refreshing accompaniment.

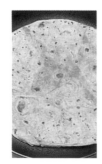

BROILED STEAK WITH TOMATOES & GARLIC

ORIGINATING IN NAPLES, WHERE IT IS DIFFICULT TO FIND ANY DISH THAT DOES NOT FEATURE THE BRILLIANTLY COLORED, RICH-TASTING TOMATOES OF THE REGION, THIS WAY OF SERVING STEAK IS NOW POPULAR THROUGHOUT ITALY—AND BEYOND.

serves
4
preparation
20 minutes
cooking
20–30 minutes

ingredients
- 3 tbsp olive oil, plus extra for brushing
- 1 lb 9 oz/700 g tomatoes, peeled and chopped
- 1 red bell pepper, seeded and chopped
- 1 onion, chopped
- 2 garlic cloves, finely chopped
- 1 tbsp chopped fresh flat-leaf parsley
- 1 tsp dried oregano
- 1 tsp sugar
- 4 x 6 oz/175 g entrecôte (flesh from ribs) or round steaks
- salt and pepper

1 Place the oil, tomatoes, red bell pepper, onion, garlic, parsley, oregano, and sugar in a heavy-bottom pan and season to taste with salt and pepper. Bring to a boil, reduce the heat, and let simmer for 15 minutes.

2 Meanwhile, preheat the broiler to high. Snip any fat around the outsides of the steaks. Season each generously with pepper (no salt) and brush with oil. Broil for 1 minute on each side, then reduce the heat to medium and cook according to taste: 1½–2 minutes each side for rare; 2½–3 minutes each side for medium; 3–4 minutes on each side for well done.

3 Transfer the steaks to warmed individual plates and spoon the sauce over them. Serve immediately.

MIXED GRILL

THIS MIXED GRILL IS A MEAT FEAST, AND IS IDEAL FOR ALFRESCO DINING. IT INCLUDES EVERYTHING A MEAT-LOVER COULD WANT—SAUSAGES, BACON, STEAK, AND KIDNEYS—AND THE BAY LEAVES ADD A WONDERFUL AROMATIC FLAVOR. SERVE IT WITH BAKED POTATOES AND A CRISP GREEN SALAD.

serves
4

preparation
20 minutes

cooking
12 minutes

ingredients
- 4 lambs' kidneys
- 6 smoked Canadian bacon slices, rinded
- 4 cherry tomatoes
- 4 small tenderloin steaks or tournedos
- 8 small pork sausages
- 4 white mushrooms
- 12 bay leaves
- salt and pepper

SPICY MARINADE
- 2 tbsp sunflower-seed oil
- 1 large onion, finely chopped
- 2 garlic cloves, finely chopped
- 2 tbsp jerk seasoning

- 1 tbsp curry paste
- 1 tsp grated fresh gingerroot
- 14 oz/400 g canned chopped tomatoes
- 4 tbsp Worcestershire sauce
- 3 tbsp brown sugar
- salt and pepper

MUSTARD BUTTER
- 4 tbsp unsalted butter, softened
- 1½ tsp tarragon mustard
- 1 tbsp chopped fresh parsley
- dash of lemon juice

1 To make the marinade, heat the oil in a heavy-bottom pan. Add the onion and garlic and cook, stirring occasionally, for 5 minutes, or until softened. Stir in the jerk seasoning, curry paste, and grated ginger and cook, stirring constantly, for 2 minutes. Add the tomatoes, Worcestershire sauce, and sugar, then season to taste with salt and pepper. Bring to a boil, stirring constantly, then reduce the heat and let simmer for 15 minutes, or until thickened. Remove the pan from the heat and let cool.

2 To make the mustard butter, mix all the ingredients together in a small bowl, beating with a fork until well blended. Cover with plastic wrap and let chill in the refrigerator until required.

3 Preheat the barbecue. Using a sharp knife, trim the kidneys, cut each one in half and, using a pair of kitchen scissors, remove the cores. Cut the bacon slices in half across the center, then wrap a piece of bacon around each kidney half and around each cherry tomato.

4 Thread the kidneys, tomatoes, steaks, sausages, mushrooms, and bay leaves alternately onto several metal skewers. Season to taste with salt and pepper and brush with the marinade.

5 Cook over medium hot coals, turning and brushing frequently with the marinade, for 12 minutes. Transfer the kabobs to a large serving plate and serve immediately with the mustard butter.

variation
If you like, you can substitute the steak with medallions or noisettes of other meats, such as lamb or chicken.

GLAZED HAM STEAKS

HAM STEAKS, WHICH ARE ALSO KNOWN AS GAMMON STEAKS, MAKE A TASTY DISH FOR A LUNCH OR LIGHT SUPPER. THESE STEAKS ARE DELICIOUSLY SWEET GLAZED WITH SUGAR AND MUSTARD. SIMPLY ADD A BAKED POTATO AND LIGHTLY COOKED GREEN BEANS AND YOU HAVE A PERFECT MEAL.

serves
4

preparation
5 minutes

cooking
10 minutes

ingredients
- 4 ham steaks
- 4 tbsp brown sugar
- 2 tsp mustard powder
- 4 tbsp butter
- 8 slices pineapple

TO SERVE
- baked potatoes
- freshly cooked green beans

1 Preheat the griddle over medium heat. Place the ham steaks on it and cook for 5 minutes, turning once. If you have room for only 2 steaks at a time, cook them completely and keep warm while cooking the second pair.

2 Combine the brown sugar and mustard in a small bowl.

3 Melt the butter in a large skillet. Add the pineapple and cook for 2 minutes to heat through, turning once. Sprinkle with the sugar and mustard mixture and continue cooking over low heat until the sugar has melted and the pineapple is well glazed. Turn the pineapple once more so that both sides are coated with sauce. Place the ham steaks on individual plates and arrange 2 pineapple slices either next to them or overlapping on top. Spoon over some of the sweet pan juices.

4 Serve with a baked potato and green beans.

LAMB KABOBS

LAMB AND ROSEMARY MAKE THE PERFECT PARTNERSHIP. THESE LAMB KABOBS ARE FULL OF FLAVOR. THEY ARE ALSO RICH IN PROTEIN, AND MAKE MOUTHWATERING BARBECUE FARE. YOU CAN SERVE THEM ON THEIR OWN, OR WITH RICE AND A SIDE SALAD FOR A SATISFYING MEAL.

serves
4
preparation
15 minutes
cooking
10 minutes

ingredients
- 1 lb 6 oz/625 g fresh ground lamb
- 3 1/4 oz/90 g Gruyère cheese, grated
- 4 tbsp thick plain yogurt
- 2 garlic cloves, chopped
- 1 tbsp chopped fresh rosemary
- 16 white mushrooms
- 16 cherry tomatoes
- 1 tbsp olive oil
- salt and pepper
- fresh rosemary sprigs, to garnish
- freshly cooked rice, to serve

1 Preheat the broiler or light a barbecue. Place the lamb, cheese, yogurt, and garlic in a large bowl and mix well. Stir in the rosemary and season with salt and pepper. Using your hands, shape the mixture into small balls.

2 Thread the lamb balls onto several metal skewers, alternating them with the mushrooms and cherry

tomatoes. When the skewers are full (leave a small space at either end), brush them with oil. Transfer them to the hot broiler or barbecue and cook for 10 minutes, or until cooked through, turning them frequently and brushing with more oil if necessary.

3 Remove the kabobs from the heat and serve with freshly cooked rice, garnished with rosemary sprigs.

SHEPHERD'S PIE

SHEPHERD'S PIE IS AN OLD ENGLISH DISH, AND WAS ORIGINALLY CREATED TO USE UP LEFTOVERS FROM THE SUNDAY ROAST. IT USUALLY CONTAINS GROUND LAMB OR BEEF COOKED WITH ONIONS, CARROTS, HERBS, AND TOMATOES IN GRAVY, AND IS TOPPED WITH PIPED MASHED POTATOES.

serves
4–5
preparation
10 minutes
cooking
1½ hours

ingredients
- 1 lb 9 oz/700 g fresh lean ground lamb or beef
- 2 onions, chopped
- 8 oz/225 g carrots, diced
- 1–2 garlic cloves, crushed
- 1 tbsp all-purpose flour
- scant 1 cup beef stock
- 7 oz/200 g canned chopped tomatoes
- 1 tsp Worcestershire sauce
- 1 tsp chopped fresh sage or oregano or ½ tsp dried sage or oregano
- 1 lb 10 oz–2 lb/750 g–1 kg potatoes
- 2 tbsp margarine
- 3–4 tbsp skim milk
- 4½ oz/125 g white mushrooms, sliced (optional)
- salt and pepper

1 Preheat the oven to 400°F/200°C. Place the meat in a large, heavy-bottom pan with no extra fat and cook gently until the meat begins to brown.

2 Add the onions, carrots, and garlic and continue to cook gently for 10 minutes. Stir in the flour and cook for 1–2 minutes, then gradually stir in the stock and tomatoes and bring to a boil.

3 Add the Worcestershire sauce, seasoning, and herbs, cover and let simmer gently for 25 minutes, giving an occasional stir.

4 Cook the potatoes in boiling salted water until tender, then drain thoroughly and mash, beating in the margarine, seasoning, and enough milk to give a piping consistency. Place in a pastry bag fitted with a large star tip.

5 Stir the mushrooms (if using) into the meat and taste and adjust the seasoning if necessary. Turn into a shallow ovenproof dish.

6 Pipe the potatoes evenly over the meat. Cook in the preheated oven for 30 minutes, or until piping hot and the potatoes are golden brown.

variation

If liked, a mixture of boiled potatoes and parsnips or rutabaga may be used for the topping.

MOUSSAKA

MOUSSAKA ORGINATED IN GREECE, BUT ITS POPULARITY IS NOW WIDESPREAD THROUGHOUT THE EASTERN MEDITERRANEAN. THERE ARE MANY VARIATIONS OF THIS DISH, BUT IT USUALLY CONTAINS SLICES OF EGGPLANT AND GROUND BEEF OR LAMB, COVERED WITH BÉCHAMEL SAUCE AND CHEESE.

serves
4
preparation
40 minutes
cooking
45 minutes

ingredients
- 2 eggplants, thinly sliced
- 1 lb/450 g fresh lean ground beef
- 2 onions, thinly sliced
- 1 tsp finely chopped garlic
- 14 oz/400 g canned tomatoes
- 2 tbsp chopped fresh parsley
- 2 eggs
- 1¼ cups lowfat plain yogurt
- 1 tbsp freshly grated Parmesan cheese
- salt and pepper

1 Preheat the oven to 350°F/180°C. Dry-fry the eggplant slices, in batches, in a nonstick skillet on both sides until browned. Remove from the skillet.

2 Add the beef to the skillet and cook for 5 minutes, stirring, until browned. Stir in the onions and garlic and cook for 5 minutes, or until browned. Add the tomatoes, parsley, salt and pepper, then bring to a boil and let simmer for 20 minutes, or until the meat is tender.

3 Arrange half the eggplant slices in a layer in an ovenproof dish. Add the meat mixture, then a final layer of the remaining eggplant slices.

4 Beat the eggs in a bowl, then beat in the yogurt and add salt and pepper to taste. Pour the mixture over the eggplants and sprinkle the grated cheese on top. Bake the moussaka in the oven for 45 minutes, or until golden brown. Serve straight from the dish.

cook's tip

Try experimenting with your own combinations of ingredients to vary the flavor and texture. For example, you can use ground lamb instead of the beef, and add sliced artichokes or potatoes to the eggplants.

RACK OF LAMB

IF YOU WANT A ROAST FOR TWO, A RACK OF LAMB IS IDEAL. IT IS SIMPLE TO COOK AND PROVIDES DELICIOUS MEAT, FULL OF FLAVOR. LAMB IS BEST IN SPRING, FROM EASTER ONWARD, WHEN IT IS AT ITS SWEETEST AND MOST SUCCULENT. FRESH MINT IS ALSO AT ITS BEST AROUND THIS TIME.

serves
2

preparation
20 minutes,
plus 3–8 hours'
marinating

cooking
30–35 minutes

ingredients
- 1 trimmed rack of lamb (about 9–10½ oz/ 250–300 g rack)
- 1 garlic clove, crushed
- ²/3 cup red wine
- 1 fresh rosemary sprig, crushed to release the flavor
- 1 tbsp olive oil
- ²/3 cup lamb stock
- 2 tbsp red currant jelly
- salt and pepper

MINT SAUCE
- small bunch of fresh mint leaves, chopped
- 2 tsp superfine sugar
- 2 tbsp boiling water
- 2 tbsp white wine vinegar

1 Place the rack of lamb in a nonmetallic bowl and rub all over with the garlic. Pour over the wine and place the rosemary sprig on top. Cover and let marinate in the refrigerator for 3 hours, or overnight if possible.

2 To make the mint sauce, combine the mint leaves with the sugar in a small bowl. Add the boiling water and stir to dissolve the sugar. Add the white wine vinegar and let stand for 30 minutes before serving with the lamb.

3 Preheat the oven to 425°F/220°C. Remove the lamb from the marinade, reserving the marinade. Dry the meat with paper towels, and season well with salt and pepper.

Place in a small roasting pan, drizzle with the oil, and roast in the oven for 15–20 minutes, depending on whether you like your meat rare or medium. Remove the lamb from the oven and let rest in a warm place, covered with foil, for 5 minutes.

4 Place the marinade in a small pan, bring to a boil over medium heat and bubble away for 2–3 minutes. Add the lamb stock and red currant jelly and let simmer until a syrupy consistency is achieved.

5 Carve the lamb into chops and serve on warmed plates with the stock and red currant jelly sauce spooned over the top. Serve the mint sauce separately.

cook's tip
Rack of lamb is an impressive dish for entertaining, too. Just double or treble the ingredients, depending on the number of guests.

PROVENÇAL BARBECUED LAMB

PROVENÇAL DISHES ARE PREPARED IN THE STYLE OF PROVENCE, A REGION IN FRANCE, AND ARE MOST OFTEN ASSOCIATED WITH GARLIC, TOMATOES, AND OLIVE OIL. BE GENEROUS WITH THE FRESH HERBS AND THE AROMAS WILL TRANSPORT YOU TO THE PROVENÇAL COUNTRYSIDE!

serves
4–6
preparation
30 minutes,
plus 6–24 hours'
marinating and 10
minutes' resting
cooking
20–25 minutes

ingredients
- 1 leg of lamb, about 3 lb 5 oz/1.5 kg, boned
- olive oil, for brushing

MARINADE
- 1 bottle full-bodied red wine
- 2 large garlic cloves, chopped
- 2 tbsp extra virgin olive oil
- large handful of fresh rosemary sprigs, plus extra to garnish
- fresh thyme sprigs, plus extra to garnish

BLACK OLIVE TAPENADE
- 1½ cups black Niçoise olives in brine, rinsed and pitted
- 1 large garlic clove
- 2 tbsp walnut pieces
- 4 canned anchovy fillets, drained
- ½ cup extra virgin olive oil
- lemon juice, to taste
- pepper

1 Place the boned lamb on a cutting board. Holding the knife almost flat, slice horizontally into the pocket left by the leg bone, taking care not to cut all the way through, so the boned meat can be opened out flat, like a book.

2 Place the lamb in a large nonmetallic bowl and add all the marinade ingredients. Cover with plastic wrap and let marinate in the refrigerator for at least 6 hours, but preferably up to 24 hours, turning the meat over several times.

3 Preheat the barbecue. To make the tapenade, place the olives, garlic, walnut pieces, and anchovies in a food processor and process until blended. With the motor running, slowly add the olive oil through the feed tube. Add lemon juice and pepper to taste. Transfer to a bowl, cover and let chill until required.

4 When ready to cook, remove the lamb from the marinade and pat dry. Lay the lamb flat and thread 2–3 long metal skewers through the flesh, so that the meat remains flat while it cooks. Spread the tapenade all over the lamb on both sides.

5 Brush the barbecue rack with oil. Place the lamb on the rack about 4 inches/10 cm above hot coals and cook for 5 minutes. Turn the meat over, and continue cooking for an additional 5 minutes. Turn twice more at 5-minute intervals, brushing with extra tapenade. Raise the rack to 6 inches/15 cm if the meat begins to look charred—it should be medium-cooked after 20–25 minutes.

6 Remove the lamb from the heat and let stand for 10 minutes before carving into thin slices and serving, garnished with rosemary and thyme sprigs.

LAMB SHANKS WITH ROASTED ONIONS

IN THIS RECIPE SLOW-ROASTED LAMB IS INFUSED WITH THE FLAVORS OF GARLIC AND ROSEMARY AND
SERVED WITH SWEET RED ONIONS AND GLAZED CARROT STICKS. YOU WON'T REQUIRE ANYTHING
MORE EXCEPT A BOTTLE OF FRUITY RED WINE.

serves
4

preparation
20 minutes

cooking
2–2¼ hours

ingredients

- 4 x 12 oz/350 g lamb shanks
- 6 garlic cloves
- 2 tbsp virgin olive oil
- 1 tbsp fresh rosemary, very finely chopped
- 4 red onions
- 12 oz/350 g carrots, cut into thin sticks
- 4 tbsp water
- salt and pepper

1 Preheat the oven to 350°F/180°C. Trim off any excess fat from the lamb. Using a small, sharp knife, make 6 incisions in each shank. Cut the garlic cloves lengthwise into 4 slices. Insert 6 garlic slices in the incisions in each lamb shank.

2 Place the lamb in a single layer in a roasting pan, drizzle with the olive oil, sprinkle with the rosemary, and season with pepper. Roast in the preheated oven for 45 minutes.

3 Wrap each of the onions in a piece of foil. Remove the roasting pan from the oven and season the lamb with salt. Return to the oven and place the wrapped onions on the shelf next to it. Roast for an additional 1–1¼ hours until the lamb is very tender.

4 Meanwhile, bring a large pan of water to a boil. Add the carrot sticks and blanch for 1 minute. Drain and refresh in cold water.

5 Remove the roasting pan from the oven when the lamb is meltingly tender and transfer it to a warmed serving dish. Skim off any fat from the roasting pan and place it over medium heat. Add the carrots and cook for 2 minutes, then add the water, bring to a boil and let simmer, stirring constantly and scraping up the glazed bits from the base of the roasting pan.

6 Transfer the carrots and sauce to the serving dish. Remove the onions from the oven and unwrap. Cut off and discard about ½ inch/1 cm of the tops and add the onions to the dish. Serve immediately.

ROGAN JOSH

THIS INDIAN DISH OF CHUNKS OF LAMB BRAISED IN CREAM AND SPICES IS A KASHMIRI SPECIALTY. THE TURMERIC GIVES IT A LOVELY GOLDEN COLOR. IT IS DELICIOUS SERVED WITH COOKED RICE, BUT IT CAN ALSO BE SERVED WITH NAAN BREAD TO SOAK UP THE WONDERFULLY CREAMY SAUCE.

serves
4

preparation
20 minutes,
plus 15 minutes'
cooling

cooking
50–55 minutes

ingredients
- ½ cup ghee or vegetable oil
- 1 lb 2 oz/500 g boneless lamb, cut into bite-size chunks
- 4 garlic cloves, chopped
- 3 fresh green chilies, chopped
- 1-inch/2.5-cm piece fresh gingerroot, grated
- 1 tsp poppy seeds
- 1 cinnamon stick, ground
- 1 cardamom pod, ground
- 4 cloves, ground
- 1 tsp coriander seeds, ground
- 1 tsp cumin seeds, ground
- generous 1 cup sour cream
- ½ tsp turmeric
- ½ tsp chili powder
- 2 large tomatoes, chopped
- 1 bay leaf
- fresh cilantro leaves, to garnish
- freshly cooked rice, to serve

1 Heat half of the ghee in a large pan over high heat. Add the lamb and cook, stirring, for 5 minutes. Lift out the meat with a slotted spoon and drain on paper towels. Add the garlic, chilies, ginger, poppy seeds, and ground spices to the pan and cook over medium heat, stirring, for 4 minutes. Remove from the heat, let cool for a few minutes, then transfer the spice mixture to a food processor. Stir in the sour cream, turmeric, and chili powder and process the mixture until smooth.

2 Heat the remaining ghee in the pan over low heat. Add the chopped tomatoes and cook, stirring, for 3 minutes. Add the sour cream mixture and cook, stirring, until the oil separates. Remove from the heat and add the lamb. Add the bay leaf, return the pan to the heat, and cover. Let simmer gently for 35–40 minutes, or until most of the liquid has been absorbed. Remove from the heat and discard the bay leaf. Garnish with cilantro leaves and serve with freshly cooked rice.

POT-ROAST PORK

BEEF AND CHICKEN ARE THE MOST POPULAR CHOICES FOR POT-ROASTING, BUT A LOIN OF PORK WORKS SUPERBLY WELL, TOO. THIS IS A RICH AND FLAVORSOME DISH THAT IS IDEAL FOR ENTERTAINING. SERVE IT WITH BOILED, BAKED, OR ROAST POTATOES AND FRESHLY COOKED PEAS.

serves
4

preparation
20 minutes

cooking
1½ hours

ingredients
- 1 tbsp sunflower-seed oil
- 4 tbsp butter
- 2 lb 4 oz/1 kg boned and rolled pork loin joint
- 4 shallots, chopped
- 6 juniper berries
- 2 fresh thyme sprigs, plus extra to garnish
- ⅔ cup hard cider
- ⅔ cup chicken stock or water
- 8 celery stalks, chopped
- 2 tbsp all-purpose flour
- ⅔ cup heavy cream
- salt and pepper

TO SERVE
- freshly cooked peas
- boiled potatoes

1 Heat the oil with half the butter in a large, heavy-bottom pan or ovenproof casserole. Add the pork and cook over medium heat, turning frequently, for 5–10 minutes, or until browned. Transfer to a plate.

2 Add the shallots to the pan and cook, stirring frequently, for 5 minutes, or until softened. Add the juniper berries and thyme sprigs and return the pork to the pan, with any juices that have collected on the plate. Pour in the cider and stock, season to taste with salt and pepper, then cover and let simmer for 30 minutes. Turn the pork over and add the celery. Re-cover the pan and cook for an additional 40 minutes.

3 Meanwhile, make a beurre manié by mashing the remaining butter with the flour in a small bowl. Transfer the pork and celery to a platter with a slotted spoon and keep warm. Remove and discard the juniper berries and thyme. Whisk the beurre manié, a little at a time, into the simmering cooking liquid. Cook, stirring constantly, for 2 minutes, then stir in the cream and bring to a boil.

4 Slice the pork and spoon a little of the sauce over it. Garnish with thyme sprigs and serve immediately with the celery, freshly cooked peas, and potatoes. Hand around the remaining sauce separately.

  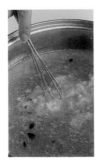

variation
Substitute 2 thinly sliced fennel bulbs for the chopped celery if you would prefer an anise flavor in this dish.

CITRUS PORK CHOPS

THE ADDITION OF JUNIPER AND FENNEL TO THE PORK CHOPS GIVES AN UNUSUAL AND DELICATE FLAVOR TO THIS DISH. WHEN COMBINED WITH THE SWEET, CITRUS TASTE OF ORANGE, THE RESULT IS AN UNFORGETTABLE, MOUTHWATERING EXPERIENCE THAT WILL LEAVE YOU YEARNING FOR MORE.

serves
4

preparation
25 minutes, plus 2 hours' marinating

cooking
10–15 minutes

ingredients
- ½ fennel bulb
- 1 tbsp juniper berries, lightly crushed
- about 2 tbsp olive oil
- finely grated rind and juice of 1 orange
- 4 pork chops, about 5½ oz/150 g each

TO SERVE
- crisp salad
- fresh bread

1 Using a sharp knife, finely chop the fennel bulb, discarding the fronds and green parts.

2 Grind the juniper berries in a mortar and pestle. Mix the crushed juniper berries with the fennel flesh, olive oil, and orange rind.

3 Using a sharp knife, score a few cuts all over each pork chop.

4 Place the pork chops in a roasting pan or an ovenproof dish. Spoon the fennel and juniper mixture over the pork chops.

5 Carefully pour the orange juice over the top of each pork chop, cover, and let marinate in the refrigerator for 2 hours.

6 Preheat the broiler to medium. Cook the pork chops under the hot broiler for 10–15 minutes, depending on the thickness of the meat, until the meat is tender and cooked through, turning occasionally.

7 Transfer the pork chops to serving plates and serve with a crisp, fresh salad and plenty of fresh bread to mop up the cooking juices.

cook's tip

Juniper berries are usually associated with gin, but are often added to meat dishes in Italy for their delicate citrus flavor. They can be bought dried from health food stores.

SWEET-&-SOUR PORK RIBS

THIS DISH MAKES A DELICIOUS ADDITION TO ANY BARBECUE, AND THE SLICED PINEAPLE RINGS ARE
A PERFECT COMPANION TO THE RIBS. IN THIS RECIPE, THE TRADITIONAL CHINESE-STYLE SPARERIB
HAS BEEN USED, BUT BABY BACK RIBS AND LOIN RIBS ARE ALSO SUITABLE.

serves
4

preparation
15 minutes, plus 2
hours' marinating

cooking
50 minutes

ingredients
- 2 garlic cloves, crushed
- 2-inch/5-cm piece fresh
  gingerroot, grated
- ²/₃ cup soy sauce
- 2 tbsp sugar
- 4 tbsp sweet sherry
- 4 tbsp tomato paste
- 10½ oz/300 g pineapple,
  cubed
- 4 lb 8 oz/2 kg pork spareribs
- 3 tbsp honey
- 10½ oz/300 g pineapple
  rings, fresh or canned,
  to serve

1 Mix the garlic, ginger, soy sauce, sugar, sherry, tomato paste, and cubed pineapple together in a nonporous dish.

2 Place the spareribs in the dish and make sure that they are coated completely with the marinade.

3 Cover the dish with plastic wrap. Let the ribs marinate at room temperature for 2 hours.

4 Preheat the barbecue. Cook the ribs over medium-hot coals for 30–40 minutes, brushing with the honey after 20–30 minutes.

5 Baste the spareribs with the reserved marinade frequently until cooked.

6 Cook the pineapple rings over medium-hot coals for 10 minutes, turning once.

7 Transfer the cooked ribs to a serving dish and serve immediately, with the barbecued pineapple rings on the side.

cook's tip

*If a marinade contains soy sauce, the
marinating time should be limited, usually
to 2 hours. If left to marinate for too long,
the meat will dry out and become tough.*

BRAISED VEAL IN RED WINE

THIS IS A CLASSIC CASSEROLE OF MEAT BRAISED IN WINE WITH GARLIC, TOMATOES, AND A LIBERAL AMOUNT OF HERBS. YOU CAN USE STEWING VEAL OR BEEF IN THIS RECIPE, AND THIS DISH GOES PARTICULARLY WELL WITH (LONG-GRAIN) RICE.

serves

6

preparation

25 minutes

cooking

2 hours 20 minutes–2 hours 25 minutes

ingredients

- scant ¼ cup all-purpose flour
- 2 lb/900 g stewing veal or beef, cubed
- 4 tbsp olive oil
- 12 oz/350 g button onions
- 2 garlic cloves, finely chopped
- 12 oz/350 g carrots, sliced
- 1¼ cups dry red wine
- ⅔ cup beef or chicken stock
- 14 oz/400 g canned chopped tomatoes with herbs
- pared rind of 1 lemon
- 1 bay leaf
- 1 tbsp chopped fresh flat-leaf parsley
- 1 tbsp chopped fresh basil
- 1 tsp chopped fresh thyme
- salt and pepper
- freshly cooked rice, to serve

1 Preheat the oven to 350°F/180°C. Place the flour and pepper in a plastic bag, add the meat, and shake well to coat each piece. Heat the oil in a large ovenproof casserole. Add the meat and cook, in batches, for 5–10 minutes, stirring constantly, until browned on all sides. Remove with a slotted spoon and set aside.

2 Add the button onions, garlic, and carrots to the casserole and cook for 5 minutes until beginning to soften. Return the meat to the casserole.

3 Pour in the wine, stirring in any glazed bits from the bottom, then add the stock, the tomatoes with their juice, lemon rind, bay leaf, parsley, basil, thyme, salt and pepper. Bring to a boil then cover the casserole.

4 Cook in the preheated oven for 2 hours, or until the meat is tender. Serve hot with freshly cooked rice.

cook's tip

This is a perfect casserole for cooking in advance and then reheating. Once cooked, let cool and store in the refrigerator. Reheat by bringing to a boil then simmering for 15 minutes.

OSSO BUCCO WITH CITRUS RINDS

POPULAR THROUGHOUT ALL OF ITALY, YOU'LL ALSO FIND SLOW-COOKED VEAL SHINS IN MANY RESTAURANTS ALONG THE MEDITERRANEAN. THE ORANGE AND LEMON RINDS, ALONG WITH FRESH BASIL, GIVE THE DISH A REAL SOUTHERN ITALIAN FLAVOR.

serves
6

preparation
25 minutes

cooking
1½ hours

ingredients
- 1–2 tbsp all-purpose flour
- 6 meaty slices osso bucco (veal shins)
- 2 lb 4 oz/1 kg fresh tomatoes, peeled, seeded, and diced, or 1 lb 12 oz/ 800 g canned chopped tomatoes
- 1–2 tbsp olive oil
- 9 oz/250 g onions, very finely chopped
- 9 oz/250 g carrots, finely diced
- 1 cup dry white wine
- 1 cup veal stock
- 6 large basil leaves, torn
- 1 large garlic clove, very finely chopped
- finely grated rind of 1 large lemon
- finely grated rind of 1 orange
- 2 tbsp finely chopped fresh flat-leaf parsley
- salt and pepper
- crusty bread, to serve

1 Place the flour in a plastic bag and season with salt and pepper. Add the osso bucco, a couple of pieces at a time, and shake until well coated. Remove and shake off the excess flour. Continue until all the pieces are coated.

2 If using canned tomatoes, pass them through a strainer and let drain.

3 Heat 1 tablespoon of the oil in a large ovenproof casserole. Add the osso bucco and cook for 10 minutes on each slide until well browned. Remove from the casserole.

4 Add 1–2 teaspoons of oil to the casserole if necessary. Add the onions and cook for 5 minutes, stirring, until softened. Stir in the carrots and continue cooking until they become soft.

5 Add the tomatoes, wine, stock, and basil and return the osso bucco to the casserole. Bring to a boil, then reduce the heat, cover, and let simmer for 1 hour. Check that the meat is tender with the tip of a knife. If not, continue cooking for 10 minutes and test again.

6 When the meat is tender, sprinkle with the garlic and lemon and orange rinds, re-cover and cook for an additional 10 minutes.

7 Adjust the seasoning if necessary. Sprinkle with the parsley and serve with crusty bread.

4

POULTRY
AND GAME

POULTRY IS DELICIOUS, ECONOMICAL, AND VERY

VERSATILE. A ROAST CHICKEN, FOR EXAMPLE, MAKES

A WONDERFUL TABLE CENTERPIECE, AND WHEN

YOU HAVE EATEN YOUR FILL, THERE ARE ALL KINDS

OF INSPIRING DISHES YOU CAN MAKE USING THE

LEFTOVERS. GAME IS ALSO DELICIOUS, AND MAKES

IMPRESSIVE FARE FOR A DINNER PARTY.

INTRODUCTION

POULTRY IS RICH IN PROTEIN, AND QUICK AND EASY TO PREPARE AND COOK. SOME BIRDS, SUCH AS CHICKEN AND TURKEY, CAN BE A LOWFAT CHOICE AS LONG AS THE FATTY SKIN IS REMOVED, AND THEY ARE VERY VERSATILE. DUCK IS FATTIER, BUT MAKES A GOOD DINNER PARTY CHOICE. GAME BIRDS AND ANIMALS ARE BECOMING MORE WIDELY AVAILABLE.

Buying and storing poultry and game

Always buy your poultry and game as fresh as possible and from a reputable supplier. Choose plump birds that have unblemished skin, and make sure that any wrapping or packaging is intact. As soon as you get it home, remove the packaging (if it's a fresh bird) and transfer the giblets (if any) to a separate bowl. Place the bird on a rack in a dish, then cover it and any giblets loosely with plastic wrap and store in the refrigerator. Keep it well away from cooked meats to prevent any cross-contamination. Whole birds will keep for 1–2 days in the refrigerator, and giblets no longer than 1 day.

Frozen birds can be stored in the freezer in their original packaging. Thaw in the refrigerator thoroughly before cooking; you will need to allow 5 hours per 1 lb/450 g for a chicken and 6 hours per 1 lb/450 g for a turkey.

Game birds are available fresh when in season and frozen all year round. If they are truly wild birds and not farmed, they will have a lower fat content and should therefore be wrapped in bacon or pork fat during roasting. Older birds are not recommended for roasting, but are more suited to soups, casseroles, and stews. Game animals, such as venison and rabbit, tend to be less tender than farmed animals because they get more exercise in the wild. They should therefore be cooked slowly until tender, but not overcooked. Braising is a good method for keeping the meat moist, or it can be roasted if wrapped first in bacon or pork fat.

Types of bird

In addition to the flavor, the choice of bird may depend on the occasion, how many people you are catering for, and how much preparation you wish to do.

Chicken

There are many different varieties of chicken available, including free-range, organic, and corn-fed. You can buy whole birds ready prepared for the oven or frozen. You can also buy a variety of joints—wing, breast, leg, thigh, or drumstick—or you can joint a whole bird yourself. Chicken is delicious roasted, steamed, poached, broiled, casseroled, barbecued, chargrilled, stir-fried, pan-fried, or deep-fried.

Squab chicken

A squab chicken is a very young, small chicken. Squab chickens weigh up to 1 lb/450 g and you should therefore allow one whole bird per person. They are suitable for roasting, barbecuing, and broiling.

Guinea fowl

This bird is related to the chicken and the partridge, and has light and dark meat and a strong flavor. It is available fresh and frozen. As guinea fowl has a low fat content, it is most suited to moist cooking methods such as casseroling. Alternatively, you can wrap it in bacon slices or pork fat and roast it.

Turkey

These birds are much larger than chickens—some can grow to a massive 70 lb/31.5 kg—but the

Chicken

trend nowadays is for much smaller birds. This is because turkey suppliers would like to encourage their use all year round, rather than just during Christmas and other vacations. Turkeys have similar uses to chickens, and you can often interchange them with chickens in recipes. You can buy whole birds ready prepared for the oven or frozen. You can also buy separate joints, such as breast joints or drumsticks. Turkey is particularly suitable for roasting, casseroling, braising, stir-frying, or pan-frying.

Duck

Ducks are available whole, fresh, and frozen. Breast and leg joints are also available. Duck is fattier than chicken or turkey, and is therefore particularly suitable for roasting, broiling, or pan-frying. Duck is often served with a tart fruit sauce, such as orange, in order to cut through any fatty aftertaste.

Goose

Geese are larger than ducks, and can be bought fresh, although they are more often bought frozen. Although they are popular during vacations and Christmas time, especially in Europe, they have become less popular year-round because of their very high fat content. Goose is best roasted, pot-roasted, braised, or stewed. It is also a good idea to serve it with a tart fruit sauce in order to cut through any fatty aftertaste.

Grouse

These are small game birds, and you will need to allow one bird per person. If you are going to roast them, wrap the grouse in bacon or pork fat during cooking. You can also pot-roast, braise, casserole, or stew them.

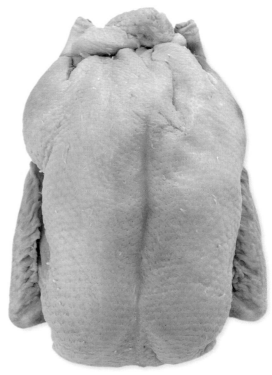

Duck

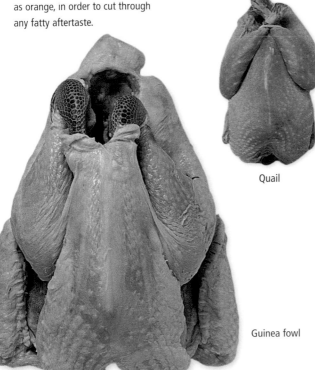

Guinea fowl

Quail

Partridge

This game bird has a dark flesh and an earthy flavor. Since its flesh can be somewhat tough, it is better braised, stewed, or casseroled. However, it can also be roasted.

Pheasant

This is a medium-size game bird. The male has more brilliant plumage than the female, but the female is juicier and more tender. Young birds can be roasted, but older ones should be wrapped in bacon or pork fat during roasting; they can also be braised, casseroled, or stewed.

Quail

This small game bird is related to the partridge. The European variety has lean, medium-dark flesh, whereas the American variety has lean but lighter flesh. Both types have a sweet flavor. Quails are suitable for roasting, pot-roasting, braising, barbecuing, casseroling, or broiling. Their small eggs have a speckled brown shell and a rich flavor.

Venison

Deer is a popular game animal and the meat is available wild or farmed. It is low in cholesterol, and usually available as leg or saddle joints, or as steaks. The best meat comes from a male deer under the age of two years. Venison meat is quite dry and is therefore more suited to casseroles.

Rabbit

This game animal has fine white meat and is available fresh or frozen; you can also buy it whole or boned and cut into pieces. Young rabbits are suitable for broiling, frying, or roasting; older rabbits should be braised, casseroled, or stewed.

Preparation and cooking techniques

Preparing a bird in the right way will help to ensure that it is presented to its best advantage. It is essential to cook poultry all the way through in order to kill off any potentially harmful bacteria.

SPATCHCOCKING A SMALL BIRD

Spatchcocking helps to flatten the bird before broiling or barbecuing, ensuring quicker and more even cooking. Place the bird breast-side down (this means the legs are under the bird, and the wings are on top) on a clean cutting board. Cut along either side of the backbone and remove it (you can save it for making chicken stock or discard it). Open the bird out and turn it over. Using your palms, press down on the bird to flatten it against the cutting board.

MAKING CHICKEN STOCK

Chicken stock is ideal for soups and sauces, and you can store it, covered with plastic wrap, in the refrigerator for 2–3 days. You can also freeze it for up to 6 months. Put the chicken carcass into a large pan with 1 chopped onion, 1 sliced carrot, 1 chopped celery stalk, and 1 chopped leek. Add 1 bay leaf and 1 sprig of thyme, 3 stalks of parsley, and some cracked black peppercorns. Cover with water and bring to a boil, then use a slotted spoon to skim off any scum from the surface. Reduce the heat, cover the pan, and let simmer for 2–3 hours. Strain the contents into a large bowl and discard the solids. Use the stock as required.

ROASTING A LARGE CHICKEN OR A TURKEY

First wipe the chicken or turkey inside and out with paper towels. If you are going to stuff it, pull back the skin around the neck cavity and insert the dressing into the neck end only (do not overfill the bird or it will not cook through properly). If you are not stuffing the bird, simply season the cavity. Pull the skin over the top, then pull up the wings and tie with string. Pull the legs together and tie with string. Rub butter or oil over the skin of the bird, then season to taste with salt and pepper. Transfer the bird to a wire rack in a roasting pan, and roast in a preheated oven, basting occasionally, until cooked through and tender. To test, insert a sharp knife or skewer into the thickest part of the bird: if the juices run clear, the bird is cooked. If not, return it to the oven and cook until done. Alternatively, if you are using a meat thermometer, the bird is cooked when the temperature reaches 194°F/90°C. Remove from the oven and let it rest, covered in kitchen foil, for 15–20 minutes before carving.

CARVING A LARGE BIRD

Place the cooked bird breast-side up on a clean cutting board. Steady the bird with a carving fork, then use a carving knife to cut between one wing and the side of the breast. Remove the wing and cut thin downward slices through the breast meat. Repeat this step on the other side and set aside the wings and the breast slices. Pull out one leg and cut through the joint. Repeat with the other side. Slice the meat from the

---

Oven temperatures and roasting times

Remember that individual oven temperatures and cooking times vary, so the following cooking times are approximate only. Always preheat the oven before cooking.

Bird	Weight	Temperature	Cooking time
Chicken	6 lb 8 oz/3 kg	400°F/200°C	2 1/4 hours
Turkey	11 lb/5 kg	350°F/180°C	3 1/2 hours
	18 lb/8 kg	350°F/180°C	4 3/4–5 hours
Quail	1 lb/450 g	400°F/200°C	30 minutes
Duck	5 lb 8 oz/2.5 kg	350°F/180°C 400°F/200°C	50 minutes at lower temperature, then 2 hours at higher temperature

thighs and drumsticks. Serve the wings, and the slices from the breast, thighs, and drumsticks.

ROASTING AND SERVING A DUCK
Place the duck breast-side up on a clean counter, then wipe it inside and out with paper towels. Duck has a high fat content, so remove any surplus fat. Season inside the tail cavity and insert a bay leaf. Transfer the bird to a wire rack in a roasting pan. Use a fork to prick holes all over it, then season with salt and freshly ground black pepper. Roast in a preheated oven until cooked through and tender (turn and baste it halfway during the cooking time). To test, insert a sharp knife or skewer into the thickest part of the bird: if the juices run clear, the bird is cooked. If not, return the bird to the oven and cook until done. Alternatively, if you are using a meat thermometer, the bird is cooked when the temperature reaches 194°F/90°C. To serve the duck, joint it by cutting it in half lengthwise. Alternatively, use a sharp knife to separate the legs from the body, then cut off the wings. Remove the breast meat and slice it. Serve the legs, wings, and breast slices.

Jointing a whole bird

1 To cut a large raw bird into joints, first remove any string and place it on a clean cutting board, breast-side up, with the legs pointing toward you.

2 Using a sharp knife, cut the skin between one leg and the side of the breast, then use your hand to press the leg down flat to the board. Do the same with the other leg. Cut through the joint attaching one of the legs and remove the leg from the body. Do the same for the other side.

3 Turn the bird to face the other way and locate the ridge along the middle of the back. Using a knife, cut away one breast, taking a wing off with it. Do the same with the other breast.

4 To divide the legs into thighs and drumsticks, put them skin-side down on the cutting board, then cut through the line to separate the joint. Set aside the carcass for making stock.

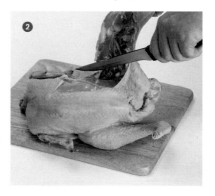

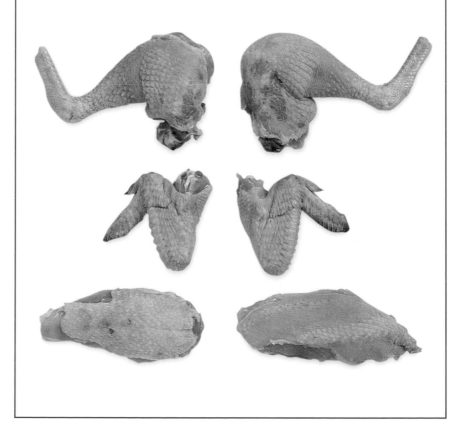

TRADITIONAL ROAST CHICKEN

ROAST CHICKEN IS A POPULAR DISH IN BRITAIN. IN THIS VERSION, A DELICIOUS MIXTURE OF GARLIC, WALNUTS, AND PARSLEY IS STUFFED UNDERNEATH THE SKIN TO CREATE A WONDERFUL FLAVOR AND TEXTURE OVER THE SURFACE OF THE BIRD. SERVE IT WITH ROAST POTATOES AND VEGETABLES.

serves
4

preparation
20 minutes,
plus 10 minutes'
resting

cooking
1 hour 50 minutes

ingredients
- 2 tbsp butter, softened
- 1 garlic clove,
  finely chopped
- 3 tbsp finely chopped
  toasted walnuts
- 1 tbsp chopped
  fresh parsley
- 1 oven-ready chicken,
  weighing 4 lb/1.8 kg
- 1 lime, cut into quarters
- 2 tbsp vegetable oil
- 1 tbsp cornstarch
- 2 tbsp water
- salt and pepper

TO GARNISH
- lime wedges
- fresh rosemary sprigs

TO SERVE
- roast potatoes
- selection of freshly
  cooked vegetables

1 Preheat the oven to 375°F/190°C. Mix 1 tablespoon of the butter with the garlic, walnuts, and parsley together in a small bowl. Season well with salt and pepper. Loosen the skin from the breast of the chicken without breaking it. Spread the butter mixture evenly between the skin and breast meat. Place the lime quarters inside the body cavity.

2 Pour the oil into a roasting pan. Transfer the chicken to the pan and dot the skin with the remaining butter. Roast for 1¾ hours, basting occasionally, until the chicken is tender and the juices run clear

when a skewer is inserted into the thickest part of the meat. Lift out the chicken and place on a serving platter to rest for 10 minutes.

3 Blend the cornstarch with the water, then stir into the juices in the pan. Transfer to the stove. Stir over low heat until thickened. Add more water if necessary. Garnish the chicken with lime wedges and rosemary sprigs. Serve with roast potatoes and a selection of freshly cooked vegetables and spoon over the thickened juices.

 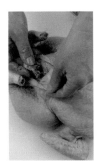 

CHICKEN BIRYANI

THIS RECIPE MAY LOOK COMPLICATED, BUT IS NOT DIFFICULT TO FOLLOW. YOU CAN SUBSTITUTE LAMB FOR THE CHICKEN, BUT IF YOU DO SO YOU WILL HAVE TO MARINATE IT OVERNIGHT FIRST. GHEE IS A CLARIFIED BUTTER. IF IT IS UNAVAILABLE, USE ORDINARY BUTTER INSTEAD.

serves
8

preparation
15 minutes,
plus 3 hours'
marinating

cooking
1½–1¾ hours

ingredients
- 1½ tsp finely chopped fresh gingerroot
- 1½ tsp crushed fresh garlic
- 1 tbsp garam masala
- 1 tsp chili powder
- ½ tsp ground turmeric
- 2 tsp salt
- 5 green/white cardamom pods, crushed
- 1¼ cups plain yogurt
- 3 lb 5 oz/1.5 kg chicken, skinned and cut into 8 pieces
- ⅔ cup milk
- 1 tsp saffron strands
- 6 tbsp ghee
- 2 onions, sliced
- 1 lb/450 g basmati rice
- 2 cinnamon sticks
- 4 black peppercorns
- 1 tsp black cumin seeds
- 4 fresh green chilies
- 4 tbsp lemon juice
- 2–3 tbsp finely chopped fresh cilantro leaves

1 Blend the ginger, garlic, garam masala, chili powder, turmeric, half the salt, and the cardamoms together in a bowl. Add the yogurt and chicken pieces and mix well. Cover and let marinate in the refrigerator for 3 hours.

2 Boil the milk in a small pan, pour over the saffron, and set aside.

3 Heat the ghee in a pan. Add the onions and cook until golden. Transfer half of the onions and ghee to a bowl and set aside.

4 Place the rice, cinnamon sticks, peppercorns, and black cumin seeds in a pan of water. Bring the rice to a boil and remove from the heat when half-cooked. Drain and place in a bowl. Mix with the remaining salt.

5 Chop the chilies and set aside. Add the chicken mixture to the pan containing the onions. Add half each of the chopped green chilies, lemon juice, cilantro, and saffron milk. Add the rice, then the rest of the ingredients, including the reserved onions and ghee. Cover tightly. Cook over low heat for 1 hour. Check that the meat is cooked through; if it is not cooked, return to the heat, and cook for an additional 15 minutes. Mix well before serving.

THAI RED CHICKEN CURRY

THAI CURRY PASTE IS A PASTE OF AROMATIC HERBS, SPICES, AND VEGETABLES THAT IS A POPULAR FLAVORING IN THAI CUISINE. IT COMES IN DIFFERENT VARIETIES: RED CURRY PASTE TENDS TO VARY IN SPICINESS, WHILE GREEN CURRY PASTE IS THE HOTTEST, AND YELLOW IS THE MILDEST.

serves
4
preparation
30 minutes
cooking
40 minutes

ingredients
- 6 garlic cloves, chopped
- 2 fresh red chilies, chopped
- 2 tbsp chopped fresh lemon grass
- 1 tsp finely grated lime rind
- 1 tbsp chopped fresh kaffir lime leaves
- 1 tbsp Thai red curry paste
- 1 tbsp coriander seeds, toasted and crushed
- 1 tbsp chili oil
- 4 skinless, boneless chicken breasts, sliced
- 1¼ cups coconut milk
- 1¼ cups chicken stock
- 1 tbsp soy sauce
- ⅓ cup shelled unsalted peanuts, toasted and ground
- 3 scallions, diagonally sliced
- 1 red bell pepper, seeded and sliced
- 3 Thai eggplants, sliced
- 2 tbsp chopped fresh Thai basil or fresh cilantro
- fresh cilantro, to garnish
- freshly cooked jasmine rice, to serve

1 Place the garlic, chilies, lemon grass, lime rind, lime leaves, curry paste, and coriander seeds in a food processor and process until the mixture is smooth.

2 Heat the oil in a preheated wok or large skillet over high heat. Add the chicken and garlic mixture and stir-fry for 5 minutes. Add the coconut milk, stock, and soy sauce and bring to a boil. Reduce the heat and cook, stirring, for an additional 3 minutes. Stir in the ground peanuts and let simmer for 20 minutes.

3 Add the scallions, bell pepper, and eggplants and let simmer, stirring occasionally, for an additional 10 minutes. Remove from the heat, stir in the basil, and garnish with cilantro. Serve immediately with freshly cooked jasmine rice.

CHICKEN FRICASSÉE

WHILE IT IS TYPICALLY COOKED IN CREAM, THE TERM "FRICASSÉE" SIMPLY MEANS COOKING THE
MEAT—OR SOMETIMES FISH—IN A WHITE SAUCE, WITHOUT BROWNING IT. SERVE THIS CREAM-FREE
VERSION WITH PLAIN BOILED RICE OR NEW POTATOES FOR A DELICIOUS, FILLING SUPPER.

serves
4
preparation
15 minutes
cooking
35–40 minutes

ingredients
- 1 tbsp all-purpose flour
- 4 skinless, boneless chicken breasts, about 5 oz/140 g each, trimmed of all visible fat and cut into ¾-inch/ 2-cm cubes
- 1 tbsp sunflower-seed or corn oil
- 8 pearl onions
- 2 garlic cloves, crushed
- 1 cup chicken stock
- 2 carrots, diced
- 2 celery stalks, diced
- 2 cups frozen peas
- 1 yellow bell pepper, seeded and diced
- 4 oz/115 g white mushrooms, sliced
- ½ cup lowfat plain yogurt
- 3 tbsp chopped fresh parsley
- salt and white pepper

1 Spread out the flour on a dish and season with salt and pepper. Add the chicken and, using your hands, coat in the flour. Heat the oil in a heavy-bottom pan. Add the onions and garlic and cook over low heat, stirring occasionally, for 5 minutes. Add the chicken and cook, stirring, for 10 minutes, or until just beginning to color.

2 Gradually stir in the stock, then add the carrots, celery, and peas. Bring to a boil, then reduce the heat, cover, and let simmer for 5 minutes. Add the bell pepper and mushrooms, cover, and let simmer for an additional 10 minutes.

3 Stir in the yogurt and chopped parsley and season to taste with salt and pepper. Cook for 1–2 minutes, or until heated through, then transfer to 4 large, warmed serving plates and serve immediately.

cook's tip
When dicing bell peppers, cut them in half and place them on a cutting board, shiny side downward, to prevent the knife from slipping.

variation
You can substitute skim milk for the yogurt and add extra flavor with 1 teaspoon of lemon juice and a pinch of freshly grated nutmeg in Step 3.

ROAST SQUAB CHICKENS

IN THIS RECIPE, SQUAB CHICKENS—BABY CHICKENS—ARE STUFFED WITH LEMON GRASS, LIME LEAVES, AND GINGER, COATED WITH A SPICY MARINADE, THEN ROASTED UNTIL GOLDEN. THE RESULT IS A DISH OF SUCCULENT GOLDEN CHICKEN, PAIRED WITH AN EXCITING FUSION OF ASIAN FLAVORS.

serves
4

preparation
10 minutes

cooking
55 minutes

ingredients
- 4 small squab chickens, weighing about 12 oz–1 lb 2 oz/350–500 g each
- 4 blades lemon grass
- 4 fresh kaffir lime leaves
- 4 slices fresh gingerroot
- about 6 tbsp coconut milk, for brushing
- a mixture of freshly cooked wild rice and basmati rice, to serve

MARINADE
- 4 garlic cloves, peeled
- 2 fresh cilantro roots
- 1 tbsp light soy sauce
- salt and pepper

TO GARNISH
- fresh cilantro leaves
- lime wedges

1 Preheat the oven to 375°F/190°C. Carefully wash the squab chickens and pat dry on paper towels.

2 Place all the ingredients for the marinade in a blender and purée until smooth. Alternatively, grind to a paste using a mortar and pestle.

3 Rub the marinade mixture into the skin of the squab chickens, using the back of a spoon to spread it evenly over the skins.

4 Place a blade of lemon grass, a lime leaf, and a piece of ginger in the cavity of each squab chicken.

5 Place the squab chickens in a roasting pan and brush lightly with the coconut milk. Roast in the preheated oven for 30 minutes.

6 Remove from the oven, brush again with coconut milk, then return to the oven and cook for an additional 15–25 minutes, or until golden and cooked through, depending upon the size of the squab chicken. The squab chickens are cooked if the juices run clear when a skewer is inserted into the thickest part of the meat.

7 Serve the squab chickens with the pan juices poured over. Garnish with cilantro leaves and lime wedges and serve with rice.

CHICKEN & GINGER STIR-FRY

THE POMEGRANATE SEEDS ADD A SHARP CHINESE FLAVOR TO THIS INDIAN STIR-FRY. SERVE IT IN THE SUMMER WITH A SPICY RICE SALAD OR A MIXED GREEN SALAD, OR IN THE WINTER ON A BED OF FRESHLY COOKED LONG-GRAIN RICE OR WITH SOME WARM NAAN BREAD.

serves
4
preparation
10 minutes
cooking
25 minutes

ingredients
- 3 tbsp vegetable oil
- 1 lb 9 oz/700 g lean skinless, boneless chicken breasts, cut into 2-inch/ 5-cm strips
- 3 garlic cloves, crushed
- 1 tsp pomegranate seeds, crushed
- 1½-inch/3.5-cm piece fresh gingerroot, cut into strips
- ½ tsp turmeric
- 1 tsp garam masala
- 2 fresh green chilies, sliced
- ½ tsp salt
- 4 tbsp lemon juice
- grated rind of 1 lemon
- 6 tbsp chopped fresh cilantro, plus extra to garnish
- ½ cup chicken stock
- naan bread, to serve

1 Heat the oil in a preheated wok or large skillet. Add the chicken and stir-fry until golden brown all over. Remove from the wok and set aside.

2 Add the garlic, pomegranate seeds, and ginger to the wok and stir-fry in the oil for 1 minute, taking care not to let the garlic burn.

3 Stir in the turmeric, garam masala, and chilies and fry for 30 seconds.

4 Return the chicken to the wok and add the salt, lemon juice, lemon rind, cilantro, and stock. Stir the chicken well to make sure it is coated in the sauce.

5 Bring the mixture to a boil, then reduce the heat and let simmer for 10–15 minutes, or until the chicken is thoroughly cooked. Garnish with chopped cilantro and serve with warm naan bread.

DUCK BREASTS WITH CHILI & LIME

THESE DUCK BREASTS ARE WONDERFULLY COMPLEMENTED BY THE LIME MARINADE AND PLUM JELLY. THE ACIDITY OF THE LIME CUTS THROUGH THE RICHNESS OF THE DUCK BEAUTIFULLY. DUCK IS A VERY FATTY MEAT, SO DRAIN OFF AS MUCH EXCESS FAT AS YOU CAN DURING COOKING.

serves
4

preparation
15 minutes,
plus 3–8 hours'
marinating

cooking
10 minutes

ingredients
- 4 boneless duck breasts
- 1 tsp vegetable oil
- ½ cup chicken stock
- 2 tbsp plum jelly
- salt and pepper

MARINADE
- 2 garlic cloves, crushed
- 4 tsp brown sugar
- 3 tbsp lime juice
- 1 tbsp soy sauce
- 1 tsp chili sauce

TO SERVE
- mixed salad greens
- freshly cooked rice

1 To make the marinade, mix together the garlic, sugar, lime juice, and the soy and chili sauces.

2 Using a small sharp knife, cut deep slashes in the skin of the duck breasts to make a diamond pattern. Place the duck breasts in a wide, nonmetallic dish.

3 Spoon the marinade over the duck breasts, turning well to coat them evenly in the mixture. Cover the dish with plastic wrap and let marinate in the refrigerator for at least 3 hours, or overnight.

4 Drain the duck, reserving the marinade. Heat a large, heavy-bottom pan until very hot and brush with the oil. Add the duck breasts, skin-side down, and cook for 4–5 minutes until the skin is browned and crisp. Pour off the excess fat.

5 Turn the duck breasts and cook on the other side for 2–3 minutes to brown. Add the reserved marinade, stock and jelly and let simmer for 2 minutes. Adjust the seasoning to taste and serve hot, with the juices spooned over the meat, salad greens, and freshly cooked rice.

PEKING DUCK

NO COOKBOOK WOULD BE COMPLETE WITHOUT THIS FAMOUS DISH. IN THIS VERSION, DELICIOUS CRISPY DUCK IS SERVED WITH PANCAKES AND A TANGY SAUCE FOR A REALLY SPECIAL MEAL. IT IS AN EXCELLENT CHOICE FOR A DINNER PARTY.

serves
4

preparation
20 minutes, plus 8 hours' standing

cooking
1½ hours

ingredients
- 4 lb/1.8 kg duck
- 7¼ cups boiling water
- 4 tbsp honey
- 2 tsp dark soy sauce
- carrot strips, to garnish

SAUCE
- 2 tbsp sesame oil
- ½ cup hoisin sauce
- scant ⅔ cup superfine sugar
- ½ cup water

TO SERVE
- Chinese pancakes
- thin cucumber sticks
- shredded scallions

1 Place the duck on a rack set over a roasting pan and pour 5 cups of the boiling water over it. Remove the duck and rack and discard the water. Pat dry with paper towels, replace the duck and rack and set aside for several hours.

2 Mix the honey, 2½ cups of boiling water and soy sauce together. Brush the mixture as a glaze over the skin and inside the duck. Set aside the remaining glaze. Set aside for 1 hour, until the glaze has dried.

3 Coat the duck with another layer of glaze. Let dry and repeat until all of the glaze is used.

4 Preheat the oven to 375°F/190°C. To make the sauce, heat the oil and add the hoisin sauce, sugar, and water. Let simmer for 2–3 minutes, until thickened. Cool and let chill until required.

5 Cook the duck in the preheated oven for 30 minutes. Turn the duck over and cook for 20 minutes. Turn

the duck again and cook for 20–30 minutes, or until the meat is cooked through and the skin is crisp.

6 Remove the duck from the oven and let stand for 10 minutes. Meanwhile, heat the Chinese pancakes in a bamboo steamer for 5–7 minutes. Cut the skin and duck meat into strips and divide betweeen individual serving plates. Garnish with carrot strips and serve with the pancakes, thin cucumber sticks, shredded scallions, and sauce.

ROAST DUCK WITH APPLE

THIS DISH MAKES AN EXCELLENT SUPPER AND IS FULL OF INTERESTING FLAVORS. THE RICHNESS OF THE DUCK MEAT IN THIS RECIPE CONTRASTS WELL WITH THE APPLES, LEMON, BAY LEAVES, AND APRICOT SAUCE. IF DUCKLING PORTIONS ARE UNAVAILABLE, USE A WHOLE BIRD CUT INTO JOINTS.

serves
4

preparation
10 minutes

cooking
1½ hours

ingredients
- 4 duckling portions, about 12 oz/350 g each
- 4 tbsp dark soy sauce
- 2 tbsp brown sugar
- 2 red-skinned apples
- 2 green-skinned apples
- juice of 1 lemon
- 2 tbsp honey
- a few bay leaves
- salt and pepper
- assorted freshly cooked vegetables, to serve

APRICOT SAUCE
- 14 oz/400 g canned apricots in fruit juice
- 4 tbsp sweet sherry

1 Preheat the oven to 375°F/190°C. Wash the duck and trim away any excess fat. Place on a wire rack over a roasting pan and prick all over with a fork or a clean, sharp needle.

2 Brush the duck with the soy sauce. Sprinkle over the sugar and season with pepper. Cook in the preheated oven, basting occasionally, for 50–60 minutes, or until the meat is cooked through and the juices run clear when a skewer is inserted into the thickest part of the meat.

3 Meanwhile, core the apples and cut each into 6 wedges, then place in a small bowl and mix with the lemon juice and honey. Transfer to a small roasting pan, add a few bay leaves, and season to taste with salt and pepper. Cook alongside the duck, basting occasionally, for 20–25 minutes until tender. Discard the bay leaves.

4 To make the sauce, place the apricots in a blender or food processor with the can juices and the sherry. Process until smooth. Alternatively, mash the apricots with a fork until smooth and mix with the juice and sherry.

5 Just before serving, heat the apricot sauce in a small pan. Remove the skin from the duck and pat the flesh with paper towels to absorb any fat. Serve the duck with the apple wedges, apricot sauce, and freshly cooked vegetables.

variation
Fruit complements duck perfectly. Use canned pineapple in natural juice for a delicious alternative.

ROAST TURKEY WITH BREAD SAUCE

ROAST TURKEY MAKES AN EXCELLENT TABLE CENTERPIECE FOR CHRISTMAS OR THANKSGIVING.
IN THIS RECIPE, CHESTNUTS, SAUSAGE, AND SAGE COMBINE TO MAKE A WONDERFUL DRESSING FOR
THE BIRD, WHICH IS COMPLEMENTED BEAUTIFULLY BY A DELICIOUSLY SMOOTH BREAD SAUCE.

serves
8

preparation
20 minutes,
plus 10 minutes'
resting

cooking
3½ hours

ingredients
- 11 lb/5 kg turkey
- 4 tbsp butter
- 5 tbsp red wine
- 1¾ cups chicken stock,
  bought fresh or made with
  a bouillon cube
- 1 tbsp cornstarch
- 1 tsp French mustard
- 1 tsp sherry vinegar
- 2 tsp water
- roast new potatoes,
  to serve

DRESSING
- 8 oz/225 g pork
  sausagemeat
- 8 oz/225 g unsweetened
  chestnut purée
- ¾ cup walnuts, chopped
- ⅔ cup no-soak dried
  apricots, chopped
- 2 tbsp chopped fresh
  parsley
- 2 tbsp chopped fresh sage
- 2 tbsp snipped fresh chives
- 4–5 tbsp heavy cream
- salt and pepper

BREAD SAUCE
- 1 onion, peeled
- 4 cloves
- 2½ cups milk
- 2 cups fresh white bread
  crumbs
- 4 tbsp butter

1 Preheat the oven to 425°F/220°C.
To make the dressing, combine the
sausagemeat and chestnut purée in a
bowl, then stir in the walnuts,
apricots, and herbs. Stir in enough
cream to make a firm, but not dry,
mixture. Season to taste with salt
and pepper.

2 Spoon the dressing into the neck
cavity of the turkey and close the
flap of skin with a skewer. Place the
bird in a large roasting pan and rub
all over with 3 tablespoons of the
butter. Roast for 1 hour, then reduce
the oven temperature to 350°F/
180°C and roast for an additional
2½ hours. You may need to pour
off the fat from the roasting
pan occasionally.

3 Meanwhile, make the bread sauce.
Stud the onion with the cloves, then
place in a pan with the milk, bread
crumbs, and butter. Bring just to
boiling point over low heat, then
remove from the heat and let stand
in a warm place to infuse. Just
before serving, remove the onion
and reheat the sauce gently, beating
well with a wooden spoon. Season to
taste with salt and pepper.

4 Check that the turkey is cooked
by inserting a skewer or the tip of
a sharp knife into the thigh; if the
juices run clear, it is ready. Transfer
the bird to a carving board, cover
loosely with foil, and let rest.

5 To make the gravy, skim off the
fat from the roasting pan then place
the pan on the top of the stove over
medium heat. Add the red wine and
stir with a wooden spoon, scraping
up all the sediment from the bottom
of the pan. Stir in the stock. Mix the
cornstarch, mustard, vinegar, and the
water together in a small bowl, then
stir into the wine and stock mixture.
Bring to a boil, stirring constantly
until thickened and smooth. Stir in
the remaining butter.

6 Carve the turkey and serve with
the warm bread sauce and all the
trimmings—including dressing, roast
potatoes, and gravy.

ROAST PHEASANT WITH RED WINE & HERBS

ROAST PHEASANT IS A DELICIOUS TREAT, AND MAKES A SPLENDID DISH FOR DINNER PARTIES AND ENTERTAINING. IN THIS RECIPE, YOU WILL NEED TO USE YOUNG PHEASANTS, BECAUSE THEIR TENDER FLESH IS JUICY ENOUGH FOR ROASTING AND WILL NOT DRY OUT. OLDER BIRDS ARE NOT SUITABLE.

serves
4

preparation
20 minutes,
plus 15 minutes'
resting

cooking
1 hour

ingredients
- 7 tbsp butter, slightly softened
- 1 tbsp chopped fresh thyme
- 1 tbsp chopped fresh parsley
- 2 oven-ready young pheasants
- 4 tbsp vegetable oil
- ½ cup red wine
- salt and pepper

TO SERVE
- roast parsnips
- sautéed potatoes
- freshly cooked Brussels sprouts

1 Preheat the oven to 375°F/190°C. Place the butter in a small bowl and mix in the chopped herbs. Lift the skins off the pheasants, taking care not to tear them, and push the herb butter under the skins. Season to taste with salt and pepper.

2 Pour the oil into a roasting pan, add the pheasants, and cook in the preheated oven for 45 minutes, basting occasionally. Remove from the oven, pour over the red wine, then return to the oven and cook for an additional 15 minutes, or until cooked through. Check that each

bird is cooked by inserting a knife between the legs and body. If the juices run clear, they are cooked.

3 Remove the pheasants from the oven, cover with foil, and let stand for 15 minutes. Divide between individual serving plates, and serve with roast parsnips, sautéed potatoes, and freshly cooked Brussels sprouts.

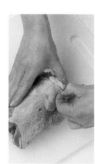

QUAILS WITH GRAPES

THIS IS A VERY POPULAR GAME DISH IN SPAIN, AND APPEARS ON MANY RESTAURANT MENUS. THE CLOVES AND BRANDY GIVE A WONDERFUL AROMATIC FLAVOR TO THE BIRDS AND GRAPES, AND THE WEDGES OF POTATO PANCAKE PROVIDE A LOVELY CONTRAST IN TEXTURE AND FLAVOR.

serves
4

preparation
30 minutes, plus
10–15 minutes'
cooling

cooking
1 hour

ingredients
- 4 tbsp olive oil
- 8 quails, cleaned
- 10 oz/280 g green seedless grapes
- 1 cup grape juice
- 2 cloves
- about ²/₃ cup water
- 2 tbsp Spanish brandy
- salt and pepper

POTATO PANCAKE
- 1 lb 5 oz/600 g unpeeled potatoes
- 2¹/₂ tbsp unsalted butter or pork fat
- 1¹/₂ tbsp olive oil

1 Preheat the oven to 450°F/230°C. To make the pancake, parboil the potatoes for 10 minutes. Drain and let cool completely, then peel, coarsely grate, and season with salt and pepper to taste. Set aside until required.

2 Heat the 4 tablespoons of oil in a heavy-bottom skillet or ovenproof casserole large enough to hold the quails in a single layer over medium heat. Add the quails and cook on all sides until they are golden brown.

3 Add the grapes, grape juice, cloves, enough water to come halfway up the side of the quails, and salt and pepper to taste. Cover and let simmer for 20 minutes. Transfer the quails and all the juices to a roasting pan, or casserole, and sprinkle with brandy. Roast, uncovered, in the preheated oven for 10 minutes.

4 Meanwhile, to make the potato pancake, melt the butter or pork fat with the oil in a 12-inch/30-cm nonstick skillet over high heat. When the fat is hot, add the grated potato and spread into an even layer. Reduce the heat and let simmer for 10 minutes. Place a plate over the skillet and, wearing oven mitts, invert them so the potato pancake drops onto the plate. Slide the potato back into the skillet and continue cooking for 10 minutes, or until cooked through and crisp. Slide out of the skillet and cut into 4 wedges. Keep the pancake warm until the quail is ready.

5 Place a potato pancake wedge and 2 quails on each individual serving plate. Taste the grape sauce and adjust the seasoning if necessary. Spoon the sauce over the quails and serve immediately.

CHARGRILLED VENISON STEAKS

VENISON HAS A GOOD STRONG FLAVOR, WHICH MAKES IT AN IDEAL MEAT TO BARBECUE OR BROIL.
IN THIS RECIPE, THE VENISON STEAKS ARE FIRST MARINATED IN A DELICIOUS COMBINATION OF WINE,
OIL, SUGAR, AND HERBS, AND THEN COOKED TO RELEASE ALL THEIR DELICIOUS FLAVOR.

serves
4
preparation
15 minutes, plus 8
hours' marinating
cooking
12–24 minutes

ingredients
- 4 venison steaks
- ⅔ cup red wine
- 2 tbsp sunflower-seed oil
- 1 tbsp red wine vinegar
- 1 onion, chopped
- fresh parsley sprigs
- 2 fresh thyme sprigs
- 1 bay leaf
- 1 tsp superfine sugar
- ½ tsp mild mustard
- salt and pepper

TO SERVE
- jacket baked potatoes
- salad greens
- cherry tomatoes

1 Place the venison steaks in a shallow, nonmetallic dish.

2 Combine the wine, oil, wine vinegar, onion, fresh parsley, thyme, bay leaf, sugar, mustard, and salt and pepper to taste in a screw-top jar and shake vigorously until well combined. Alternatively, using a fork, whisk the ingredients together in a bowl.

3 Pour the marinade mixture over the venison, cover, and let marinate in the refrigerator overnight. Turn the steaks over in the mixture occasionally so that the meat is well coated.

4 Preheat the barbecue to high. Cook the venison over hot coals, searing the meat over the hottest part of the barbecue for 2 minutes on each side. Alternatively, cook under a hot broiler.

5 Move the meat to an area with slightly less intense heat, or turn down the broiler to medium, and cook for an additional 4–10 minutes on each side, according to taste. Test the meat by inserting the tip of a knife into the meat—the juices will range from red when the meat is still rare to clear as the meat becomes well cooked.

6 Serve the steaks immediately with jacket baked potatoes, salad greens, and cherry tomatoes.

cook's tip

Farmed venison is available all year round. Look out for it in the meat section of the supermarket or order it from an independent butcher. Marinate overnight to tenderize.

5

VEGETABLES
AND SALADS

VEGETABLES AND SALADS ARE VERY GOOD FOR
YOU AND EXTREMELY VERSATILE. YOU CAN COOK
VEGETABLES IN COUNTLESS WAYS, FROM BOILING,
STEAMING, AND PAN-FRYING, TO BAKING, ROASTING,
AND STEWING. MANY OF THEM CAN BE EATEN RAW,
TOO. YOU CAN ALSO PRESENT THEM IN A MULTITUDE
OF WAYS, FROM MASHED OR PURÉED TO JULIENNED.

INTRODUCTION

VEGETABLES ARE VERY GOOD FOR YOU: THEY ARE RICH IN VITAMINS AND MINERALS AND LOW IN FAT. THEY ARE ALSO VERY QUICK AND EASY TO PREPARE AND COOK. YOU CAN ALSO USE SURPLUS OR LEFTOVER VEGETABLES IN OTHER DISHES, SUCH AS A STOCK.

Buying and storing vegetables

Choose vegetables when they are in season because this is when they are at their best. Try to buy them in small quantities on a frequent basis to ensure a constant fresh supply—the fresher the vegetables, the better they will taste, and the more nutrients they will have. Here are some of the main varieties.

ROOT VEGETABLES

Root vegetables are delicious and vary greatly in terms of flavor. They provide a colorful contrast to leafy green vegetables and are particularly good roasted or in casseroles.

Carrots

These are available all year round. Carrots should be peeled first, then you can grate them raw into salads, or slice and boil them. After boiling, you can mash them if liked. You can also steam, stir-fry, or roast them.

Beet

These are available all year round and are excellent washed and grated raw into salads. Alternatively, you can boil or roast them whole. You can also buy beet ready-cooked.

Radishes

These are available in many sizes, shapes, and colors all year round, the most common variety being the small red radish, which is either round or oval. Washed, trimmed, and served raw, they give a peppery taste to salads and make excellent garnishes, whole or sliced.

Celery root

This knobbly vegetable is usually available in the fall, winter, and spring. It is very good peeled and boiled, then mashed. You can also parboil and roast celeary root.

Parsnips

Fresh parsnips are best during the fall and winter, although they are available all year round. They should always be cooked. You can boil and mash, or parboil and roast them. You can also steam or sauté parsnips, and they are very good in soups.

Potatoes

Available all year round, and usually classified as either mealy or waxy, this versatile and popular vegetable comes in many shapes, sizes, and colors, including long white, round white, and rounded. Potatoes range in size from small new potatoes, which are ideal for boiling and for salads, to large baking potatoes, which are excellent for baking in their skins or for making fries. Sweet potatoes are not botanically related to the potato, but they have a delicious sweet flavor and can be substituted for potatoes in many recipes. When cooking potatoes, you can either peel them first, or simply scrub them and leave unpeeled.

Potato skins are very nutritious, and delicious when cooked, so it is often a good idea to leave the skins on, unless you are making mashed potatoes, when it is better to remove them. Potatoes are excellent boiled, mashed, fried, baked, and roasted. You can serve them hot or cold. After buying your potatoes, store in a cool, dark place.

Rutabaga

This root vegetable is available all year round and should always be peeled and cooked. You can boil and mash it, or parboil and roast it. It is delicious mashed with carrots.

Turnips

Although available all year round, the peak season for turnips is in winter. Like rutabagas, these root vegetables are best peeled and boiled, then mashed. You can also parboil and roast them.

Parsnips

Radishes

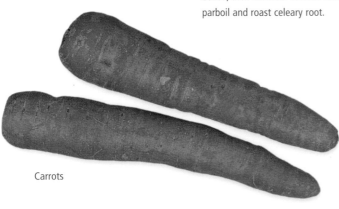

Carrots

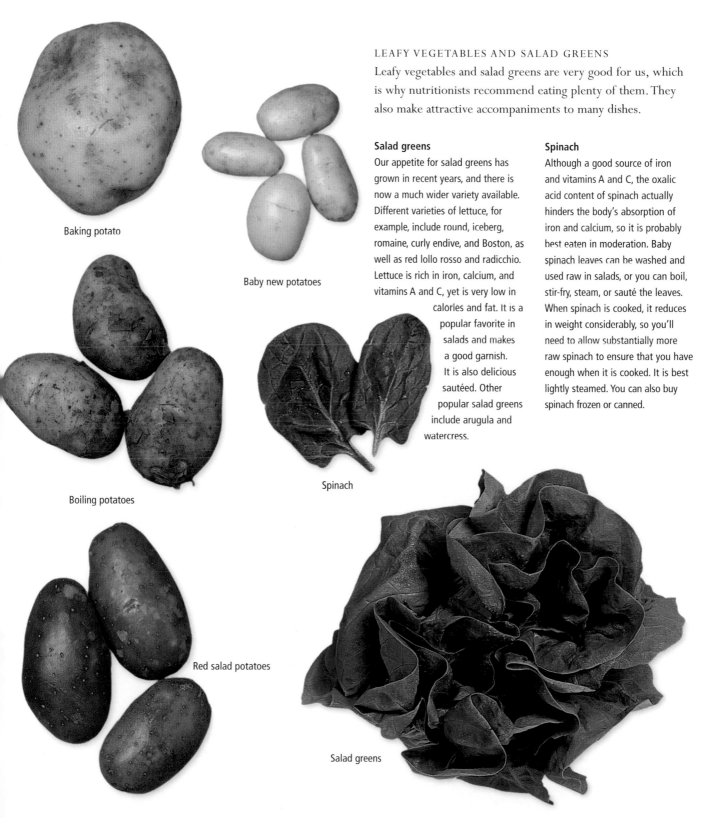

Baking potato

Baby new potatoes

Boiling potatoes

Red salad potatoes

Spinach

Salad greens

LEAFY VEGETABLES AND SALAD GREENS

Leafy vegetables and salad greens are very good for us, which is why nutritionists recommend eating plenty of them. They also make attractive accompaniments to many dishes.

Salad greens

Our appetite for salad greens has grown in recent years, and there is now a much wider variety available. Different varieties of lettuce, for example, include round, iceberg, romaine, curly endive, and Boston, as well as red lollo rosso and radicchio. Lettuce is rich in iron, calcium, and vitamins A and C, yet is very low in calories and fat. It is a popular favorite in salads and makes a good garnish. It is also delicious sautéed. Other popular salad greens include arugula and watercress.

Spinach

Although a good source of iron and vitamins A and C, the oxalic acid content of spinach actually hinders the body's absorption of iron and calcium, so it is probably best eaten in moderation. Baby spinach leaves can be washed and used raw in salads, or you can boil, stir-fry, steam, or sauté the leaves. When spinach is cooked, it reduces in weight considerably, so you'll need to allow substantially more raw spinach to ensure that you have enough when it is cooked. It is best lightly steamed. You can also buy spinach frozen or canned.

BRASSICAS

These vegetables are excellent boiled, steamed, or stir-fried. Take care not to overcook them, however—brassicas are best when tender but still slightly crisp to the bite.

Cabbages

These come in many shapes and colors, ranging from white and green to red. Look for cabbage that is crisp and fresh. You can wash and eat it raw in salads and coleslaw, or cook it in a variety of ways, such as boiling, steaming, or stir-frying.

Broccoli

This popular vegetable is available all year round and is very nutritious. It can be boiled, steamed, stir-fried, sautéed, or baked.

Napa cabbage

These crinkly, cream-colored leaves with green tips are available all year round. They can be used raw in salads, or sautéed, steamed, braised, or baked. They are also popular in stir-fries.

Brussels sprouts

These look like tiny cabbages and are, in fact, related to the cabbage family. They are available fresh during the fall and winter, or frozen all year round. They are very good boiled or steamed, or shredded and added to stir-fries. However, due to their sulfur content, they have a strong flavor that some people dislike.

Cauliflower

Like cabbage, cauliflower comes in different colors: white, green, and red, although the white variety is the most popular. You can eat it raw, or cook it by boiling, steaming, stir-frying, sautéeing, or baking.

Bok choy

This is available all year round. It looks a little like celery and has crunchy white stalks and dark green leaves. It is related to Napa cabbage botanically, and is often confused with it. However, it does have similar uses and can be used raw in salads, or stir-fried, sautéed, steamed, braised, or baked.

Napa cabbage

Broccoli

Cabbage leaf

Brussels sprouts

Cauliflower

THE ONION FAMILY

These members of the onion family contain sulfuric compounds that give them their unmistakable aroma and flavor. Their taste varies from mild to pungent.

Leeks

These have a very mild onion flavor and range in size from small baby leeks to large. They can be boiled, steamed, sautéed, stir-fried, or baked, and can be substituted for onions in most recipes.

Garlic

This versatile bulb was popular with the ancient Egyptians for its medicinal qualities and has many uses in modern cooking. It has an unmistakable taste, due to its sulfur content, and adds delicious flavor to many different recipes. It can be boiled, steamed, sautéed, stir-fried, baked, and roasted. When garlic is cooked with wine, it gives off a wonderful flavor and the combination is excellent in soups and sauces. It can also be used to liven up dressings.

Onions

These are available all year round in a variety of colors, from yellow and white to red. They also range in size from tiny pearl onions, to medium-size French onions, to the large Spanish onions, and vary in flavor from mildly pungent to very strong. Once peeled and trimmed, they can be eaten raw in salads or as a garnish, or cooked in a wide variety of dishes, from stir-fries to bakes. You can also pickle onions.

Shallots

These are small onions that resemble large garlic cloves when they are peeled. Use shallots when you need a milder onion flavor. They are particularly good in stir-fries and bakes, and in kabobs.

Scallions

These very small onions are available all year round but their peak season is during the spring and summer. They can be used raw in salads or sliced to make an attractive garnish, or they can be boiled, steamed, sautéed, or baked. Scallions are also excellent in stir-fries and soups.

Garlic

Leek

Scallions

Shallots

French onion

Red onion

VEGETABLE FRUITS

The tastes of the vegetables in this category vary from the mild, creamy flavor of avocados, to the fiery heat of chilies. They are popular in a wide range of international dishes.

Eggplants

These come in different sizes and colors, but the most popular is the large, deep-purple variety. Eggplants must always be cooked, and unless you are using them in a moist recipe with lots of liquid, you should degorge them to remove bitter the juices first. Simply cut the eggplant into slices about 1/2 inch/1 cm thick, spread them out in a large, shallow dish, and sprinkle over plenty of salt. Leave the slices for 30 minutes, then transfer to a colander and rinse off the salt with plenty of cold running water. Pat dry with paper towels, then use in your chosen recipe.

Avocados

These are green or purplish-black vegetable fruits that are shaped like pears but have a soft, buttery interior. Look for avocados that are just beginning to yield to the touch when pressed, and have no bruises. You can use them halved as an appetizer, sliced in salads, or mashed in dips. Avocados discolor quickly when cut, so use them straight away after cutting, or brush them with lemon juice to prevent discoloration.

Chilies

These fiery vegetable fruits usually come in red or green, and in many different sizes and shapes, from 1/4 inch/5 mm to 12 inches/30 cm in length. Generally, the smaller the chili, the hotter the flavor; the small ones can be so fiery that they can burn the skin. Always wear protective gloves when handling chilies, and keep them away from your eyes. Chilies add a spicy kick to many recipes and are particularly good in sauces and stir-fries, and in dishes such as chili con carne. Seed chilies before use in order to reduce their fiery heat.

Bell peppers

When sweet peppers are young they are green, then as they ripen and get sweeter they turn red. You can also get yellow, orange, purple, and brown bell peppers, or peppers in different shapes, such as the long pointed red Mediterranean peppers. Once sliced and seeded, they can be used raw in salads or as crudités, or you can cook them in a variety of dishes. Roasting or broiling brings out their sweet flavor. They can also be sautéed, stir-fried, steamed, braised, and baked.

Tomatoes

These are available all year round and come in many different sizes and shapes, from tiny cherry tomatoes to large beefsteak tomatoes. Make sure your tomatoes are firm when you buy them. Tomatoes left on the vine are particularly flavorful: in order to preserve their flavor, store them on the vine until you intend to use them. You can eat tomatoes raw in salads, or cook them. They make good sauces, soups, and pizza toppings, and are delicious sautéed, stir-fried, broiled, and baked.

Peas   Snow peas

Green beans

POD VEGETABLES

Pod vegetables have a delicious flavor, and some varieties, such as sugar snap peas, are tender enough to have an edible pod, so you can eat them whole. They are very good stir-fried.

Pods

These are young vegetables that have edible pods, such as sugar snap peas, snow peas, green beans, and string beans. They have a delicious sweet flavor and can be steamed, boiled, sautéed, or stir-fried.

Shelled peas and beans

These are seeds that are allowed to grow in the pod; they are served shelled. They include garden peas, petit pois (smaller peas), and fava beans, which are green and slightly kidney-shaped. All of them can be boiled or steamed.

OTHER VEGETABLES

Mushrooms and corn are delicious in salads, risottos, and stir-fries, but try experimenting with more exotic varieties of vegetables too, such as Asian vegetables and seaweeds.

Exotic vegetables

There is a great variety of exotic vegetables available nowadays, and they come from all over the world. Some of the most popular include kombu, which is a dried form of kelp that is used in Japanese cooking; daikon, a long white root that is used in Asian cooking; and wakame, an edible seaweed popular in Asia.

Corn

The most popular type of corn these days is the yellow corn. The husks and silks need to be removed before cooking, then you can simply cook the corn whole on the cob, or remove the kernels and cook them on their own. Corn comes into season in the summer months, but you can also buy it frozen or canned all year round. It is delicious boiled on the cob, or the kernels can be cooked and used in soups, salads, and bakes. You can also buy baby corn, which can be boiled, steamed, or stir-fried.

Mushrooms

Both cultivated or wild mushrooms are available all year round. The former include the common white or cremini and large, flat portobello mushrooms. Wild mushrooms vary enormously in size, shape, and color, and include shiitake, porcini, and pieds de moutons. They are available fresh or dried. Mushrooms can absorb a lot of water, so it is better to wipe them with a clean, damp cloth rather than wash them. They can be sautéed, stir-fried, deep-fried in batter, broiled, or baked.

SQUASHES

Squashes are becoming increasingly popular these days, and we are becoming more creative with them. Small varieties can be particularly flavorful—for example, try mini zucchini.

Zucchini

This member of the squash family is shaped like a cucumber and comes in various shades of green, sometimes with yellow stripes. It also comes in a variety of sizes, from 4 inches/10 cm to 2 feet/60 cm long (the largest are known as marrows). The smaller varieties tend to have the most flavor. Zucchini are available all year round, and are very versatile. They can be steamed, broiled, stir-fried, chargrilled, sautéed, deep-fried, baked, and roasted, or you can eat them raw in salads. Zucchini flowers, if you can get them, are wonderful stuffed and cooked, or battered and fried.

Cucumbers

Although best known as a salad vegetable, the cucumber is, in fact, a member of the squash family. It can be cut into crudités, with or without its skin, and served raw with dips, or lightly sautéed or stir-fried.

Pumpkins

This large squash is available in the fall and winter. The large variety is popular at Hallowe'en, when it is carved out and made into a mask or lantern. The smaller, orange variety has a sweeter flavor and is more suitable for cooking. Pumpkin pie is a particular favorite. You can also use pumpkin in soups and casseroles.

Squashes

Butternut, acorn, and spaghetti squashes are classed as winter squashes. They are large and have thick skins and firm flesh. Once seeded, they can be roasted, baked, or steamed. Summer squashes, such as patty pans, are smaller and can be cooked fairly quickly by sautéeing, steaming, or baking.

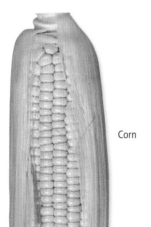

Corn

White mushrooms

Butternut squash

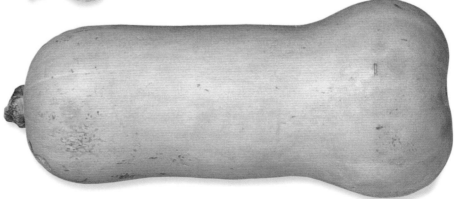

BORSCHT

ANTONIN CARÊME, CHEF TO CZAR ALEXANDER I, IS CREDITED WITH INTRODUCING THIS
TRADITIONAL RUSSIAN BEET SOUP TO FRANCE AND SO TO THE REST OF EUROPE. THIS IS A LIGHTER,
EASIER VERSION OF HIS RATHER ELABORATE RECIPE AND IS SUITABLE FOR VEGETARIANS.

serves
6

preparation
30 minutes

cooking
1¼ hours

ingredients
- 1 onion
- 4 tbsp butter
- 12 oz/350 g raw beet,
  cut into thin sticks, and
  1 raw beet, grated
- 1 carrot, cut into
  thin sticks
- 3 celery stalks, thinly sliced
- 2 tomatoes, peeled,
  seeded, and chopped
- generous 6⅓ cups
  vegetable stock
- 1 tbsp white wine vinegar
- 1 tbsp sugar
- 2 large fresh dill
  sprigs, snipped
- 4 oz/115 g white
  cabbage, shredded
- salt and pepper
- ⅔ cup sour cream, to
  garnish
- rye bread, to serve
  (optional)

1 Slice the onion into rings. Melt the butter in a large, heavy-bottom pan over low heat. Add the onion and cook, stirring occasionally, for 3–5 minutes, or until softened. Add the beet sticks, carrot, celery, and chopped tomatoes. Cook, stirring frequently, for 4–5 minutes.

2 Add the stock, vinegar, and sugar and add a tablespoon of dill to the pan. Season to taste with salt and pepper. Bring to a boil, reduce the heat, and let simmer for 35–40 minutes, or until the vegetables are tender.

3 Stir in the cabbage, cover, and let simmer for 10 minutes. Stir in the grated beet, with any juices, and cook for an additional 10 minutes. Ladle into warmed bowls. Garnish with a spoonful of sour cream and remaining snipped dill, and serve with rye bread, if liked.

variation

For a more substantial soup, add 2 diced potatoes along with the cabbage in Step 3. Cook for an additional 10 minutes before adding the grated beet.

LEEK & POTATO SOUP

LEEK AND POTATO IS A WONDERFUL COMBINATION, ESPECIALLY WHEN TEAMED WITH HERBS AND CREAM. IN THIS DISH, A DELICIOUS SMOKY FLAVOR HAS BEEN INTRODUCED WITH THE ADDITION OF THE SMOKED CHEESE. IT MAKES A SATISFYING, WARMING SOUP FOR ANY OCCASION.

serves
4

preparation
15–20 minutes,
plus 10 minutes'
cooling

cooking
35 minutes

ingredients
- 2 tbsp butter
- 2 garlic cloves, chopped
- 3 large leeks, trimmed and sliced
- 1 lb/450 g potatoes, peeled and chopped into bite-size chunks
- 1 tbsp chopped fresh parsley
- 1 tbsp chopped fresh oregano
- 1 bay leaf
- 3¹/₂ cups vegetable stock
- scant 1 cup sour cream
- 3¹/₂ oz/100 g smoked firm cheese, grated
- salt and pepper
- thick slices of fresh crusty bread, to serve

TO GARNISH
- fresh chives
- chopped fresh parsley

1 Melt the butter in a large pan over medium heat. Add the garlic and cook, stirring, for 1 minute. Add the leeks and cook, stirring, for an additional 2 minutes. Add the potatoes, herbs, and stock and season to taste with salt and pepper. Bring to a boil, then reduce the heat, cover the pan, and let simmer for 25 minutes. Remove from the heat, let cool for 10 minutes, then remove and discard the bay leaf.

2 Transfer half of the soup to a food processor and process until smooth (you may need to do this in batches). Return to the pan with the rest of the soup, stir in the sour cream, and reheat gently. Season to taste with salt and pepper.

3 Remove from the heat and stir in the cheese. Ladle into serving bowls and garnish with chives and chopped fresh parsley. Serve with slices of fresh crusty bread.

LES HALLES ONION SOUP

MORE LIKE A THICK ONION STEW THAN A SOUP, THIS TRADITIONAL RECIPE, WHICH INCLUDES A SLUG OF BRANDY, RECALLS THE DAYS WHEN THE LES HALLES DISTRICT OF PARIS WAS HOME TO THE CITY'S MEAT, SEAFOOD, AND FRUIT AND VEGETABLE MARKETS, AND KNOWN AS THE "BELLY OF PARIS."

serves
4

preparation
20 minutes

cooking
1 hour 10 minutes–1 hour 15 minutes

ingredients
- 6 tbsp butter
- 2 tbsp olive oil
- 1 lb 10 oz/750 g onions, thinly sliced
- 1 tsp sugar
- ½ tsp salt
- 1½ tbsp all-purpose flour
- 2½ cups hot beef stock
- 4 tbsp brandy
- 4½ oz/125 g Gruyère cheese, or half Gruyère and half Parmesan cheese, grated
- salt and pepper

CROÛTES
- 8 slices French bread, about ½ inch/1 cm thick
- 1 garlic clove, halved

1 Melt the butter with the oil in a large, heavy-bottom pan with a tight-fitting lid, or an ovenproof casserole, over medium–high heat. Stir in the onions, sugar, and salt, then reduce the heat to low. Cover the surface with a piece of wet waxed paper or the lid and cook for 20–30 minutes, stirring occasionally, until the onions are a rich, dark golden brown. Uncover and stir constantly when they begin to darken, as they can burn easily.

2 Sprinkle the flour over the onions and continue cooking, stirring for 2 minutes. Stir in the hot stock and let simmer, partially covered, for an additional 15 minutes, skimming the surface if necessary.

3 To make the croûtes, preheat the broiler to high and the oven to 400°F/200°C. Arrange the bread slices on the broiler rack and toast for 1–2 minutes, or until golden and crisp. Flip the slices over and repeat on the other side. Rub the top of each bread slice while it is still hot with the garlic halves, then set aside until required.

4 Stir the brandy into the soup and season to taste with salt and pepper. At this point, the soup can be left for up to a day, but reheat it before proceeding.

5 Divide the toasted bread between 4 heatproof soup bowls. Ladle over the soup, then top each with a quarter of the cheese. Place the bowls in the oven for 20 minutes, or until the cheese is golden and bubbling. Let the soup stand for a couple of minutes before serving.

cook's tip
The toasted croûtes are a good way to use up day-old French bread. Take care, however, not to cut the bread too thick, or it will absorb all the liquid.

RATATOUILLE

RATATOUILLE IS A WONDERFULLY VERSATILE DISH, AND IS ESPECIALLY USEFUL WHEN CATERING FOR VEGETARIANS. IT GOES WELL WITH JACKET BAKED POTATOES, PERHAPS TOPPED WITH A LITTLE SOUR CREAM, OR PILE IT ONTO A PLATTER OF FRESHLY COOKED RICE OR COUSCOUS.

serves
4
preparation
15 minutes,
plus 30 minutes'
standing
cooking
45 minutes

ingredients
- 1 eggplant, about
  9 oz/250 g
- 4 tbsp olive oil
- 2 garlic cloves, chopped
- 1 large onion, chopped
- 2 red bell peppers, seeded
  and cut into bite-size
  chunks
- 1 lb 12 oz/800 g canned
  chopped tomatoes
- 2 zucchini, sliced
- 1 celery stalk, sliced
- 1 tsp sugar
- 2 tbsp chopped fresh thyme
- salt and pepper
- fresh thyme sprigs,
  to garnish

TO SERVE
- baked potatoes with butter
- fresh crusty bread

1 Trim the eggplant and cut it into bite-size chunks, then place it in a colander. Sprinkle with salt and let stand for 30 minutes.

2 Heat the oil in a large pan over medium heat. Add the garlic and onion and cook, stirring, for 3 minutes until softened slightly. Rinse the eggplant and drain well, then add it to the pan with the red bell peppers. Reduce the heat and cook gently, stirring frequently, for an additional 10 minutes.

3 Stir in the tomatoes, zucchini, celery, sugar, and thyme, and season to taste with salt and pepper. Bring to a boil, then reduce the heat, cover the pan, and let simmer gently for 30 minutes.

4 Remove the pan from the heat, transfer to serving plates, and garnish with fresh thyme sprigs. Serve with buttered hot baked potatoes and fresh crusty bread.

variation
You can substitute the canned tomatoes with 1 lb/450 g peeled and seeded fresh tomatoes and replace the fresh thyme with fresh basil, if you prefer.

CLASSIC ROAST POTATOES

THERE IS NOTHING QUITE LIKE LOVINGLY COOKED ROAST POTATOES, GOLDEN AND CRISP ON THE
OUTSIDE, AND WONDERFULLY FLUFFY ON THE INSIDE. THESE POTATOES HAVE A LITTLE PAPRIKA FOR
ADDED SPICE AND COLOR. SIMPLY PILE THEM INTO A BOWL AND WATCH THEM DISAPPEAR.

serves
4
preparation
10 minutes
cooking
1½ hours

ingredients
- 2 lb/900 g medium–large mealy potatoes, peeled
- ½ tsp salt
- paprika
- generous ⅓ cup vegetable oil
- pepper

1 Preheat the oven to 400°F/200°C. Using a sharp knife, cut the potatoes in half, or into quarters if very large, then arrange in a roasting pan. Sprinkle over the salt, then season to taste with pepper and paprika.

2 Pour the oil over the potatoes, then turn them in the oil until well coated. Transfer to the preheated oven and roast, basting occasionally, for 1½ hours, or until golden brown and tender. Remove from the oven and serve immediately.

variation

To ring the changes, try adding 1 crushed garlic clove and 1 tablespoon of lemon juice to the oil before pouring over the potatoes. They will add a deliciously different flavor and the aroma will be irresistible.

ROASTED GARLIC MASHED POTATOES

HERE ARE MASHED POTATOES WITH A DIFFERENCE. TANTALIZE EVERY MEMBER OF YOUR HOUSEHOLD WITH THESE DELICIOUS POTATOES MASHED WITH JUICY BULBS OF ROASTED GARLIC AND GARNISHED WITH SPRIGS OF FRAGRANT, FRESH PARSLEY. AN UNFORGETTABLE COMBINATION.

serves
4
preparation
20 minutes
cooking
1 hour

ingredients
- 2 whole bulbs of garlic
- 1 tbsp olive oil
- 2 lb/900 g mealy potatoes, peeled
- ½ cup milk
- 4 tbsp butter
- salt and pepper
- fresh parsley sprigs, to garnish

1 Preheat the oven to 350°F/180°C. Separate the garlic cloves, place on a large piece of foil, and drizzle with the oil. Wrap the garlic loosely in the foil and roast in the preheated oven for 1 hour, or until very tender. Let cool slightly.

2 Twenty minutes before the end of the cooking time, cut the potatoes into chunks, then cook in salted boiling water for 15 minutes, or until tender.

3 Meanwhile, squeeze the cooled garlic cloves out of their skins and push through a strainer into a pan. Add the milk, butter, and salt and pepper to taste. Heat gently, until the butter has melted.

4 Drain the cooked potatoes, then mash in the pan until smooth. Pour in the garlic mixture and heat gently, stirring, until the ingredients are combined. Serve hot garnished with fresh parsley sprigs.

DAUPHINOIS POTATOES

COOKING THE HUMBLE POTATO IN THIS CLASSIC WAY ELEVATES IT TO GOURMET HEIGHTS. THIS DELICIOUS, CREAMY DISH MAKES AN EXCELLENT ACCOMPANIMENT FOR A VEGETABLE BAKE—THEY CAN BE COOKED IN THE OVEN AT THE SAME TIME AND SERVED TOGETHER.

serves
4

preparation
20 minutes

cooking
1–1½ hours

ingredients
- 2 tbsp butter, diced, plus extra for greasing
- 2 lb/900 g waxy potatoes, peeled and very thinly sliced
- 1 large onion, finely chopped
- 8 oz/225 g Emmental or Gruyère cheese, grated
- ⅔ cup light cream
- salt and pepper

1 Preheat the oven to 375°F/190°C. Grease an ovenproof casserole with butter. Make a layer of potato slices in the bottom, dot with a little butter, sprinkle with onion and cheese, and season to taste with salt and pepper. Pour in 2 tablespoons of the cream. Continue making layers in this way, ending with a layer of cheese. Pour over any remaining cream.

2 Cover and bake in the preheated oven for 1–1½ hours, or until the potatoes are tender.

3 Preheat the broiler to medium. Remove the lid and place the casserole under the hot broiler for 5 minutes, or until the top of the bake is golden brown and bubbling. Serve immediately.

variation
For Anna Potatoes, pour 1 cup of melted butter between 2 lb/900 g of seasoned, layered potato slices. Bake at 425°F/220°C for 1 hour.

STUFFED BAKED POTATOES

THESE WONDERFUL BAKED POTATOES MAKE AN EXCELLENT LUNCH OR SUPPER DISH. THEY ARE SUITABLE FOR VEGETARIANS IF YOU OMIT THE HAM AND USE A CHEESE MADE WITH NONANIMAL RENNET. THEY ARE EASY TO PREPARE AND THE IDEAL SOLUTION FOR COOKS ON A TIGHT BUDGET.

serves
4

preparation
10 minutes

cooking
1¼ hours

ingredients
- 2 lb/900 g baking potatoes, washed
- 2 tbsp vegetable oil
- 1 tsp coarse sea salt
- ½ cup butter
- 1 small onion, chopped
- 1 cup grated Cheddar cheese or crumbled blue cheese
- salt and pepper
- fresh chives, to garnish

OPTIONAL INGREDIENTS
- 4 tbsp cooked ham or bacon, diced
- 4 tbsp corn kernels
- 4 tbsp cooked mushrooms, zucchini, or bell peppers

1 Preheat the oven to 375°F/190°C. Prick the potatoes with a fork, brush with oil, sprinkle with the salt, and bake on an oven tray for 1 hour, or until the skins are crispy and the inside is soft when pierced with a fork.

2 Melt 1 tablespoon of butter in a small skillet. Add the onion and cook gently for 4–5 minutes, or until softened and golden. Set aside.

3 Remove the potatoes from the oven and cut in half lengthwise. Scoop the insides into a large mixing bowl and keep the shells. Increase the oven temperature to 400°F/200°C.

4 Coarsely mash the potato and mix in the onion and remaining butter. Add salt and pepper and 1 or more of the optional ingredients, if using. Spoon the mixture back into the empty shells. Top with cheese.

5 Return the potatoes to the oven for 10 minutes, or until the cheese melts and begins to brown. Garnish with chives to serve.

ROAST SUMMER VEGETABLES

THIS APPETIZING AND COLORFUL MIXTURE OF MEDITERRANEAN VEGETABLES MAKES A SENSATIONAL SUMMER LUNCH FOR VEGETARIANS AND MEAT-EATERS ALIKE. ROASTING BRINGS OUT THE FULL FLAVOR AND SWEETNESS OF THE BELL PEPPERS, EGGPLANTS, ZUCCHINI, AND ONIONS.

serves
4
preparation
10 minutes
cooking
20–25 minutes

ingredients
- 2 tbsp olive oil
- 1 fennel bulb
- 2 red onions
- 2 beefsteak tomatoes
- 1 eggplant
- 2 zucchini
- 1 yellow bell pepper
- 1 red bell pepper
- 1 orange bell pepper
- 4 garlic cloves
- 4 fresh rosemary sprigs
- pepper
- crusty bread, to serve (optional)

1 Preheat the oven to 400°F/200°C. Brush a large ovenproof dish with a little of the oil. Prepare the vegetables. Cut the fennel, red onions, and tomatoes into wedges. Slice the eggplant and zucchini thickly, then seed all the bell peppers and cut into chunks. Arrange the vegetables in the dish and tuck the garlic cloves and rosemary sprigs among them. Drizzle with the remaining oil and season to taste with pepper.

2 Roast the vegetables in the preheated oven for 10 minutes. Remove the dish from the oven and turn the vegetables over with a slotted spoon. Return to the oven and roast for an additional 10–15 minutes until tender and beginning to turn golden brown.

3 Serve the vegetables straight from the dish, or transfer to a warmed serving plate. Serve with crusty bread, if liked.

variation

You can substitute a herb-flavored oil, such as tarragon or garlic and rosemary, for the plain olive oil, if liked.

OVEN-DRIED TOMATOES

WHEN YOU CAN'T TAKE ADVANTAGE OF THE INTENSE MEDITERRANEAN SUN, USE THIS EASY
TECHNIQUE TO PRESERVE THE RICH FLAVOR OF TOMATOES. MAKE SURE YOU USE ONLY RIPE,
FULL-FLAVORED TOMATOES FOR THIS, IN ORDER TO GET THE BEST FLAVOR POSSIBLE.

serves
4

preparation
15 minutes

cooking
2½ hours

ingredients
- 2 lb 4 oz/1 kg large, juicy full-flavored tomatoes
- sea salt and pepper
- 1 lb 2 oz/500 g buffalo mozzarella, sliced
- basil leaves, to garnish
- extra virgin olive oil for drizzling and storing (if required)

1 Preheat the oven to 250°F/120°C. Using a sharp knife, cut each of the tomatoes into quarters lengthwise.

2 Using a teaspoon, scoop out the seeds and discard. If the tomatoes are large, cut each quarter in half lengthwise again.

3 Sprinkle sea salt in a roasting pan and arrange the tomato slices, skin side down, on top. Roast in the preheated oven for 2½ hours, or until the edges are just beginning to look charred and the flesh is dry but still pliable. The exact roasting time and yield will depend on the size and juiciness of the tomatoes. Check the tomatoes at 30-minute intervals after 1½ hours.

4 Remove the dried tomatoes from the roasting pan and let cool completely. Serve with slices of buffalo mozzarella—drizzle with olive oil and sprinkle with pepper and basil leaves.

cook's tip

To preserve, place in a 1-cup preserving jar and pour over enough olive oil to cover. Seal tightly and store in the refrigerator for up to 2 weeks.

CRISP NOODLE & VEGETABLE STIR-FRY

THE CHINESE CAREFULLY SELECT VEGETABLES TO ACHIEVE A HARMONIOUS BALANCE OF
CONTRASTING COLORS AND TEXTURES. ONCE YOU HAVE CHOPPED THE VEGETABLES, THIS DISH
IS QUICK AND EASY TO PUT TOGETHER, AND MAKES AN ATTRACTIVE AND NUTRITIOUS MEAL.

serves
4
preparation
5 minutes
cooking
15–20 minutes

ingredients
- peanut or sunflower-seed oil, for deep-frying
- 4 oz/115 g rice vermicelli, broken into 3-inch/7.5-cm lengths
- 4 oz/115 g green beans, cut into short lengths
- 2 carrots, cut into thin sticks
- 2 zucchini, cut into thin sticks
- 4 oz/115 g shiitake mushrooms, sliced
- 1-inch/2.5-cm piece fresh gingerroot, shredded
- ½ small head Napa cabbage, shredded
- 4 scalllions, shredded
- ½ cup bean sprouts
- 2 tbsp dark soy sauce
- 2 tbsp Chinese rice wine
- large pinch of sugar
- 2 tbsp coarsely chopped fresh cilantro

1 Half-fill a wok or deep, heavy-bottom skillet with oil. Heat to 350–375°F/180–190°C, or until a cube of bread browns in 30 seconds.

2 Add the noodles, in batches, and cook for 1½–2 minutes, or until crisp and puffed up. Remove and drain on paper towels. Pour off all but 2 tablespoons of oil from the wok.

3 Heat the remaining oil over high heat. Add the green beans and stir-fry for 2 minutes.

4 Add the carrot and zucchini sticks, sliced mushrooms, and ginger and stir-fry for an additional 2 minutes.

5 Add the shredded Napa cabbage, scallions, and bean sprouts and stir-fry for an additional 1 minute.

6 Add the soy sauce, rice wine, and sugar and cook, stirring constantly, for 1 minute.

7 Add the noodles and chopped cilantro and toss well. Serve immediately.

cook's tip

This dish also looks attractive if you serve the noodles in a small nest on top of the stir-fried vegetables, rather than tossing them with the vegetables in Step 3.

GRATIN OF MIXED VEGETABLES

THIS MIXED VEGETABLE GRATIN IS VERY EASY TO PREPARE AND MAKES AN ECONOMICAL SUPPER DISH
FOR A GROUP OF PEOPLE. ONCE YOU HAVE IT ASSEMBLED IN THE DISH, IT NEEDS LITTLE ATTENTION:
SIMPLY POP IT IN THE OVEN AND BRING IT OUT WHEN IT IS READY TO SERVE.

serves
6
preparation
15 minutes
cooking
1¼ hours

ingredients
- 2 parsnips, sliced
- 2 tbsp olive oil
- 1 eggplant, diced
- 1 garlic clove, finely
  chopped
- 2 tsp chopped
  fresh thyme
- ½ tbsp butter
- 2 shallots, chopped

- 4 canned artichoke hearts,
  drained
- 4 canned celery hearts,
  sliced
- 2 oz/55 g Emmental cheese,
  grated
- ½ cup freshly grated
  romano cheese
- salt

1 Preheat the oven to 350°F/180°C.
Steam the parsnips over a pan of
simmering water for 4 minutes,
or until just tender. Drain, then
let cool.

2 Heat the oil in a heavy-bottom
skillet. Add the diced eggplant and
cook, stirring frequently, for
5 minutes. Add the chopped garlic
and thyme, season to taste with salt,
and cook for 3 minutes. Transfer the
eggplant mixture to a large dish with
a slotted spoon. Place the butter in
the skillet. When it has melted, add

the shallots and a pinch of salt, and
cook over very low heat, stirring
occasionally, for 7–10 minutes.

3 Mix the shallots and eggplant
mixture together. Cut each artichoke
heart into 8 pieces and add to the
mixture with the parsnips, celery
hearts, Emmental, and half the
romano cheese. Mix well, then
sprinkle over the remaining romano
cheese. Bake in the preheated oven
for 45 minutes. Serve immediately.

STUFFED RED BELL PEPPERS WITH BASIL

STUFFED BELL PEPPERS ARE POPULAR WITH VEGETARIANS AND MEAT-EATERS ALIKE. THEY ARE EASY TO PREPARE AND NUTRITIOUS: THE WALNUTS AND CHEESE ALONE ARE A RICH SOURCE OF PROTEIN. THIS DISH IS ALSO RICH IN IRON AND VITAMIN C. SERVE THESE BELL PEPPERS FOR LUNCH OR SUPPER.

serves
4
preparation
15–20 minutes
cooking
1¼–1½ hours

ingredients
- ¾ cup long-grain white or brown rice
- 4 large red bell peppers
- 2 tbsp olive oil
- 1 garlic clove, chopped
- 4 shallots, chopped
- 1 celery stalk, chopped
- 3 tbsp chopped toasted walnuts
- 2 tomatoes, peeled and chopped
- 1 tbsp lemon juice
- ⅓ cup raisins
- 4 tbsp freshly grated Cheddar cheese
- 2 tbsp chopped fresh basil
- salt and pepper
- fresh basil sprigs, to garnish
- lemon wedges, to serve

1 Preheat the oven to 350°F/180°C. Cook the rice in a pan of lightly salted boiling water for 20 minutes if using white rice, or 35 minutes if using brown. Drain, rinse under cold running water, then drain again.

2 Using a sharp knife, cut the tops off the bell peppers and set aside. Remove the seeds and white cores, then blanch the bell peppers and reserved tops in boiling water for 2 minutes. Remove from the heat and drain well. Heat half the oil in a large skillet. Add the garlic and shallots and cook, stirring, for

3 minutes. Add the celery, walnuts, tomatoes, lemon juice, and raisins and cook for an additional 5 minutes. Remove from the heat and stir in the cheese, chopped basil, and seasoning.

3 Stuff the bell peppers with the rice mixture and arrange them in a baking dish. Place the tops on the bell peppers, drizzle over the remaining oil, loosely cover with foil, and bake in the preheated oven for 45 minutes. Remove from the oven. Garnish with basil sprigs and serve with lemon wedges.

BRAISED RED CABBAGE

BRAISED RED CABBAGE MAKES A COLORFUL ACCOMPANIMENT TO A VARIETY OF HOT AND COLD DISHES. TRY SERVING IT WITH TARTS AND QUICHES, AND FRESHLY BAKED PIES. THIS CABBAGE HAS A LOVELY FLAVOR, WITH HINTS OF AROMATIC CLOVES AND THE SWEETNESS OF RAISINS.

serves
6
preparation
15 minutes
cooking
55 minutes

ingredients
- 2 tbsp sunflower-seed oil
- 2 onions, thinly sliced
- 2 eating apples, peeled, cored, and thinly sliced
- 2 lb/900 g red cabbage, cored and shredded
- 4 tbsp red wine vinegar
- 2 tbsp sugar
- ¼ tsp ground cloves
- ⅓ cup raisins
- ½ cup red wine
- 2 tbsp red currant jelly
- salt and pepper

1 Heat the oil in a large pan. Add the onions and cook, stirring occasionally, for 10 minutes, or until softened and golden. Stir in the apple slices and cook for 3 minutes.

2 Add the cabbage, vinegar, sugar, cloves, raisins, and red wine and season to taste with salt and pepper. Bring to a boil, stirring occasionally. Reduce the heat, cover, and cook, stirring occasionally, for 40 minutes, or until the cabbage is tender and most of the liquid has been absorbed.

3 Stir in the red currant jelly, transfer the cabbage to a warmed dish, and serve.

variation

You can vary the flavor and texture of this dish by substituting 2 tablespoons honey for the sugar, and replacing half of the raisins with golden raisins.

BAKED EGGPLANTS

THIS DELICIOUS RECIPE IS FROM PARMA, AND CONTAINS LAYERS OF SLICED EGGPLANTS BAKED
WITH TOMATO SAUCE AND MOZZARELLA CHEESE. YOU MAY NEED TO REDUCE THE TOMATO SAUCE
A LITTLE BY BOILING IT DOWN BEFORE USING, SO THAT THE END RESULT IS NOT TOO RUNNY.

serves
4

preparation
15 minutes

cooking
1¼ hours

ingredients
- 4 eggplants, trimmed
- 3 tbsp olive oil, plus extra
  for oiling
- 5½ oz/300 g mozzarella
  cheese, thinly sliced
- 4 slices prosciutto,
  shredded
- 1 tbsp chopped fresh
  marjoram
- 1 oz/25 g Parmesan
  cheese, grated
- fresh sage sprigs,
  to garnish

TOMATO SAUCE
- 4 tbsp olive oil
- 1 large onion, sliced
- 4 garlic cloves, crushed
- 14 oz/400 g canned
  chopped tomatoes
- 1 lb/450 g fresh tomatoes,
  peeled and chopped
- 4 tbsp chopped
  fresh parsley
- 2½ cups hot
  vegetable stock
- 1 tbsp sugar
- 2 tbsp lemon juice
- ⅔ cup dry
  white wine
- salt and pepper

BÉCHAMEL SAUCE
- 2 tbsp butter
- scant ½ cup all-purpose flour
- 1 tsp mustard powder
- 1¼ cups milk
- freshly grated nutmeg
- salt and pepper

1 Preheat the oven to 375°F/190°C.
To make the tomato sauce, heat the
oil in a large skillet. Add the onion
and garlic and fry until just beginning
to soften. Add the canned and fresh
tomatoes, parsley, stock, sugar, and
lemon juice. Cover and let simmer
for 15 minutes. Stir in the wine and
season to taste with salt and pepper.

2 Slice the eggplants thinly
lengthwise. Bring a large pan
of water to a boil and cook the
eggplant slices for 5 minutes.
Drain on paper towels and pat dry.

3 Pour half of the fresh tomato
sauce into a large, oiled ovenproof
dish. Cover with half of the cooked
eggplants and drizzle with a
little oil. Cover with half of the
mozzarella, prosciutto, and herbs.
Season to taste with salt and pepper.
Repeat the layers until the tomato
sauce is used up.

4 To make the béchamel sauce,
heat the butter in a large pan. When
it has melted, add the flour and
mustard powder. Stir until smooth
and cook over low heat for
2 minutes. Slowly beat in the milk.
Let simmer gently for 2 minutes.
Remove from the heat and season
with a large pinch of nutmeg and salt
and pepper to taste.

5 Sprinkle the béchamel sauce
with Parmesan cheese. Bake in the
preheated oven for 35–40 minutes
until golden on top. Garnish with
sage sprigs and serve.

CAESAR SALAD

THIS SALAD WAS THE INVENTION OF A CHEF AT CAESAR'S, A RESTAURANT IN TIJUANA, MEXICO. IT HAS RIGHTLY EARNED AN INTERNATIONAL REPUTATION. CAESAR SALAD MAKES AN EXCELLENT LUNCH AS WELL AS AN ACCOMPANIMENT, AND IS FULL OF NUTRIENTS, ESPECIALLY PROTEIN.

serves
4
preparation
25 minutes
cooking
15–20 minutes

ingredients
- 1 large romaine lettuce or 2 Boston lettuces
- 4 canned anchovies in oil, drained and halved lengthwise
- Parmesan shavings, to garnish

DRESSING
- 2 garlic cloves, crushed
- 1½ tsp Dijon mustard
- 1 tsp Worcestershire sauce
- 4 canned anchovies in olive oil, drained and chopped
- 1 egg yolk
- 1 tbsp lemon juice
- ⅔ cup olive oil
- 4 tbsp freshly grated Parmesan cheese
- salt and pepper

CROUTONS
- 4 thick slices day-old bread
- 2 tbsp olive oil
- 1 garlic clove, crushed

1 Preheat the oven to 350°F/180°C. To make the dressing, place the garlic, mustard, Worcestershire sauce, anchovies, egg yolk, lemon juice, and seasoning in a food processor or blender and process for 30 seconds until foaming. With the machine still running, add the olive oil, drop by drop, until the mixture begins to thicken. Continue adding the oil in a steady stream until all the oil has been incorporated. Transfer to a bowl. Add a little hot water if the dressing is too thick. Stir in the grated Parmesan cheese. Season to taste with salt and pepper and let chill until required.

2 To make the croutons, cut the bread into ½ inch/1 cm cubes. Toss with the oil and garlic in a bowl. Spread out on a baking sheet in a single layer. Bake in the preheated oven for 15–20 minutes, stirring occasionally, until browned and crisp. Remove from the oven and let cool.

3 Separate the lettuce into individual leaves and wash and spin dry in a salad spinner or pat dry on paper towels. (Excess moisture will dilute the dressing.) Transfer to a plastic bag and place in the refrigerator.

4 To assemble the salad, tear the lettuce into pieces and place in a large serving bowl. Add the dressing and toss well. Top with the halved anchovies, croutons, and Parmesan shavings. Serve immediately.

ROAST CHICKEN SALAD WITH ORANGE DRESSING

THIS COLORFUL SALAD MAKES A DELICIOUS SUMMER LUNCH, AND IS AN EXCELLENT WAY OF USING UP ANY LEFTOVER ROAST CHICKEN. IT IS ALSO MOUTHWATERING FARE FOR A PICNIC. THE SUCCULENT ROAST CHICKEN AND SWEET TANG OF ORANGE MAKE A LOVELY COMBINATION.

serves
4

preparation
20 minutes

cooking
none

ingredients
- 5⅝ cups young spinach leaves
- handful of fresh parsley leaves
- ½ cucumber, thinly sliced
- generous ¾ cup walnuts, toasted and chopped
- 12 oz/350 g boneless lean roast chicken, thinly sliced
- 2 red apples
- 1 tbsp lemon juice

ORANGE DRESSING
- 2 tbsp extra virgin olive oil
- juice of 1 orange
- finely grated rind of ½ orange
- 1 tbsp sour cream
- fresh flat-leaf parsley sprigs, to garnish
- orange wedges, to serve

1 Wash and drain the spinach and parsley leaves, if necessary, then arrange on a large serving platter. Top with the cucumber and walnuts. Arrange the chicken slices on top of the leaves.

2 Core the apples, then cut them in half. Cut each half into slices and brush with the lemon juice to prevent discoloration. Arrange the apple slices over the salad.

3 Place all the dressing ingredients in a screw-top jar, screw on the lid tightly, and shake well until thoroughly combined. Drizzle the dressing over the salad, garnish with parsley sprigs, and serve immediately with orange wedges.

GREEK SALAD

WALK INTO ANY TAVERNA OR CAFÉ IN GREECE OR SOUTHERN CYPRUS AND YOU WILL SEE THIS SALAD, OR A VARIATION OF IT, ON THE MENU. IT MAKES A DELICIOUS ACCOMPANIMENT TO OTHER GREEK DISHES, OR A SATISFYING LUNCH IN ITS OWN RIGHT IF SERVED WITH FRESH PITA BREAD.

serves
4

preparation
15 minutes

cooking
none

ingredients
- 4 tomatoes, cut into wedges
- 1 onion, sliced
- ½ cucumber, sliced
- 1⅓ cups kalamata olives, pitted
- 8 oz/225 g feta cheese, cubed (drained weight)
- 2 tbsp fresh cilantro leaves
- fresh flat-leaf parsley, to garnish
- pita bread, to serve

DRESSING
- 5 tbsp extra virgin olive oil
- 2 tbsp white wine vinegar
- 1 tbsp lemon juice
- ½ tsp sugar
- 1 tbsp chopped fresh cilantro
- salt and pepper

1 To make the dressing, place the oil, vinegar, lemon juice, sugar, and cilantro in a large bowl. Season with salt and pepper and mix together well.

2 Add the tomatoes, onion, cucumber, olives, feta cheese, and cilantro. Toss all the ingredients together, then divide between individual serving bowls. Garnish with fresh parsley and serve with pita bread.

cook's tip

For an authentic Greek salad you need to use kalamata olives, but if they are unavailable then the same quantity of pitted green or black olives will work well in this recipe.

SPICY TOMATO SALAD

TOMATO SALAD MAKES A COLORFUL ACCOMPANIMENT TO MANY DISHES. THIS VERSION HAS A DELICIOUS SPICY FLAVOR AND MAKES AN EXCELLENT SALAD FOR A PICNIC OR BUFFET. IT IS ALSO SUITABLE FOR VEGANS AND WILL SUIT ANYONE ON A MEAT-FREE OR DAIRY-FREE DIET.

serves
4
preparation
5 minutes, plus 10 minutes' cooling
cooking
2–4 minutes

ingredients
- 4 large ripe tomatoes
- 1 small fresh red chili
- 1 garlic clove
- 1 oz/25 g fresh basil
- 4 tbsp extra virgin olive oil
- 1 tbsp lemon juice
- 2 tbsp balsamic vinegar
- salt and pepper
- fresh crusty bread, to serve

TO GARNISH
- fresh basil sprigs
- lemon wedges

1 Bring a tea kettle of water to a boil. Place the tomatoes in a heatproof bowl, then pour over enough boiling water to cover them. Let them soak for 2–4 minutes, then lift out of the water and cool slightly.

2 When the tomatoes are cool enough to handle, gently pierce the skins with the tip of a knife. The skins should now be easy to remove. Discard the skins, then chop the tomatoes and place them in a large salad bowl.

3 Seed and finely chop the chili, then chop the garlic. Rinse and finely chop the basil, then add it to the tomatoes in the bowl with the chili and the garlic.

4 Mix the oil, lemon juice, and balsamic vinegar together in a separate bowl, then season to taste with salt and pepper. Pour the mixture over the salad and toss together well. Garnish with basil sprigs and lemon wedges, and serve immediately with fresh crusty bread.

cook's tip

If possible, choose ripe tomatoes that are still on the vine. Their flavor is unmistakable, and will really enhance the taste of the salad. If you can't find tomatoes on the vine, then any tomatoes will work, but try to find some that have a good flavor.

6

HERBS AND
SPICES

HERBS AND SPICES HAVE A VERY WIDE RANGE OF
WONDERFUL FLAVORS, AND THE MEREST PINCH OF A
WELL-CHOSEN HERB OR SPICE CAN ELEVATE THE TASTE
OF A DISH TO AN ALTOGETHER NEW AND INSPIRING
LEVEL. TAKE YOUR INSPIRATION FROM THE RECIPES
FEATURED HERE, OR EXPERIMENT WITH YOUR OWN
COMBINATIONS FOR NEW AND EXCITING RESULTS.

INTRODUCTION

THERE IS A WIDE RANGE OF FRESH HERBS AVAILABLE ALL YEAR ROUND IN YOUR LOCAL SUPERMARKET, AS WELL AS A TEMPTING ARRAY OF FRAGRANT AND EXOTIC SPICES. YOU CAN ALSO BUY FROZEN HERBS, WHICH ARE A GOOD SUBSTITUTE WHEN FRESH HERBS ARE UNAVAILABLE. IT IS A GOOD IDEA TO KEEP SOME POTS OF FRESH HERBS ON A WINDOWSILL AND A SELECTION OF DRIED HERBS AND SPICES IN YOUR PANTRY. NOTE THAT IF YOU ARE SUBSTITUTING A DRIED HERB FOR FRESH, YOU WILL NEED ONLY HALF THE QUANTITY.

Buying and storing herbs and spices

If you buy fresh herbs as pot plants, place them on a windowsill where they can get plenty of light, and water them regularly. Basil, in particular, needs lots of water, so make sure you do not let it dry out. Packaged fresh herbs should be stored in their wrapping in the refrigerator. If you grow herbs in your garden, after picking, keep them in a pitcher of clean water until you are ready to use them. Store dried herbs and ground spices in a cool, dark place—an airy pantry is ideal. Use all fresh herbs by their "best before" date, and go through your pantry regularly and throw out any dried herbs and spices that are past their best.

Types and uses of herbs

Shown here are some of the most popular varieties of herbs and their uses. They are delicious served raw as garnishes or in salads, as well as chopped and added to cooked dishes.

Tarragon
The dark green, pointed leaves of tarragon have an aromatic, anise-like flavor. It adds a distinctive flavor to poultry, fish, eggs, sauces, salads, and dressings. It is best to use this herb on its own, since its strong flavor can overpower other herbs if mixed with them.

Basil
There are many species of this herb. It thrives in a warm, Mediterranean climate, and therefore in cold climates it will do better indoors on a windowsill with plenty of sunshine

and water. It has a sweet, aromatic flavor, and is particularly good with tomatoes and mozzarella cheese. It is also delicious with poultry, fish and seafood, salads, and sauces. This herb is fragile and should therefore be added to recipes toward the end of the cooking time.

Thyme
This herb comes in different varieties, and several of them are commonly used in cooking. The leaves add a pungent, aromatic flavor to meat, poultry, egg, and potato dishes, and are good in soups, sauces, roasts, casseroles, and stews.

Basil

How to make a bouquet garni

You can use this combination of herbs to flavor soups and stews. Take a bay leaf and a sprig each of parsley and thyme. Tie them together at one end with kitchen string, or enclose the herbs in a cheesecloth bag. Add the bouquet garni to your chosen dish to flavor it during cooking, then, when the dish is cooked, remove and discard it before serving.

Thyme

Oregano

Oregano

This green herb is related to marjoram. It has a pungent flavor and should be used sparingly. It is popular in Italian cooking, particularly on pizzas, and adds an aromatic flavor to meat and poultry, eggs, and cheese.

Cilantro

This pungent herb has bright green leaves and is very popular in Mediterranean and Asian cooking. It adds a distinctive flavor to salads, cooked vegetables, and stir-fries.

Fennel

There are two types of fennel. One has a bulbous base, which can be cooked and used like a vegetable; the other variety has no bulb. Fennel has a strong anise flavor. The leaves of both types can be snipped into soups and sauces, and are excellent with fish and egg dishes.

Marjoram

This ancient herb has pale green leaves and a delicate, sweet flavor. It is ideal with meat, poultry, cheese, tomatoes, eggs, and dressings.

Rosemary

The silvery, needle-shaped leaves of rosemary have a strong aromatic flavor. It is used in soups, salads, roasts, dressing, and marinades, as well as on pizzas. The herb also makes delicious skewers for kabobs. It pairs particularly well with potatoes and bread, as well as meat, poultry, fish, and eggs.

Bay

The leaves of this aromatic herb come from the Mediterranean laurel tree. The fresh leaves, if you can get them, have more flavor than the dried, but either type will add a good, pungent flavor to soups, sauces, stocks, and casseroles. They are usually discarded once the food has absorbed their flavor.

Sage

This herb has grayish oval leaves and a pungent, slightly bitter taste. It is very common in dresssings, especially those containing onion, and is excellent with pork, poultry, beans, cheese, rice, and pasta. It is also used to flavor drinks.

Chervil

The dark green, curly leaves of chervil have an aromatic flavor with a hint of anise. It is especially good in chicken, fish, and egg dishes.

Mint

There are many species of mint, the two most well known being peppermint and spearmint. Peppermint has a more peppery flavor, while spearmint has a fresher, mint taste. Mint is a hardy plant and can take over a herb garden if not carefully controlled. Use it to flavor cooked potatoes, peas, sauces, soups, meat dishes, desserts, and drinks.

Dill

This herb has feathery green leaves and a mild flavor. Dill is excellent with fish, as well as in salads, cheese dishes, and sauces.

Chives

These relatives of the onion family have long, hollow stems and edible purple flowers. The fresh stems are snipped into small pieces and added to salads, soups, cream cheese, and egg dishes. You can also buy them frozen and dried.

Parsley

This versatile herb is rich in vitamins A and C and comes in many varieties. The two most popular types have green leaves that are either curly or flat. Curly parsley is common all year round, while flat-leaf parsley may be found only in some supermarkets and specialist delicatessens. Parsley is used in a wide range of dishes, including soups, salads, sauces, stir-fries, and bakes, as well as dressings and marinades. It adds a spicy, lingering flavor to meat, poultry, fish, eggs, and vegetables, and helps to offset the sulfur aftertaste of garlic. It also makes an attractive garnish, particularly the flat-leaf variety.

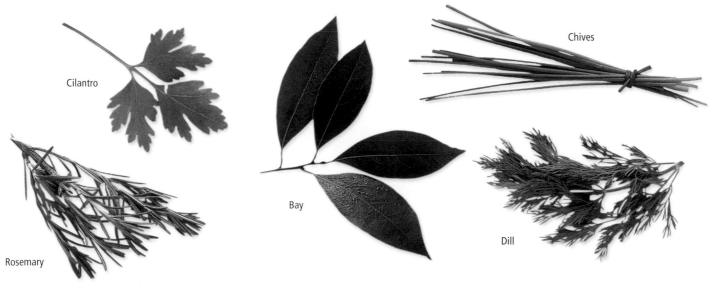

Cilantro

Chives

Bay

Dill

Rosemary

Types and uses of spices

Spices used to be costly when international travel was comparatively slow and difficult—now they are both less expensive and also more widely available.

Paprika

This spice is made from ground red pepper pods and its flavor can vary from mild, sweet, and pungent to fiery hot. It is good in salads and as a garnish. It also goes well with meat, poultry, eggs, vegetables, cream cheese, pasta, rice, and beans.

Cardamom

This aromatic spice is related to ginger and has a pungent lemon flavor. You can grind and use the whole pod, or just the seeds inside. Cardamom is widely used in Asian and Middle Eastern dishes, and adds a distinctive flavor to soups, stews, curries, pastry, bread, and cakes.

Allspice

This small berry comes from the West Indies and South America and has a sweet flavor of nutmeg, cinnamon, and cloves. You can buy it whole or ground. It is used with meat, onions, and fruit desserts, as well as cakes and bread.

Cardamom pods

Mustard

This hot, acrid spice is available in three forms: whole seeds, ground, or processed into a paste. It goes well with meat, poultry, seafood, eggs, beans, potatoes, cheese, cream and butter sauces, bread, marinades, chutneys, and relishes.

Chili powder

This is a powdered mixture of spices that includes dried chilies, cumin, coriander, and cloves. It has a fiery heat but you can also buy mild chili powder. Use it to flavor soups and stews. It goes well with seafood, meat, poultry, vegetables (especially potatoes), beans, and eggs.

Fennel seeds

You can buy fennel seeds whole or ground. They have a sweet, mildly anise flavor and can be used in savory and sweet dishes, including marinades, pizzas, dressings, bread, cakes, cookies, and a variety of desserts and drinks. Fennel goes particularly well with meat, poultry, fish, beet, onions, potatoes, tomatoes, cucumber, beans, pasta, rice, cheese, eggs, and fruit.

Star anise

This star-shaped brown pod comes from an Asian tree. It has a warm, aromatic, slightly bitter anise flavor and is available whole or ground. It is popular in Chinese cooking, and is used in marinades, stir-fries, bakes, cakes, fruit, and some drinks. It goes particularly well with pork, poultry, and fish.

Caraway

These seeds have a nutty, anise flavor and can be bought whole or ground. They are popular in German and Austrian cooking, and are used to flavor soups, stews, meat, cheese, vegetables, sauerkraut, bread, cakes, and the liqueur kümmel.

Juniper

These berries are available dried and are usually crushed to release their pungent pine flavor. Use them to flavor various meats as well as pâtés, dressings, and sauces.

Mace

This sweet, fragrant spice is most often sold ground and is used to flavor a wide range of savory and sweet dishes, including beef, chicken, fish, vegetables, pasta, beans, cheese, chocolate, fruit, cakes, marinades, cookies, chutneys, and mulled wine.

Cayenne pepper

This type of pepper is made from tropical chilies and has a hot, spicy flavor. Use it to add a kick to South American and Caribbean dishes. It is especially good with seafood and chutneys.

Peppercorns

The dried berries from the pepper plant come in black, white, and green. Black peppercorns are the most widely used, and are available whole, cracked, or ground. They deteriorate quickly when ground, so it is best to buy them whole and grind them yourself. They have an aromatic flavor and can be used in almost every savory recipe and some sweet fruit dishes, such as balsamic strawberries.

Cinnamon

This spice comes from the bark of a tropical tree. The bark is dried and curled into quills or sticks; it can also be bought ground. Cinnamon has a sweet, aromatic smell and flavor, and is popular in Middle Eastern dishes. It is used to flavor a wide range of savory and sweet dishes, such as stews, curries, pies, bread, and cakes, and a whole host of desserts and drinks.

Chili powder

Ground cinnamon

Cinnamon sticks

Nutmeg

Nutmeg has a sweet, fragrant flavor and is available whole or ground. It is used in a wide variety of savory and sweet dishes, from meat, poultry, vegetables, beans, rice, cheese, and eggs to chocolate, fruit, cream sauces, and drinks.

Cilantro

The dried seeds of the cilantro plant are fragrant and lemony and can be used whole or ground. They are popular in marinades, chutneys, curries, and bakes, and go particularly well with meat, poultry, fish, cheese, vegetables, beans, chocolate, and jelly.

Saffron

This spice has a pungent, slightly bitter flavor. It comes from the purple crocus and is available in threads or powdered. It is used to tint and flavor marinades, soups, stews, rice dishes, breads, and bakes. This is the spice that gives the rice in Spanish paella its characteristic yellow color. Saffron is expensive, so the less expensive turmeric is often used in its place.

Cloves

These come from the buds of the tropical clove tree. The dried brown buds are sold whole or ground, and have a sweet, pungent flavor. Push whole cloves into ham, pork, onions, and oranges to flavor them, or use them ground in soups, stews, bread, cakes, desserts, and chutneys. You can also use them whole in drinks such as mulled wine (always remove whole cloves before serving).

Pumpkin pie spice

This blend of spices commonly used in pumpkin pie usually consists of allspice, cinnamon, cloves, ginger, coriander, and nutmeg. It has a warm, sweet flavor and is delicious in fruit desserts, bread, cakes, cookies, and drinks.

Cumin

These dried seeds have a pungent, nutty flavor and are also available ground. Cumin is popular in Asian and Mexican cooking, and goes well with beef, pork, salmon, shellfish, beans, pasta, eggs, cheese, and rice.

Five spice

Chinese five-spice powder is, as its name implies, a blend of five spices, usually cloves, cinnamon, fennel seeds, Szechuan peppercorns, and star anise. It has a sweet, pungent flavor and is popular in Chinese and Vietnamese cooking. It is especially good in stir-fries. There is also a Tunisian version, which consists of cloves, cinnamon, nutmeg, pepper, and grains of paradise (which are also known as melegueta pepper).

Curry powder

This powder contains a mixture of spices including cardamom, chilies, cloves, coriander, fenugreek, and turmeric. It is available mild or hot, and is used in curries, cream sauces, and chutneys. It also goes well with beef, chicken, turkey, seafood, root vegetables, rice, eggs, and cheese.

Turmeric

This spice comes from the root of a tropical plant and has a pungent, somewhat bitter flavor. The powdered variety has a bright orange-yellow color, so is used to tint foods as well as to flavor them. Turmeric is often used as a cheaper alternative to saffron to color food. Use this spice to color or flavor seafood, poultry, pasta, cheese, eggs, curries, risottos, chutneys, marinades, bread, and beans.

Garam masala

The blend of spices in garam masala varies, but it often includes cumin, cinnamon, cloves, cardamom, chilies, fennel, fenugreek, garlic, ginger, and black pepper. It is popular in Indian cooking, especially in curries, and also goes well with vegetables, eggs, cheese, and rice.

Ginger

Ginger is available fresh or dried. The fresh root has a warm, lemon flavor and can be used chopped or grated. It is especially useful in marinades, salads, soups, stews, and stir-fries; it can also be preserved in syrup. Ground ginger has a more pungent, spicy flavor, and is particularly good with chocolate, cream, fruit, gingerbread, cakes, cookies, jellies, chutneys, and drinks.

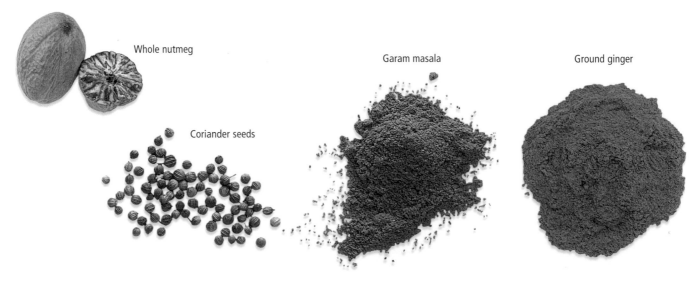

Whole nutmeg

Coriander seeds

Garam masala

Ground ginger

PEA & MINT SOUP

THE SWEETNESS OF GARDEN PEAS AND THE FRESH TASTE OF MINT PAIR TOGETHER BEAUTIFULLY IN THIS DISH, AND THE SHALLOTS AND LEEKS ADD AN APPEALING DEPTH. THIS SOUP IS IDEAL FOR VEGETARIANS BUT ENJOYABLE FOR ALL. IT MAKES A DELICOUS APPETIZER OR LIGHT LUNCH.

serves
4

preparation
15 minutes,
plus 10 minutes'
cooling

cooking
40 minutes

ingredients
- 1 tbsp butter
- 3 shallots, chopped
- 2 leeks, trimmed and finely chopped
- 1 potato, peeled and chopped
- 1 lb/450 g frozen peas
- 2 tbsp chopped fresh mint
- 3½ cups vegetable stock
- salt and pepper
- fresh mint sprigs, to garnish
- slices of fresh whole wheat bread, to serve

1 Melt the butter in a large pan over medium heat. Add the shallots and cook, stirring, for 2 minutes. Add the leeks and cook, stirring, for an additional 2 minutes. Add the potato, peas, chopped mint, and stock, and season with salt and pepper. Bring to a boil, then reduce the heat, cover the pan, and let simmer for 30 minutes. Remove the pan from the heat and let cool for 10 minutes.

2 Transfer the soup to a food processor and process until smooth (you may need to do this in batches).

3 Return to the pan, season to taste with salt and pepper, and reheat gently. Remove from the heat and pour into serving bowls. Garnish with fresh mint sprigs and serve with slices of fresh whole wheat bread.

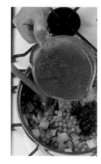

BASIL & PINE NUT PESTO

PESTO IS DELICIOUS STIRRED INTO PASTA, SOUPS, AND SALAD DRESSINGS. IT IS AVAILABLE IN MOST SUPERMARKETS, BUT MAKING YOUR OWN GIVES A CONCENTRATED FLAVOR. YOU CAN MAKE THIS PESTO A DAY AHEAD AND KEEP IT IN THE REFRIGERATOR UNTIL YOU ARE READY TO COOK THE PASTA.

serves
4

preparation
15 minutes

cooking
10 minutes

ingredients
- about 40 fresh basil leaves
- 3 garlic cloves, crushed
- ⅛ cup pine nuts
- 1¾ oz/50 g Parmesan cheese, finely grated
- 2–3 tbsp extra virgin olive oil
- 1 lb 8 oz/675 g fresh pasta or 12 oz/350 g dried pasta
- salt and pepper

1 Rinse the basil leaves and pat them dry with paper towels.

2 Place the basil leaves, garlic, pine nuts, and grated Parmesan cheese in a food processor and process for 30 seconds, or until smooth. Alternatively, pound all of the ingredients by hand, using a mortar and pestle.

3 If you are using a food processor, keep the motor running and slowly add the olive oil. Alternatively, add the oil drop by drop while stirring briskly. Season to taste with salt and pepper.

4 Bring a large, heavy-bottom pan of water to a boil. Add the pasta, return to a boil, and cook for 3–4 minutes for fresh pasta or 8–10 minutes for dried, until tender but still firm to the bite. Drain the pasta thoroughly, then transfer to a serving plate and serve with the pesto. Toss to mix well and serve hot.

cook's tip

Only buy pine nuts in small quantities as their high oil content means they quickly turn rancid. Pine nuts are available in most large supermarkets or health food stores.

TARRAGON CHICKEN

THIS IS A CLASSIC FRENCH RECIPE AND IS SUCH A STYLISH, YET UNDERSTATED DISH THAT IT WOULD BE AN EXCELLENT CHOICE FOR A MAIN COURSE AT AN INFORMAL DINNER PARTY. TARRAGON HAS A POWERFUL FLAVOR, SO USE IT SPARINGLY OR IT WILL DOMINATE THE OTHER FLAVORS.

serves
4
preparation
5 minutes
cooking
20 minutes

ingredients
- 4 skinless, boneless chicken breasts, about 6 oz/175 g each
- 1/2 cup dry white wine
- 1–1 1/4 cups chicken stock
- 1 garlic clove, finely chopped
- 1 tbsp dried tarragon
- 3/4 cup heavy cream
- 1 tbsp chopped fresh tarragon
- salt and pepper
- fresh tarragon sprigs, to garnish

1 Season the chicken with salt and pepper and place in a single layer in a large, heavy-bottom skillet. Pour in the wine and enough chicken stock just to cover and add the garlic and dried tarragon. Bring to a boil, reduce the heat, and cook gently for an additional 10 minutes, or until the chicken is tender and cooked through.

2 Remove the chicken with a slotted spoon or tongs, cover, and keep warm. Strain the poaching liquid into a clean skillet and skim off any fat from the surface. Bring to a boil and cook for 12–15 minutes, or until reduced by about two-thirds.

3 Stir in the cream, return to a boil, and cook until reduced by about half. Stir in the fresh tarragon. Slice the chicken breasts and arrange on warmed plates. Spoon over the sauce, garnish with tarragon sprigs, and serve immediately.

cook's tip

Tongs are the easiest way to remove the chicken breasts from the skillet. Make sure that the chicken is completely cooked through before serving.

OMELETS WITH FINES HERBES

FINES HERBES ARE SIMPLY A MIXTURE OF VERY FINELY CHOPPED FRESH HERBS, AND THE CLASSIC
COMBINATION IS PARSLEY, TARRAGON, CHERVIL, AND CHIVES. THIS SUBTLY FLAVORED OMELET PAIRS
WELL WITH A TOMATO SALAD OR MIXED SALAD GREENS FOR A LIGHT, SUMMERY LUNCH.

serves
2

preparation
10 minutes

cooking
4 minutes

ingredients
- 6 eggs
- 4 tbsp chopped fresh parsley
- 4 tbsp chopped fresh tarragon
- 4 tbsp chopped fresh chervil
- 2 tbsp snipped fresh chives
- 2 tbsp butter
- salt and pepper
- mixed salad greens, to serve

1 Beat the eggs with the parsley, tarragon, chervil, and chives. Season to taste with salt and pepper.

2 Melt half the butter in an omelet pan or small, heavy-bottom skillet. Add half the egg mixture and stir with a fork. As the egg sets, draw it towards the center, and tilt the omelet pan so that the uncooked egg runs underneath. Cook until the underside of the omelet is golden and set, but the top is still moist.

3 Remove the omelet pan from the heat and slide the omelet onto a plate, flipping the pan gently so that the omelet folds. Keep the omelet warm. Melt the remaining butter and cook a second omelet in the same way. Serve immediately with mixed salad greens.

cook's tip

If you cannot find any of the four herbs normally used to make "fines herbes," use marjoram, oregano, or dill instead.

SALMON COOKED WITH DILL

SALMON ALWAYS GOES DOWN WELL AT PARTIES, AND THE COMBINATION OF THE HERBS AND FENNEL, AND THE SMOKY BARBECUE TASTE, GIVES THIS DISH A MOUTHWATERING FLAVOR THAT YOUR GUESTS WILL FIND DIFFICULT TO RESIST. SERVE IT WITH CRUSTY BREAD FOR A SATISFYING MEAL.

serves
4

preparation
5 minutes

cooking
30 minutes

ingredients
- ½ large bunch dried thyme
- 5 fresh rosemary branches, 6–8 inches/15–20 cm long
- 8 bay leaves
- 2 lb 4 oz/1 kg salmon fillet
- 1 bulb fennel, cut into 8 pieces
- 2 tbsp lemon juice
- 2 tbsp olive oil

TO SERVE
- crusty bread
- green salad

1 Preheat the barbecue. Make a base on the hot barbecue with the dried thyme, rosemary branches, and bay leaves, overlapping them so that they cover a slightly bigger area than the salmon.

2 Carefully place the salmon on top of the herbs.

3 Arrange the fennel around the edge of the fish.

4 Combine the lemon juice and oil and brush the salmon with it.

5 Cover the salmon loosely with a piece of foil, to keep it moist.

6 Cook for about 20–30 minutes, basting frequently with the lemon juice mixture.

7 Remove the salmon from the barbecue, cut it into slices, and serve with the fennel.

8 Serve with slices of crusty bread and a green salad.

variation

Use whatever combination of herbs you may have to hand—but avoid the stronger tasting herbs, such as sage and marjoram, which are unsuitable for fish.

TAGINE OF LAMB

THIS IS A TYPICAL MOROCCAN MIXTURE OF MEAT, VEGETABLES, AND APRICOTS, FLAVORED WITH PLENTY OF FRESH HERBS AND SPICES. IT IS DELICIOUS—AND AUTHENTIC—IF SERVED WITH COUSCOUS, WHICH CAN BE COOKED IN A STEAMER SET OVER THE STEW FOR 6–7 MINUTES.

serves
4
preparation
10 minutes
cooking
1 hour 40 minutes

ingredients
- 1 tbsp sunflower-seed or corn oil
- 1 onion, chopped
- 12 oz/350 g boneless lamb, trimmed of all visible fat and cut into 1-inch/ 2.5-cm cubes
- 1 garlic clove, finely chopped
- 2½ cups vegetable stock
- grated rind and juice of 1 orange
- 1 tsp clear honey
- 1 cinnamon stick
- ½-inch/1-cm piece fresh gingerroot, finely chopped
- 1 eggplant
- 4 tomatoes, peeled and chopped
- ⅔ cup no-soak dried apricots
- 2 tbsp chopped fresh cilantro
- salt and pepper
- freshly cooked couscous, to serve

1 Heat the oil in a large, heavy-bottom skillet or ovenproof casserole over medium heat. Add the onion and lamb cubes and cook, stirring frequently, for 5 minutes, or until the meat is lightly browned all over. Add the garlic, stock, orange rind and juice, honey, cinnamon stick, and ginger. Bring to a boil, then reduce the heat, cover, and let simmer for 45 minutes.

2 Using a sharp knife, halve the eggplant lengthwise and slice thinly. Add to the skillet with the chopped tomatoes and apricots. Cover and cook for an additional 45 minutes, or until the lamb is tender.

3 Stir in the cilantro and season to taste with salt and pepper. Serve immediately, straight from the skillet, with freshly cooked couscous.

7

RICE, PASTA, AND

THE SLOW RELEASING CARBOHYDRATES IN PASTA,
PULSES, AND GRAINS MAKE THEM A GOOD SOURCE
OF ENERGY. THEY ARE ALSO VERY VERSATILE AND CAN
BE USED IN A WIDE VARIETY OF DISHES. SIMPLY ADD A
TASTY SAUCE AND YOU HAVE A VERY SATISFYING MEAL.

PULSES,
GRAINS

INTRODUCTION

CARBOHYDRATES SUCH AS PASTA, NOODLES, AND GRAINS PROVIDE A GOOD, INEXPENSIVE SOURCE OF ENERGY, ESPECIALLY THE WHOLE WHEAT / WHOLE GRAIN VARIETIES, AND ARE A VALUABLE SOURCE OF DIETARY FIBER. COMBINE THEM WITH PROTEIN-RICH PULSES, AND YOU HAVE A DELICIOUS MEAL THAT IS NUTRITIOUS, SATISFYING, AND HEALTHY.

Buying and storing pasta

You can buy fresh and dried pasta in a wide variety of colors, shapes, and sizes. It is usually made with durum wheat or whole wheat flour. Fresh pasta usually keeps for up to 2 days in the refrigerator, and dried pasta for up to 2 years in the pantry, but always use them by their "best before" date.

Buying and storing noodles

In addition to Italian pasta, there are also different types of Asian noodles. Asian noodles should be stored in a cool, dry place, and used by their "best before" date.

How to cook pasta

Cooking pasta is quick and easy. Simply bring a large pan of lightly salted water to a boil, add the pasta, and return to a boil, stirring at intervals to prevent it sticking together. Reduce the heat slightly and cook until it is tender but still firm to the bite; this is known as al dente. Remove from the heat, drain, and serve tossed with olive oil or accompanied by your chosen sauce or recipe.

Fine egg noodle

Medium egg noodle

Thick egg noodle

Cellophane noodles

These thread-like noodles are also known as Chinese vermicelli and are made from the starch of mung beans. Dried cellophane noodles should be soaked briefly before use, although this isn't necessary in dishes that contain a lot of liquid, such as soups.

Egg noodles

These are very popular in Asian cooking, especially in Chinese stir-fries. Check cooking instructions on the package: some need to be soaked in hot water for about 4–5 minutes, while others can be put straight into the wok.

Ramen noodles

These noodles are deep-fried and sold packaged, often accompanied by ready-to-use broth mix.

Rice noodles

These delicate, fine, white noodles are very easy to prepare. Simply soak them in hot water for 4–5 minutes. They are very good added to soups and stir-fries, and when deep-fried they become deliciously crunchy.

Soba noodles

These thin noodles are made from wheat flour and buckwheat. They are popular in Japanese cooking.

Udon noodles

These thick Japanese noodles are like spaghetti, except that they can be square as well as round. They are made from cornstarch or wheat flour, and are available fresh or dried.

Pasta names

Anelli Very small rings

Cannelloni Large, hollow tubes

Conchiglie Ridged shells

Farfalle Bows

Fettuccine Long, narrow ribbons

Fusilli Spirals

Lasagna Large, flat rectangular sheets

Linguine Long, narrow ribbons with flattened edges

Lumaconi Snail shapes

Macaroni Long or short narrow tubes, often curved

Penne Hollow quills

Ravioli Square cushions

Spaghetti Long, narrow strings

Tagliatelle Long ribbons, a little wider than fettucine

Vermicelli Long, very fine, hair-like strings

Making your own fresh pasta

You can buy good-quality fresh pasta nowadays, but if you prefer to make your own, the process is simple. You might also like to invest in a pasta machine in order to create perfect pasta shapes of your choice.

Homemade pasta

Serves 6

2 cups all-purpose flour,
 plus extra for dusting
1 tsp salt
2 eggs, lightly beaten
3 tbsp tomato paste (optional—
 use if you want a red, tomato-
 flavored pasta)

Lightly dust a clean counter with flour. Sift the flour and salt into a mound on the counter. ❶ Make a well in the center of the flour, add the beaten eggs and tomato paste, if using, and mix to a stiff dough. If necessary, stir in a few tablespoons of water. ❷ Knead the dough vigorously for about 8 minutes, then wrap it in plastic wrap and let it rest for 30 minutes, or for up to 2 days if not required straight away.

Roll out the dough to the desired thickness, then use a sharp knife to cut it into pieces of the required shape and size. ❸ Alternatively, use a pasta machine to cut the dough. The pasta is now ready to be cooked.

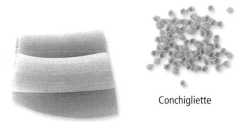

Cannelloni

Conchigliette

Lumaconi

Penne

Rigatoni

Fusilli

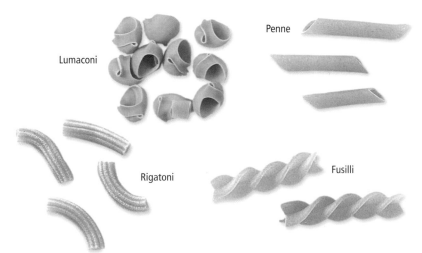

Pasta cooking times

Use a large pan for cooking pasta and bring lightly salted water to a boil. Add 1 tablespoon olive oil and the pasta and return to a boil. When the pasta is tender but still firm to the bite, drain and use as soon as possible.

Type of pasta	Unfilled/filled	Cooking time
Fresh	Unfilled	3 minutes
Fresh	Filled	10 minutes
Dried	Unfilled	10 minutes
Dried	Filled	15–20 minutes

Buying and storing pulses

Beans, lentils, and peas all fall into the category of pulses. You can buy these protein-rich foods dried, or ready to use in cans if you are short of time. When buying dried pulses, store them in airtight containers in a cool, dry place and use by the "best before" date, or, if there is no date on the package, within 1 year for best results. Do not mix old and new beans because they will take different lengths of time to cook. Once cooked, refrigerate leftover beans and use within 3 days, or freeze them in an airtight container and use within 6 months.

Preparing and cooking pulses

Most pulses need soaking for at least 8 hours, then boiling rapidly for 10 minutes, followed by further cooking for at least 45 minutes or until they are tender. The main exceptions are soybeans, which need 12 hours soaking and 4 hours to cook, and chickpeas, which need 8 hours to soak and 2 hours to cook. Haricot beans, like navy beans, need soaking overnight and need 1½ hours to cook. Lentils and split peas usually need no soaking and can be cooked in 25–30 minutes.

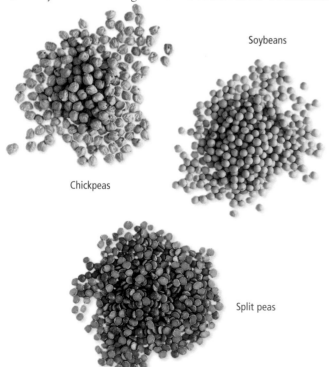

Chickpeas

Soybeans

Split peas

Black-eye peas

Chickpeas

These round and cream-colored peas have a nutty flavor, and are excellent in soups, salads, dips, and stews, as well as pasta or grain dishes. Chickpeas can also be roasted for snacks, and are used in falafel, a Middle Eastern dish in which the mashed beans are formed into balls and deep-fried. Soak chickpeas for at least 8 hours before use. After soaking, drain and rinse them, then cover with fresh water and bring to a boil. Reduce the heat and let simmer for 2 hours until they are thoroughly cooked.

Soybeans

The most common color of soybeans is pale yellow. These beans are good in soups and other savory dishes, such as curries. Remember that they need to be soaked for at least 12 hours. After soaking, drain and rinse them, then cover with fresh water and bring to a boil. Boil them for the first hour of cooking, then let simmer for another 3 hours until they are thoroughly cooked.

Azuki beans

These small red beans are good in soups and salads.

Cannellini beans

Add these long creamy-white beans to soups and salads.

Split peas

These small peas are disk-shaped like lentils, but they are split along a natural seam. Split peas are yellow or green. They can be cooked and puréed, and used in soups, bakes, and other savory dishes.

Lentils

These are small, disk-shaped pulses. Use red or orange lentils puréed and in soups and sauces; green or brown lentils are best in salads, sauces, stews, and other savory dishes.

Red kidney beans

These red kidney-shaped beans can be added to soups, salads, and stews, and other savory dishes such as chili con carne.

Haricot beans

These white beans, such as navy beans and Great Northern beans can be used in a wide variety of savory dishes, including soups, salads, stews, and casseroles.

Lima beans

These white kidney-shaped beans are excellent in soups and salads.

Flageolet beans

These small green beans are excellent in salads and also make a delicious accompaniment to meat dishes.

Cranberry beans

These oval beans vary in color from pale pink to maroon-streaked skin. Use them in soups, dips, and other savory dishes.

Black-eye peas

These beans are small and beige and have a circular black "eye." Use them in sauces, stir-fries, and soups.

Long-grain rice   Pudding rice

Buying and storing rice

There are many different varieties of rice available. Store rice in airtight containers for up to 3 years in a cool, dry place, or use by the "best before" date if sooner.

Short-grain rice
This rice has short, fat grains that are more starchy and moist than medium- and long-grain rice. Varieties of short-grain rice include arborio and carnaroli rice, which are used in risottos.

Medium-grain rice
These grains are a little shorter than long-grain rice. They are more moist and therefore tend to clump together when cooked. Medium-grain rice is used in savory dishes.

Long-grain rice
Both white and brown long-grain rice are excellent for savory dishes because the grains stay dry and separate when cooked.

Basmati rice
This Himalayan long-grain rice has a nutty flavor and is excellent in savory dishes. It is available in white or brown and the grains stay dry and separate when cooked.

Jasmine rice
This tender rice has a delicate, fragrant, aromatic flavor. It is popular in both Vietnamese and Thai cooking.

Arborio rice
This starchy, short-grain creamy rice is ideal in risottos.

Carnaroli rice
This short-grain rice has often been called "the king of Italian rice." It has a high starch content and makes a lovely creamy risotto.

Easy-cook rice
These rice grains are polished and partly boiled so that they are quick to cook. They stay fluffy and separate when cooked, but have less flavor than white or brown rice.

Red rice
This rice is grown in the Camargue region of France and in China. It has a pale red color and a nutty flavor that is similar to brown rice.

Wild rice
This rice is in fact a marsh grass, not a rice. The grains are long and black, with a nutty flavor. It is often mixed with brown long-grain rice for reasons of economy.

How to cook long-grain and basmati rice

To cook rice for four people, put $1\frac{1}{2}$ cups rice into a strainer and rinse under cold running water. Transfer to a large pan and pour in $2\frac{1}{2}$ cups cold water. Add a large pinch of salt, then bring to a boil. Reduce the heat, stir briefly, then cover the pan and simmer gently until the rice is tender and all the liquid has been absorbed (but do not let the rice burn). As a rough guide, white rice will need 15 minutes, and brown rice will need 25–30 minutes. Remove from the heat and stand for 5 minutes with the lid on. Fluff the grains with a fork and serve.

Other grains

It is always worthwhile experimenting with other types of grain. Try using them in salads, soups, and stews, or piling them on a platter and topping them with tasty cooked vegetables.

Barley
The polished variety of barley, known as pearl barley, is the kind most widely available. You can also buy pot barley, which is unpolished, from specialist stores and health-food stores. Barley is excellent in soups, casseroles, and stews.

Millet
This protein-rich grain is a staple in Africa and Asia, and is boiled in a similar way to rice.

Couscous
This is not a true grain, but pieces of semolina. Steam it in accordance with the instructions on the package. It makes an excellent bed of grains on which to pile meats and vegetables.

Cornmeal
This yellow grain is made from cornmeal and features widely in Italian cooking. Follow the cooking instructions on the package because methods and cooking times vary. To serve cold, once the mixture pulls away from the pan, pour it onto a baking sheet, let cool, then cut it into squares and serve. To serve hot, at the same stage stir in a generous tablespoon of butter, then remove from the heat and stir vigorously until the cornmeal stays firm.

Bulgur wheat
This comprises wheat kernels that have been precooked. It is a golden-brown grain with a nutty flavor. Since it has already been cooked, you simply need to soak it in plenty of cold water for 20–30 minutes, then strain it in a strainer, pressing out as much water as possible. This grain is excellent in salads, especially the Middle Eastern dish known as tabbouleh. It is also good in pilaus.

SPAGHETTI BOLOGNESE

THE CLASSIC MEAT SAUCE IN THIS RECIPE IS MOST OFTEN PARTNERED WITH SPAGHETTI, AS SHOWN
HERE. HOWEVER, IT ALSO GOES WELL WITH LASAGNA, CANNELLONI, OR ANY OTHER BAKED PASTA
DISHES. YOU CAN ALSO SERVE IT WITH A JACKET BAKED POTATO FOR A TASTY LUNCH OR SUPPER.

serves

4

preparation

15 minutes

cooking

1¼ hours

ingredients

- 3 tbsp olive oil
- 2 garlic cloves, crushed
- 1 large onion, finely
  chopped
- 1 carrot, diced
- 1 cup fresh lean ground
  beef or chicken
- 3 oz/85 g chicken livers,
  finely chopped
- 3½ oz/100 g lean
  prosciutto, diced
- ⅔ cup Marsala wine
- 10 oz/280 g canned
  chopped plum tomatoes
- 1 tbsp chopped fresh
  basil leaves
- 2 tbsp tomato paste
- 1 lb/450 g dried spaghetti
- salt and pepper

1 Heat 2 tablespoons of the oil in a
large pan. Add the garlic, onion, and
carrot and cook for 6 minutes.

2 Add the ground meat, chicken
livers, and prosciutto to the pan
and cook over medium heat for
12 minutes, or until well browned.

3 Stir in the Marsala, tomatoes,
basil, and tomato paste and cook for
4 minutes. Season to taste with salt
and pepper. Cover and let simmer
for 30 minutes.

4 Remove the lid from the pan, stir,
and let simmer for an additional
15 minutes.

5 Meanwhile, bring a large pan of
lightly salted water to a boil. Add the
spaghetti and the remaining oil,
return to a boil, and cook for
12 minutes, or until tender but still
firm to the bite. Drain and transfer
to a serving dish. Pour the sauce over
the pasta, toss, and serve hot.

variation

*Chicken livers are considered an essential
ingredient in a classic Bolognese sauce,
adding richness. However, you can substitute
them with the same quantity of ground beef
or chicken, if you prefer.*

VEGETABLE LASAGNA

THIS COLORFUL AND TASTY LASAGNA HAS LAYERS OF DICED AND SLICED VEGETABLES IN TOMATO SAUCE, ALL TOPPED WITH A RICH CHEESE SAUCE. IN THIS RECIPE, VERDI (GREEN) SHEETS OF PASTA HAVE BEEN USED, BUT IF YOU PREFER YOU COULD USE NO PRECOOK WHITE PASTA SHEETS INSTEAD.

serves
4

preparation
15 minutes,
plus 20 minutes'
standing

cooking
55 minutes

ingredients
- 1 eggplant, sliced
- 3 tbsp olive oil
- 2 garlic cloves, crushed
- 1 red onion, halved and sliced
- 3 mixed bell peppers, seeded and diced
- 8 oz/225 g mixed mushrooms, sliced
- 2 celery stalks, sliced
- 1 zucchini, diced
- 1/2 tsp chili powder
- 1/2 tsp ground cumin
- 2 tomatoes, chopped
- 1 1/4 cups strained canned tomatoes

- 2 tbsp chopped fresh basil
- 8 no-precook lasagna verdi sheets
- salt and pepper

CHEESE SAUCE
- 2 tbsp butter or margarine
- 1 tbsp flour
- 2/3 cup vegetable stock
- 1 1/4 cups milk
- scant 3/4 cup grated Cheddar cheese
- 1 tsp Dijon mustard
- 1 tbsp chopped fresh basil
- 1 egg, beaten

1 Place the eggplant slices in a colander, sprinkle with salt, and leave for 20 minutes. Rinse under cold water, drain, and set aside.

2 Preheat the oven to 350°F/180°C. Heat the oil in a pan. Add the garlic and onion and sauté for 1–2 minutes. Add the bell peppers, mushrooms, celery, and zucchini and cook, stirring constantly, for 3–4 minutes.

3 Stir in the spices and cook for 1 minute. Mix in the tomatoes, strained canned tomatoes, and basil and season to taste with salt and pepper.

4 To make the sauce, melt the butter in a pan. Stir in the flour and cook for 1 minute. Remove from the heat, stir in the stock and milk, return to the heat, and add half the cheese and the mustard. Boil, stirring, until thickened. Stir in the basil. Remove from the heat and stir in the egg.

5 Place half the lasagna in an ovenproof dish. Top with half the vegetables, half the tomato sauce, then half the eggplants. Repeat and then spoon the cheese sauce on top. Sprinkle with the remaining cheese and bake for 40 minutes, or until golden brown and bubbling.

GNOCCHI WITH QUICK TOMATO SAUCE

THE WORD "GNOCCHI" IS ITALIAN FOR "DUMPLINGS," AND IS USED TO DESCRIBE SMALL BALLS OR CONCAVE OVAL DISKS MADE FROM A DOUGH OF POTATOES AND/OR FLOUR. THEY ARE USUALLY BOILED OR BAKED, AND SERVED WITH A SAUCE OR JUST SOME PARMESAN CHEESE.

serves
4
preparation
25 minutes
cooking
20 minutes

ingredients
- 2 lb/900 g mealy potatoes
- 1 tbsp olive oil
- 1²/₃–2 cups all-purpose flour, plus extra for dusting
- 1 tsp salt
- 1 tsp baking powder
- 1 egg, beaten
- freshly grated Parmesan cheese, to serve

TOMATO SAUCE
- 2 tbsp vegetable oil
- 1 large onion, chopped
- 2 garlic cloves, chopped
- 14 oz/400 g canned chopped tomatoes
- ½ vegetable bouillon cube dissolved in generous ⅓ cup boiling water
- 2 tbsp fresh basil, shredded

1 Peel the potatoes and cut into chunks. Cook in lightly salted boiling water for 15 minutes, or until tender. Drain well, then push through a strainer into a large bowl. Mix in the oil.

2 Stir the flour, 1 teaspoon of salt, and the baking powder together. Add half to the potatoes, with the egg, and mix together. Gradually knead in the remaining flour to form a smooth, slightly sticky dough.

3 For the tomato sauce, heat the oil in a pan. Add the onions and garlic and cook for 3–4 minutes. Add the tomatoes and stock and cook, uncovered, for 10 minutes. Season with salt and pepper to taste.

4 Shape the dough on a floured counter into 1-inch/2.5-cm thick rolls, then cut into ¾-inch/2-cm pieces. Using the tines of a fork, roll each piece toward you to curl in the sides and mark the top.

5 Bring a large pan of water to a boil, then reduce to a simmer. Add about 30 gnocchi and cook for 1–2 minutes until they float to the surface. Repeat until all the gnocchi are cooked.

6 Stir the basil into the tomato sauce and pour over the gnocchi. Toss to coat and season with pepper to taste. Sprinkle with grated Parmesan and serve immediately.

GOLDEN CORNMEAL, ITALIAN-STYLE

CORNMEAL, ALSO CALLED POLENTA, IS STAPLE FOOD OF NORTHERN ITALY. ONCE COOKED, IT CAN
BE EATEN HOT OR COLD. THIS RECIPE MAKES A DELICIOUS APPETIZER OR TASTY ACCOMPANIMENT
TO A MAIN MEAL. IT ALSO MAKES A SATISFYING BREAKFAST.

serves
4

preparation
20 minutes, plus
2½ hours' cooling
and standing

cooking
1 hour

ingredients
- 6⅓ cups water
- 1½ tsp salt
- scant 2 cups cornmeal
- vegetable oil, for cooking
  and oiling
- 2 beaten eggs (optional)
- 2¼ cups fresh fine white
  bread crumbs (optional)

TOMATO SAUCE
- 2 tbsp olive oil
- 1 small onion, chopped
- 1 garlic clove, chopped
- 14 oz/400 g canned
  chopped tomatoes
- 2 tbsp chopped fresh
  parsley
- 1 tsp dried oregano
- 2 bay leaves
- 2 tbsp tomato paste
- 1 tsp sugar
- salt and pepper

1 Bring the water and salt to a boil
in a large pan and gradually sprinkle
in the cornmeal, stirring constantly
to prevent lumps forming. Simmer
gently, stirring frequently, for
30 minutes, or until the cornmeal
becomes very thick and begins to
draw away from the sides of the pan.

2 Oil an 11 x 7-inch/28 x 18-cm
shallow pan, then spoon in the
cornmeal. Spread out evenly, using a
wet wooden spoon or spatula. Let
cool, then let stand for 2 hours at
room temperature, if possible.

3 Cut the cornmeal into 30–36
squares. Heat the oil in a skillet. Add
the pieces and cook until golden

brown all over, turning several times,
for about 5 minutes. Alternatively,
dip each piece of cornmeal in beaten
egg and coat in bread crumbs before
cooking in the hot oil. Keep warm.

4 To make the tomato sauce, heat the
oil in a pan over medium heat. Add
the onion and sauté for 2 minutes
until translucent. Add the garlic and
sauté for 1 minute. Stir in the
chopped tomatoes, herbs, tomato
paste, sugar, and salt and pepper to
taste. Bring to a boil, then simmer,
uncovered, for 20 minutes, or until
the sauce has reduced by half.
Discard the bay leaf.

5 Serve the cornmeal pieces with the
hot tomato sauce.

CHINESE FRIED RICE

THIS IS A DELICIOUS ADAPTATION OF A POPULAR CHINESE RECIPE. THE STRIPS OF BACON ARE A MOUTHWATERING ADDITION AND GIVE AN IRRESISTIBLE FLAVOR TO THE RICE. TO MAKE THIS DISH WORK REALLY WELL, MAKE SURE YOU USE COLD, DRY RICE WITH GRAINS THAT ARE WELL SEPARATED.

serves

4

preparation

5 minutes, plus 20 minutes' cooling

cooking

30 minutes

ingredients

- 3 cups water
- ½ tsp salt
- 1½ cups long-grain rice
- 2 eggs
- 4 tsp cold water
- 3 tbsp sunflower-seed oil
- 4 scallions, sliced diagonally
- 1 red, green, or yellow bell pepper, cored, seeded, and thinly sliced
- 3–4 lean bacon slices, rinded and cut into strips
- 1⅓ cups fresh bean sprouts
- 1⅛ cups frozen peas, thawed
- 2 tbsp soy sauce (optional)
- salt and pepper

1 Pour the water into the wok with the salt and bring to a boil. Rinse the rice in a strainer under cold running water until the water runs clear, drain thoroughly, and add to the boiling water. Stir well, then cover the wok tightly with the lid, and let simmer gently for 12–13 minutes. (Do not remove the lid during cooking or the steam will escape and the rice will not be cooked.)

2 Remove the lid, give the rice a good stir, and spread out on a large plate or baking sheet to cool and dry.

3 Meanwhile, beat each egg separately with salt and pepper and 2 teaspoons of cold water. Heat 1 tablespoon of oil in a preheated wok, pour in the first egg, swirl it around, and let cook undisturbed

until set. Transfer to a cutting board and cook the second egg. Cut the omelets into thin slices.

4 Add the remaining oil to the wok and when really hot add the scallions and bell pepper and stir-fry for 1–2 minutes. Add the bacon and continue to stir-fry for an additional 2 minutes. Add the bean sprouts and peas and toss together thoroughly. Stir in the soy sauce, if using.

5 Add the rice and salt and pepper to taste and stir-fry for 1 minute, then add the strips of omelet and continue to stir-fry for 2 minutes, or until the rice is piping hot. Serve immediately.

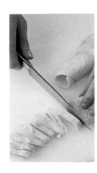

RISOTTO MILANESE

RISOTTO IS A DELICIOUS ITALIAN DISH AND VERY EASY TO MAKE, BUT IT DOES REQUIRE CONSTANT ATTENTION AND STIRRING WHILE COOKING. MAKE SURE YOU USE A STARCHY, SHORT-GRAIN RICE SUCH AS ARBORIO OR CARNAROLI, BECAUSE THIS WILL GIVE A LOVELY CREAMY CONSISTENCY.

serves

4

preparation

5 minutes

cooking

20 minutes

ingredients

- 4 cups chicken stock
- 4 cups white wine
- 1 tsp saffron strands
- 1 tbsp olive oil
- 3 tbsp butter
- 1 small onion, finely chopped
- 1 lb/400 g arborio rice
- ½ cup freshly grated Parmesan cheese
- salt and pepper

1 Bring the stock and white wine to a boil, then reduce the heat and simmer. Infuse the saffron strands in the stock and continue to simmer while preparing the risotto.

2 Heat the oil with 2 tablespoons of butter in a deep pan over medium heat until the butter has melted. Stir in the onion and cook gently until soft and beginning to turn golden but not brown.

3 Add the rice and mix to coat in oil and butter. Cook, stirring, for 2–3 minutes, or until the grains are translucent.

4 Gradually add the stock and saffron mixture, a ladleful at a time. Stir constantly, adding more liquid as the rice absorbs it. Increase the heat slightly so that the liquid bubbles. Cook for 20 minutes, or until all the liquid is absorbed.

5 Remove the risotto from the heat. Add the remaining butter, mix well, then stir in the Parmesan cheese. Season to taste with salt and pepper and serve immediately.

BROWN RICE VEGETABLE PILAF

PILAFS ARE POPULAR AROUND THE EASTERN MEDITERRANEAN AND IN ASIA. THE COOKING METHOD INVOLVES SAUTÉEING THE RICE IN HOT BUTTER OR OIL, THEN POURING IN THE STOCK AND SIMMERING. PILAF INGREDIENTS VARY—THEY CAN CONTAIN VEGETABLES, MEATS, POULTRY, OR FISH.

serves
4

preparation
30 minutes

cooking
15 minutes

ingredients

- 4 tbsp vegetable oil
- 1 red onion, finely chopped
- 2 tender celery stalks, leaves included, quartered lengthwise, and diced
- 2 carrots, coarsely grated
- 1 fresh green chili, seeded and finely chopped
- 3 scallions, green part included, finely chopped
- generous ¼ cup whole almonds, sliced lengthwise
- 1¾ cups cooked brown basmati rice
- ¾ cup cooked split red lentils
- ¾ cup chicken or vegetable stock
- 5 tbsp fresh orange juice
- salt and pepper
- fresh celery leaves, to garnish

1 Heat 2 tablespoons of the oil in a high-sided skillet with a lid over medium heat. Add the onion. Cook for 5 minutes, or until softened.

2 Add the celery, carrots, chili, scallions, and almonds. Stir-fry for 2 minutes, or until the vegetables are al dente but still brightly colored. Transfer to a bowl and set aside until required.

3 Add the remaining oil to the skillet. Stir in the rice and lentils. Cook over medium–high heat, stirring, for 1–2 minutes, or until heated through. Reduce the heat. Stir in the stock and orange juice. Season to taste with salt and pepper.

4 Return the vegetables to the skillet. Toss with the rice for a few minutes until heated through. Transfer to a warmed dish, garnish with celery leaves, and serve.

VEGETABLE COUSCOUS

COUSCOUS IS A SEMOLINA GRAIN THAT IS WIDELY EATEN IN NORTH AFRICA. IT IS VERY QUICK AND EASY TO COOK, AND MAKES A PLEASANT CHANGE FROM RICE OR PASTA. IT CAN ALSO BE COOKED WITH MILK TO MAKE A PORRIDGE, OR MIXED WITH FRUITS AND SERVED AS A DESSERT.

SERVES
4
preparation
20 minutes
cooking
40 minutes

ingredients
- 2 tbsp vegetable oil
- 1 large onion, coarsely chopped
- 1 carrot, chopped
- 1 turnip, chopped
- 2½ cups vegetable stock
- scant 1 cup couscous
- 2 tomatoes, peeled and quartered
- 2 zucchini, chopped
- 1 red bell pepper, seeded and chopped
- 4½ oz/125 g green beans, chopped
- grated rind of 1 lemon
- pinch of turmeric (optional)
- 1 tbsp finely chopped fresh cilantro or parsley
- salt and pepper
- fresh flat-leaf parsley sprigs, to garnish

1 Heat the oil in a large pan. Add the onion, carrot, and turnip and sauté for 3–4 minutes. Add the stock, bring to a boil, cover, and let simmer for 20 minutes.

2 Meanwhile, place the couscous in a bowl and moisten with a little boiling water, stirring, until the grains have swollen and separated.

3 Add the tomatoes, zucchini, bell pepper, and green beans to the pan and stir.

4 Stir the lemon rind into the couscous and add the turmeric, if using, and mix thoroughly. Place the couscous in a steamer and position it over the pan of vegetables. Let simmer the vegetables so that the couscous steams for 8–10 minutes.

5 Pile the couscous onto warmed serving plates. Ladle the vegetables and some of the liquid over the top. Sprinkle over the cilantro and serve immediately, garnished with parsley sprigs.

TABBOULEH

THIS MIDDLE EASTERN SALAD IS BECOMING INCREASINGLY FASHIONABLE IN OTHER PARTS OF THE
WORLD. IT IS A CLASSIC ACCOMPANIMENT TO LAMB, BUT IT ALSO GOES WELL WITH MOST BROILED
MEATS. ALTERNATIVELY, SERVE IT WITH HUMMUS AND PITA BREAD FOR A VEGETARIAN LUNCH.

serves
4

preparation
10 minutes,
plus 1½ hours'
marinating and
standing

cooking
none

ingredients
- scant 1 cup bulgur wheat
- 3 tbsp extra virgin olive oil
- 4 tbsp lemon juice
- 4 scallions
- 1 green bell pepper,
  seeded and sliced
- 4 tomatoes, chopped
- 2 tbsp chopped
  fresh parsley
- 2 tbsp chopped fresh mint
- 8 black olives, pitted
- salt and pepper
- fresh mint sprigs, to garnish

1 Place the bulgur wheat in a large
bowl and add enough cold water to
cover. Let stand for 30 minutes, or
until the wheat has doubled in size.
Drain well and press out as much
liquid as possible. Spread out the
wheat on paper towels to dry.

2 Place the wheat in a serving bowl.
Mix the olive oil and lemon juice
together in a pitcher and season to
taste with salt and pepper. Pour the
lemon mixture over the wheat and
let marinate for 1 hour.

3 Using a sharp knife, finely chop the
scallions, then add to the salad with
the green bell pepper, tomatoes,
parsley, and mint and toss lightly to
mix. Top the salad with the olives and
garnish with fresh mint sprigs, then
serve immediately.

cook's tip
*The bulgar wheat grains have been cracked
by boiling and so are already partially
cooked, meaning it just needs to be
rehydrated. Don't make this salad too far
in advance as it may go soggy.*

CASSOULET

A STICK-TO-THE-RIBS WINTER WARMER, THIS TRADITIONAL GASCONY BEAN FEAST HAS SO MANY VARIATIONS THAT IT IS ALMOST IMPOSSIBLE TO GIVE A DEFINITIVE RECIPE. WHAT IS IMPORTANT, HOWEVER, IS TO USE SMALL, WHITE KIDNEY BEANS THAT HOLD THEIR SHAPE DURING COOKING.

serves
6–8

preparation
30 minutes,
plus 5–8 hours'
soaking

cooking
5½ hours

ingredients
- scant 2 cups dried white kidney beans, soaked for at least 5 hours or according to the package instructions
- 5 oz/140 g plain or smoked belly of pork, rind removed, cut into thick pieces
- 4 large garlic cloves, chopped
- 1 large bouquet garni of 4 fresh parsley sprigs, 6 fresh thyme sprigs, and 1 bay leaf
- large pinch of quatre épices
- 8 Toulouse sausages
- 4 pieces of goose or duck confit, about 14 oz/400 g
- 14 oz/400 g boneless shoulder of pork, cut into 2-inch/5-cm chunks
- 7 oz/200 g day-old French bread, made into fine bread crumbs
- 8 tbsp finely chopped fresh flat-leaf parsley
- chicken or vegetable stock, if needed
- salt and pepper

1 Rinse the beans, then place them in a large, heavy-bottom pan with water to cover, over high heat. Bring to a boil, boil rapidly for 10 minutes, then drain. Return the beans to the wiped-out pan with 2 inches/5 cm of water to cover and bring to a boil. Reduce the heat to a simmer and skim the surface until the gray foam stops rising.

2 Add the belly of pork, garlic, bouquet garni, quatre épices, and pepper to taste. Adjust the heat so that bubbles just appear around the edge, then partially cover the pan and let the beans simmer for 1–½ hours, or according to the package instructions, until the beans are just slightly less than tender. The older the beans are, the longer they will take to cook. Do not let them boil or the skins will split.

3 Meanwhile, preheat the broiler to high. Broil the sausages, turning them frequently, just until the casings are browned, then set aside.

4 Heat 2 tablespoons of fat from the confit in a skillet over medium–high heat. Add the pork chunks and sauté until brown on each side. Set aside.

5 Preheat the oven to 300°F/150°C. When the beans are almost tender, place a large strainer over a large bowl and strain the beans, discarding the bouquet garni, but reserving the cooking liquid.

6 Place half the beans in a large ovenproof casserole. Add the sausages, confit, and pork chunks. Season to taste with salt and pepper, then cover with the remaining beans.

7 Pour in enough of the reserved cooking liquid to cover all the ingredients, topping up with stock if necessary. Mix the bread crumbs and parsley together, then spread half thickly over the surface.

8 Bake, uncovered, for 4 hours. After 1 hour, use the back of a spoon to lightly push the bread crumbs into the liquid, repeating this twice more at hourly intervals.

9 After 4 hours, sprinkle the top with the remaining bread crumbs but do not press into the liquid. Return the casserole to the oven and continue baking for 1 hour, or until the top is golden and crisp. If the liquid appears to evaporate too quickly, pour in a little extra stock at the edges. Serve from the casserole.

CHILI CON CARNE

THIS TEX-MEX FAVORITE IS OFTEN SERVED WITH RICE, BUT IT IS JUST AS DELICIOUS EATEN WITH A
BAKED POTATO, THICK SLICES OF FRESH CRUSTY BREAD, OR TORTILLAS. YOU CAN BUY READY-MADE
SOFT FLOUR TORTILLAS AND HEAT THEM THROUGH BRIEFLY IN A DRY SKILLET BEFORE SERVING.

serves
4

preparation
15 minutes

cooking
30–35 minutes

ingredients

- 2 tbsp sunflower-seed oil
- 1 lb 2 oz/500 g fresh ground beef
- 1 large onion, chopped
- 1 garlic clove, finely chopped
- 1 green bell pepper, seeded and diced
- 1 tsp chili powder
- 1 lb 12 oz/800 g canned chopped tomatoes
- 1 lb 12 oz/800 g canned red kidney beans, drained and rinsed
- 2 cups beef stock
- salt
- handful of fresh cilantro sprigs, plus a few to garnish
- 2 tbsp sour cream, to serve

1 Heat the oil in a large, heavy-bottom pan or ovenproof casserole. Add the beef and cook over medium heat, stirring frequently, for 5 minutes, or until broken up and browned.

2 Reduce the heat, add the onion, garlic, and bell pepper and cook, stirring frequently, for 10 minutes.

3 Stir in the chili powder, tomatoes with their juices, and kidney beans. Pour in the stock and season to taste with salt. Bring to a boil, reduce the heat, and let simmer, stirring frequently, for 15–20 minutes, or until the meat is tender.

4 Chop the cilantro sprigs, reserving a few for a garnish, and stir into the chili. Adjust the seasoning, if necessary. Either garnish with cilantro sprigs and serve immediately with a splash of sour cream or let cool, then store in the refrigerator overnight. Reheating it the next day makes the dish even more flavorsome.

variation

Substitute 1–2 finely chopped, seeded fresh chilies for the chili powder in Step 3. Anaheim (mild) or jalapeño (hot) chilies are both classic Tex-Mex varieties.

CHINESE NOODLES

THIS DISH IS USUALLY SERVED AS A SNACK OR LIGHT MEAL, BUT IT MAY ALSO BE SERVED AS AN
ACCOMPANIMENT TO PLAIN MEAT AND FISH DISHES. STIR-FRYING IS QUICK, EASY, AND INEXPENSIVE.
IT IS ALSO A HEALTHY WAY TO COOK BECAUSE IT USES A MINIMUM OF FAT.

serves
4

preparation
5 minutes

cooking
15 minutes

ingredients
- 12 oz/350 g egg noodles
- 3 tbsp vegetable oil
- 1 lb 8 oz/675 g lean beef
  steak, cut into thin strips
- 4½ oz/125 g green
  cabbage, shredded
- 2¾ oz/75 g bamboo shoots
- 6 scallions, sliced
- 1 oz/25 g green
  beans, halved
- 1 tbsp dark soy sauce
- 2 tbsp beef stock
- 1 tbsp dry sherry
- 1 tbsp brown sugar
- 2 tbsp fresh chopped
  parsley, to garnish

1 Cook the noodles in a pan of
boiling water for 2–3 minutes. Drain
well, rinse under cold running
water, and drain thoroughly again.

2 Heat 1 tablespoon of the oil in
a preheated wok or large skillet,
swirling it around until it begins
to smoke.

3 Add the noodles and stir-fry for
1–2 minutes. Drain the noodles and
set aside until required.

4 Heat the remaining oil in the wok.
Add the beef and stir-fry for 2–3
minutes. Add the cabbage, bamboo
shoots, scallions, and beans to the
wok and stir-fry for 1–2 minutes.

5 Add the soy sauce, stock, dry
sherry, and sugar to the wok, stirring
to mix well. Stir the noodles into the
mixture in the wok, tossing to mix
well. Transfer to serving bowls,
garnish with chopped parsley, and
serve immediately.

FRUIT

FRUIT IS DELICIOUS. IT CAN BE EATEN RAW OUT OF
YOUR HAND OR COOKED IN A MULTITUDE OF WAYS,
BOTH SAVORY AND SWEET. IN THE FOLLOWING PAGES
YOU WILL FIND AN INSPIRING COLLECTION OF RECIPES
TO WHET YOUR APPETITE, WHETHER YOU ARE LOOKING
FOR A LOWFAT DESSERT FOR A SLIMMER, OR A
SUMPTUOUS CREATION FOR ENTERTAINING.

INTRODUCTION

FRUIT IS A HEALTHY CHOICE BECAUSE IT IS FULL OF VITAMINS AND VERY LOW IN FAT. IT IS ALSO VERY VERSATILE—DELICIOUS IN SAVORY DISHES AND CHUTNEYS, AND DELIGHTFUL IN A WIDE RANGE OF DESSERTS AND CAKES.

Buying and storing fruit

Some fruits, such as apples and pears, are available fresh all year round, whereas others, such as cherries, have a limited season. Always buy your fruit as fresh as possible from a reputable supplier. Avoid any fruits that are bruised or damaged, or that are showing signs of mold. Choose fruits that are plump and free from blemishes: they should feel firm to the touch and not too soft. Many fruits, such as apples, pears, and oranges, can be stored for around a week at room temperature, or even longer in the refrigerator. Other fruits, such as blueberries, have a short shelf life and should be kept in the refrigerator and eaten by the "best before" date, but usually within a couple of days.

You can also freeze a wide range of fruits, such as bananas and mangoes (peel and slice them first)—even grapes are excellent frozen whole and used instead of ice cubes in drinks.

Orchard fruits

Orchard fruits, such as apples, pears, and peaches, are delicious and very versatile. They can be eaten raw on their own and in fruit salads, or in cooked dishes such as fruit tarts and pies.

Apples

There are countless different varieties of apple in existence, in a range of colors from pale yellow to deep red. Some have a sweet flavor, while others are more acidic. Some apples, such as Golden Delicious and Braeburn, are excellent eaten raw as a snack or in salads. They also pair very well with cheese. Other varieties of apple are excellent for cooking, such as Cox's Orange Pippin and Granny Smith. They make excellent desserts, and are delicious stuffed and baked, or made into pie fillings. They can also be used in some savory dishes, such as curries, and make very good sauces and purées.

Pears

Like apples, there are thousands of different types of pear, although we see only a selection of these in our stores. Pears bruise easily, so buy them while they are still hard and let them ripen at home. Many varieties, such as Comice pears, are delicious eaten as a snack, and they are excellent in salads and with cheese. Some types, such as Bartlett, are also very good for cooking. They can be stuffed and baked like apples, and are excellent peeled and poached in red wine.

Nectarines

These fruits are usually available in summer and the fall. Their smooth skins should be yellow with patches of red, with no green areas and no bruises. They will keep in the refrigerator for 5–6 days. You can eat nectarines raw as a snack or sliced in desserts. You can also poach or bake them. If they need further ripening, leave them out at room temperature for 1–2 days. If they

Golden Delicious apple

Braeburn apple

Pear

Nectarine

Apricot

Plum

do not soften during this time, they will not be suitable for eating raw, so cook them instead.

Peaches

These fruits are similar to nectarines except that they have downy instead of soft skin. Store and use them in the same way as nectarines.

Cherries

There are two main varieties of cherry: the larger sweet cherries, which are delicious eaten raw, and the smaller sour cherries, which are too tart to eat raw but can be cooked and made into excellent desserts and jellies. Cherries are usually available during late spring and early summer, and should be stored in the refrigerator before use.

Apricots

These fruits are usually yellow or orange and have a large central pit. Some varieties are sweet enough to eat raw as a snack, while others need to be cooked. Cooked apricots make excellent desserts and jellies, and can also be used in some savory dishes. Dried apricots are also very popular. The deep orange varieties have been treated with sulfur dioxide in order to preserve their color. Untreated dried apricots are dark brown, so some people may find them less attractive, but they have just as much, if not more, flavor and goodness.

Plums

Hundreds of varieties of plum exist, and all tend to have a large, central pit. Their color varies from yellow or green to red or purple, and they can grow to up to 3 inches/7.5 cm in diameter. They are in season through the summer months until early fall, and will keep at room temperature for several days, or a little longer if stored in the refrigerator. Ripe plums are deliciously sweet and juicy and can be eaten raw as a snack or in a salad. They can also be cooked. Plum crumble is a popular baked dessert, and consists of a dish of plums covered with a crunchy topping. Plums also make excellent jelly.

Citrus fruits

The fragrance and juicy tang of a ripe citrus fruit is irresistible, and wonderful in a whole host of chilled and cooked desserts. These fruits are also rich sources of vitamin C.

Oranges

These round, orange citrus fruits are available all year round and come in many different varieties, such as the sweet oranges that can be eaten as a snack and sliced in salads and desserts. A variation of these is the blood orange, which is just as sweet and juicy, but which has redder flesh. Some oranges are seedless, while others have many seeds. You can also buy bitter oranges, such as Seville oranges: they are too sour to eat but they make excellent marmalade. Oranges will keep at room temperature for up to a week, but are better stored in the refrigerator to preserve their Vitamin C content. They will keep in the refrigerator for up to 2 weeks. Oranges make excellent garnishes, and are popular in a wide range of savory and sweet dishes.

Grapefruits

Grapefruits can be seeded or seedless, and vary in color from yellow to pink to red. They are available all year round, and are usually eaten raw. However, they can also be sprinkled with sugar and lightly broiled.

Lemons

These oval, yellow fruits have a tart flavor but a wide range of uses. They are available all year round and will keep at room temperature for around a week, and in the refrigerator for up to 3 weeks (but less time if cut). Lemons make an excellent flavoring and a good garnish or decoration for a wide range of savory and sweet dishes. You can use the juice, grated zest or the flesh.

Limes

These green citrus fruits are smaller than lemons and have a milder flavor, but can replace lemons in many savory and sweet dishes. They will keep whole in the refrigerator for up to 10 days.

Mandarin orange family

These small, round, orange fruits include mandarins, clementines, satsumas, and tangerines. They are generally available in the winter months. Mandarins and tangerines have thick skins that are easy to peel. Clementines have thinner skins, and no seeds. Satsumas are also easy to peel, and are seedless. They are delicious eaten raw as a snack and in salads, and they all pair well with cream cheese.

Lemon

Orange

Grapefruit

Lime

Soft fruits

Juicy berries are delicious in desserts such as sherbets, ice creams, puddings, fruit crumbles, and pies, but they can also be used in savory dishes, such as chicken with blackberries.

Strawberries

These juicy red berries are available all year round, but peak season for strawberries is spring and early summer. Fresh strawberries will keep for up to 3 days in the refrigerator, and are delicious eaten raw, perhaps with whipped cream or marinated in balsamic vinegar. They also make excellent jellies and syrups, and are very popular in a range of desserts. Dried strawberries have a deliciously tangy flavor and are wonderful in granola.

Gooseberries

These large berries are usually green, but can also come in white and yellow. They are available in the summer months and are usually cooked before eating. Gooseberries make excellent jellies and fillings for sweet pies. They will keep in the refrigerator for up to 4 days.

Blackberries

Blackberries are also known as "brambles," and they grow wild on bushes. They are also cultivated. Blackberries come into season in the summer months. Use them straight away, or refrigerate them for up to 2 days. You can eat blackberries raw or cooked in sweet pies and desserts. They are often paired with apples. Blackberries also make good jelly.

Raspberries

The most common color of raspberry is red. These fruits are very popular with dieters, since they are very low in calories and fat, and yet have a delicious flavor. They will keep in the refrigerator for up to 3 days, and are delicious raw in a wide range of desserts. They can also be cooked, and make good coulis and fillings for desserts, as well as excellent jellies.

Blueberries

These small, round dark-blue berries are sweet and can be eaten raw or cooked in sweet pies and other desserts. Like most berries, they make excellent jelly. They are available during the summer and early fall, and will keep in the refrigerator for 4–5 days.

Cranberries

These small, shiny red berries are available in late fall and will keep in the refrigerator for 6–8 weeks and in the freezer for around 9 months. They have a tart flavor and therefore are usually mixed with sweeter fruits, such as apple—cranberry and apple juice is very popular. Cranberries can be cooked and make an excellent sauce. They can be used in sweet pies and other cooked desserts.

Currants

Fresh currants are tiny berries that can be white, red, or black. White and red currants can be eaten raw and make excellent decorations for sweet dishes. Black currants are quite tart and are better cooked and made into syrup or jelly. Fresh currants are available in summer and will keep in the refrigerator for 3–4 days. They should not be confused with dried currants, which are like dark raisins.

Grapes

Other fruits

Other well-known fruits, such as bananas, grapes, and melons, are widely available. They are very popular as snacks in their own right, and are also used in a wide range of desserts and cakes.

Grapes

These small oval fruits range in color from yellowish-green to purplish-black, and can be seeded or seedless. The eating varieties are sweet and juicy, and are delicious eaten raw as a snack or added to salads. They also make excellent decorations and are wonderful paired with cheese. Other varieties of grapes are made into grape juice, wine, jelly, or raisins.

Bananas

These long fruits start off green, but turn yellow when they have ripened. Contrary to popular opinion, very fresh bananas can be stored in the refrigerator: the skins will turn brown but the flesh will be unaffected. If you prefer your bananas to stay yellow, store them at room temperature for a day or two. Bananas are delicious peeled and eaten as they are or added to a wide range of desserts. They can also be lightly broiled or baked.

Strawberries

Raspberries

Rhubarb

Rhubarb has edible red stalks, and comes into season in spring. The stalks will keep in the refrigerator for up to 3 days. Rhubarb has a tart flavor but, once cooked and sweetened, will make a good jelly, sweet pie filling, or other dessert. It also pairs well with ginger.

Melons

These fruit come in many sizes and colors. The popular edible types include galia, charentais, watermelon, and cantaloupe. They are delicious eaten fresh on their own, or as an appetizer, perhaps combined with figs and ham, or alternatively port wine. They are also good in fruit salads.

Pineapples

This golden oval fruit has a tough, prickly exterior and spearlike leaves. Large pineapples are the most common, but baby pineapples are also available. The flesh is juicy with a tangy flavor, and is delicious sliced and eaten on its own or added to fruit salads or other desserts. It is also good when cooked. It can be lightly broiled, or baked in a cake. Fresh pineapple will keep in the refrigerator for up to 3 days. You can also buy it canned.

Exotic fruits

There is a wonderfully wide range of exotic fruits available nowadays, from Cape gooseberries to dragon fruit. Here is a selection of some of the popular ones—there are many more.

Mango

These large oval fruits vary in color from yellow to red. Eat them raw, perhaps in a fruit salad, or frozen in a sherbet.

Carambola

These star-shaped yellow fruits make beautiful decorations when cut across in slices.

Dates

These oval fruits are available fresh or dried. Chopped dried dates are delicious in granola and desserts.

Kiwifruit

These oval fruits have brown "hairy" skin and soft green flesh. Eat the flesh with a teaspoon. Alternatively, peel and slice them and add them to fruit salads and other desserts.

Litchis

These small fruits are available fresh or canned. They have a rough, pink, inedible skin, but the flesh inside is juicy and fragrant. You can eat them raw or lightly poached.

Figs

These soft, pear-shaped fruits are delicious eaten raw or poached. Dried figs are also good.

Passion fruit

Cut these brown-skinned, wrinkly fruits in half and eat the pulp by scooping it out with a teaspoon.

Papaya

This large, pear-shaped fruit is cooked when green and unripe, or eaten raw when it is ripe and golden-yellow. Papaya is good in salads.

Pineapple

Banana

Carambola

Litchis

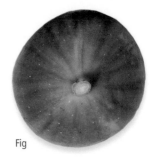

Fig

BERRY YOGURT ICE

THIS REFRESHING ICE MAKES A WONDERFUL SUMMER DESSERT AFTER A FILLING MEAL,
AS IT IS LIGHT AND COOLING WITHOUT THE RICHNESS—OR FAT—OF ICE CREAM. SERVE
WITH A SELECTION OF FRESH SUMMER BERRIES.

serves
4

preparation
15 minutes,
plus 4 hours'
freezing

cooking
5 minutes

ingredients
- 1⅛ cups raspberries
- ¾ cup blackberries
- ¾ cup strawberries
- 1 large egg
- ¾ cup strained plain yogurt
- ½ cup red wine
- 2¼ tsp powdered gelatin
- fresh berries, to decorate

1 Place the raspberries, blackberries, and strawberries in a blender or food processor and process until a smooth purée forms. Rub the purée through a strainer into a bowl to remove the seeds.

2 Break the egg and separate the yolk and white into separate bowls. Stir the egg yolk and yogurt into the berry purée and set the egg white aside.

3 Pour the wine into a heatproof bowl set over a pan of water. Sprinkle the gelatin on the surface of the wine and let stand for 5 minutes to soften. Heat the pan of water and simmer water until the gelatin has dissolved. Pour the mixture into the berry purée in a steady stream, whisking constantly. Transfer the mixture to a freezerproof container and freeze for 2 hours, or until slushy.

4 Whisk the egg white in a spotlessly clean, grease-free bowl until very stiff. Remove the berry mixture from the freezer and fold in the egg white. Return to the freezer and freeze for 2 hours, or until firm. To serve, scoop the berry yogurt ice into glass dishes, and decorate with fresh berries of your choice.

cook's tip

Vegetarians can use a vegetarian gelatin, which is available in health food stores, to make this ice. Follow the instructions on the package and proceed as in the main recipe.

ORANGE SHERBET

SHERBETS HELP TO CLEANSE THE PALATE AFTER A MEAL, AND ARE DELICIOUSLY REFRESHING IN HOT WEATHER. THEY ARE ALSO INVALUABLE TO THE HEALTH-CONSCIOUS OR AS PART OF A SLIMMING DIET BECAUSE THEY ARE VIRTUALLY FAT-FREE. THE LIQUEUR IN THIS SHERBET IS AN ADDED TREAT.

serves
4

preparation
20 minutes, plus
4 hours' chilling
and freezing

cooking
4 minutes

ingredients
- scant 2½ cups water
- 1 cup superfine sugar
- 4 large oranges
- 2 tbsp orange liqueur, such as Cointreau
- 4 scooped-out oranges, to serve

1 Heat the water and sugar in a pan over low heat, stirring, until dissolved. Boil without stirring for 2 minutes. Pour into a heatproof bowl. Cool to room temperature.

2 Grate the rind from 2 oranges and extract the juice. Extract the juice from 2 more oranges. Mix the juice and rind in a bowl, cover with plastic wrap, and set aside. Discard the squeezed oranges. Stir the orange juice, grated rind, and orange liqueur into the cooled syrup. Cover with plastic wrap and let chill for 1 hour. Transfer to an ice-cream machine and churn for 15 minutes.

3 If you do not have an ice-cream machine, place the mixture in a freezerproof container. Freeze for 1 hour, then transfer to a bowl. Beat to break up the crystals, then return it to the freezerproof container and freeze for 30 minutes. Repeat twice more, freezing for 30 minutes and whisking each time.

4 Divide the frozen sherbet between the scooped-out orange cups and serve immediately.

TROPICAL FRUIT SALAD

A TROPICAL FRUIT SALAD IS DELIGHTFULLY REFRESHING DURING HOT SUMMER DAYS OR SULTRY EVENINGS. THIS ONE CONTAINS A LITTLE PUMPKIN PIE SPICE FOR A TANTALIZING HINT OF AROMATIC SWEETNESS. YOU CAN ALSO SERVE THIS WITH HALF-FAT SOUR CREAM, IF YOU PREFER.

serves
6
preparation
20 minutes, plus
1 hour's chilling
cooking
3 minutes

ingredients
- 6 tbsp superfine sugar
- 1¾ cups water
- ½ tsp pumpkin pie spice
- grated rind of ½ lemon
- 1 papaya
- 1 mango
- 1 pineapple
- 4 oranges, peeled and cut into segments
- ¾ cup strawberries, hulled and quartered
- light or heavy cream, to serve (optional)

1 Place the sugar, water, pumpkin pie spice, and lemon rind in a pan. Bring to a boil, stirring constantly, then continue to boil for 1 minute. Remove from the heat and let cool to room temperature.

2 Transfer to a pitcher or bowl, cover with plastic wrap and chill in the refrigerator for at least 1 hour.

3 Peel and halve the papaya and remove the seeds. Cut the flesh into small chunks or slices, and place in a large bowl.

4 Cut the mango twice lengthwise, close to the seed. Remove and discard the seed. Peel and cut the flesh into small chunks or slices, and add to the bowl.

5 Cut off the top and bottom of the pineapple and remove the hard skin. Cut the pineapple in half lengthwise, then into quarters and remove the tough core. Cut the remaining flesh into small pieces and add to the bowl.

6 Add the orange segments and strawberries. Pour over the chilled syrup, cover with plastic wrap, and let chill until required. Serve with cream, if liked.

TRADITIONAL APPLE PIE

THIS SWEET APPLE PIE HAS A DELICIOUS DOUBLE CRUST. IT IS A SUBSTANTIAL DESSERT AND MAKES AN IMPRESSIVE FINISH TO ANY MEAL. IT CAN BE SERVED EITHER HOT OR COLD, ON ITS OWN, OR WITH CREAM OR CUSTARD. YOU CAN ADJUST THE AMOUNT OF SUGAR ACCORDING TO YOUR TASTE.

serves
6

preparation
25 minutes,
plus 30 minutes'
chilling

cooking
50 minutes

ingredients
- 1 lb 10 oz–2 lb/750 g–1 kg 4 oz cooking apples, peeled, cored, and sliced
- about ²⁄₃ cup brown or white sugar, plus extra for sprinkling
- ¹⁄₂–1 tsp ground cinnamon, pumpkin pie spice, or ground ginger
- 1–2 tbsp water

UNSWEETENED PIE DOUGH
- generous 2³⁄₈ cups all-purpose flour, plus extra for dusting
- pinch of salt
- 6 tbsp butter or margarine
- 6 tbsp white vegetable fat
- about 6 tbsp cold water
- beaten milk or beaten egg, to glaze

1 To make the pie dough, sift the flour and salt into a large bowl. Add the butter and fat and rub it in with your fingertips until the mixture resembles fine bread crumbs. Add enough water to mix to a dough. Wrap the dough in plastic wrap and let chill for 30 minutes.

2 Preheat the oven to 425°F/220°C. Roll out almost two-thirds of the pie dough thinly on a lightly floured counter and use to line an 8–9-inch/20–23-cm deep pie plate or shallow pie pan.

3 Mix the apples with the sugar and spices and pack into the pastry shell; the filling can come up above the rim. If the apples are a dry variety add a little water to moisten.

4 Roll out the remaining dough to form a lid. Dampen the edges of the pie rim with water and position the lid, pressing the edges firmly together. Trim and crimp the edges.

5 Use the pie dough trimmings to cut out leaves or other shapes to decorate the top of the pie. Dampen the shapes and attach. Glaze the top of the pie with milk or beaten egg, make 1–2 slits in the top, and put the pie on a baking sheet.

6 Bake in the oven for 20 minutes, then reduce the oven temperature to 350°F/180°C and cook for 30 minutes, or until the pastry is a light golden brown. Serve hot or cold, sprinkled with sugar.

STUFFED BAKED APPLES

BAKED APPLES ARE A TRADITIONAL FAMILY FAVORITE AND ARE USUALLY STUFFED WITH A TASTY COMBINATION OF GOLDEN RAISINS, RAISINS, BROWN SUGAR, AND SWEET SPICES. THIS GINGER-FLAVORED OATY FILLING IS MORE UNUSUAL, AND MAKES A WELCOME CHANGE.

serves
4

preparation
10 minutes

cooking
45 minutes

ingredients
- ⅛ cup blanched almonds
- ⅓ cup no-soak dried apricots
- 1 piece preserved ginger, drained
- 1 tbsp honey
- 1 tbsp syrup from the preserved ginger jar
- 4 tbsp rolled oats
- 4 large cooking apples

1 Preheat the oven to 350°F/180°C. Using a sharp knife, chop the almonds very finely. Chop the apricots and preserved ginger very finely. Set aside.

2 Place the honey and syrup in a pan and heat until the honey has melted. Stir in the oats and cook gently over low heat for 2 minutes. Remove the pan from the heat and stir in the almonds, apricots, and preserved ginger.

3 Core the apples, widen the tops slightly, and score around the circumference of each to prevent the skins bursting during cooking. Place the apples in an ovenproof dish and fill the cavities with the filling. Pour just enough water into the dish to come about one-third of the way up the apples. Bake in the preheated oven for 40 minutes, or until tender. Serve immediately.

variation
Use an extra tablespoon of honey instead of the preserved ginger and syrup, replace the almonds with walnuts, and add ½ teaspoon of ground cinnamon.

TARTE AU CITRON

FEW DESSERTS CAN BE MORE APPEALING TO ROUND OFF A MEAL ON A HOT EVENING THAN THIS
DELICIOUSLY TANGY TART. IT LOOKS WONDERFULLY INVITING AND SERVES UP BEAUTIFULLY, MAKING
IT THE IDEAL DESSERT TO TEMPT YOUR DINNER GUESTS OR MEMBERS OF YOUR HOUSEHOLD.

serves
6–8
preparation
25 minutes, plus
1 hour's chilling
cooking
35 minutes

ingredients
- grated rind of 2–3 large lemons
- $^2/_3$ cup lemon juice
- $^1/_2$ cup superfine sugar
- $^1/_2$ cup heavy cream or sour cream, plus extra to serve
- 3 large eggs
- 3 large egg yolks
- confectioners' sugar, for dusting

PIE DOUGH
- scant $1^1/_4$ cups all-purpose flour, plus extra for dusting
- $^1/_2$ tsp salt
- $^1/_2$ cup cold unsalted butter, diced
- 1 egg yolk beaten with 2 tbsp ice-cold water

TO SERVE
- candied citrus peel
- fresh strawberries, halved

1 To make the pie dough, sift the flour and salt into a large bowl. Add the butter and rub it in with your fingertips until the mixture resembles fine bread crumbs. Add the egg yolk and water and stir to mix to a dough.

2 Gather the dough into a ball, wrap in plastic wrap, and let chill for at least 1 hour.

3 Preheat the oven to 400°F/200°C. Roll the dough out on a lightly floured counter and use to line a 9–10-inch/23–25-cm fluted tart pan with a removable bottom. Prick the bottom all over with a fork and line with parchment paper and baking beans.

4 Bake in the preheated oven for 15 minutes until the dough looks set. Remove the paper and beans. Reduce the oven temperature to 375°F/190°C.

5 Beat the lemon rind, lemon juice, and sugar together until blended. Slowly beat in the cream, then beat in the eggs and yolks, one by one.

6 Set the pastry shell on a baking sheet and pour in the filling. Transfer to the preheated oven and bake for 20 minutes until the filling is set.

7 Let cool completely on a wire rack. Dust with confectioners' sugar. Serve with a spoonful of cream, candied citrus peel, and halved strawberries.

GOLDEN BAKED APPLE PUDDING

THIS IS A WARM AND SATISFYING DESSERT DURING COLD WEATHER, YET IT IS SURPRISINGLY LOW IN FAT, MAKING IT THE IDEAL CHOICE FOR SLIMMERS AND THE HEALTH-CONSCIOUS. YOU CAN ADJUST THE AMOUNT OF SUGAR ACCORDING TO YOUR TASTE. TRY SERVING IT WITH LOWFAT CUSTARD.

serves
4
preparation
15 minutes
cooking
30–35 minutes

ingredients
- 1 lb/450 g cooking apples
- 1 tsp ground cinnamon
- 2 tbsp golden raisins
- 4 oz/115 g whole wheat bread
- generous ½ cup lowfat cottage cheese
- 4 tbsp brown sugar
- generous 1 cup lowfat milk

1 Preheat the oven to 425°F/220°C. Peel and core the apples and chop the flesh into ½-inch/1-cm pieces. Place in a bowl and toss with the cinnamon and golden raisins.

2 Remove the crusts and cut the bread into ½-inch/1-cm cubes. Add to the apples with the cottage cheese and 3 tablespoons of the brown sugar and mix together. Stir in the milk.

3 Turn the mixture into an ovenproof dish and sprinkle with the remaining sugar. Bake in the preheated oven for 30–35 minutes, or until golden brown. Serve hot.

variation
Replace the cheese with cream cheese or ricotta and the golden raisins with raisins, if liked.

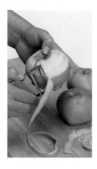

TROPICAL FRUIT DESSERT

FRUIT FOOLS ARE ALWAYS POPULAR, AND THIS LIGHTLY TANGY VERSION WILL BE NO EXCEPTION.
YOU CAN VARY THIS RECIPE BY USING YOUR FAVORITE COMBINATIONS OF FRUITS IF YOU PREFER.
FOR EXAMPLE, TRY USING PAPAYA INSTEAD OF THE MANGO, AND MELON INSTEAD OF THE KIWIFRUIT.

serves
4
preparation
20 minutes,
plus 20 minutes'
chilling
cooking
none

ingredients
- 1 ripe mango
- 2 kiwifruit
- 1 banana
- 2 tbsp lime juice
- ½ tsp finely grated lime rind, plus extra to decorate
- 2 egg whites
- scant 2 cups canned lowfat custard
- ½ tsp vanilla extract
- 2 passion fruits

1 Peel the mango and slice either side of the smooth, flat central seed. Coarsely chop the flesh and process the fruit in a food processor or blender until smooth. Alternatively, mash with a fork.

2 Peel the kiwifruit, chop the flesh into small pieces, and place in a bowl. Peel and chop the banana and add to the bowl. Toss all of the fruit in the lime juice and rind and mix well.

3 Whisk the egg whites in a grease-free bowl until stiff then gently fold in the custard and vanilla extract until thoroughly mixed.

4 Alternately layer the chopped fruit, mango purée, and custard mixture, finishing with a layer of custard in 4 tall glasses. Let chill in the refrigerator for 20 minutes.

5 Halve the passion fruits, scoop out the seeds, and spoon the passion fruit over the fruit fools. Decorate each serving with the extra lime rind and serve immediately.

variation

Other tropical fruits to try include papaya purée, with chopped pineapple and dates, and pomegranate seeds to decorate. Alternatively, make a summer fruit fool by using strawberry purée, topped with blackberries, with cherries to finish.

APPLE STRUDEL WITH WARM CIDER SAUCE

STRUDELS ARE POPULAR IN GERMANY AND AUSTRIA, AND ARE STUFFED WITH SAVORY OR SWEET FILLINGS. APPLE IS THE MOST FAMOUS SWEET STRUDEL, AND THIS VERSION HAS AN ADDED ADVANTAGE IN THAT IT IS EXTREMELY LOW IN FAT AND SUITABLE FOR THOSE WITH LOWFAT DIETS.

serves
2–4

preparation
25 minutes

cooking
15–20 minutes

ingredients
- 8 crisp eating apples
- 1 tbsp lemon juice
- ½ cup golden raisins
- 1 tsp ground cinnamon
- ½ tsp grated nutmeg
- 1 tbsp brown sugar
- 6 sheets phyllo pastry
- vegetable oil spray
- confectioners' sugar, to serve

CIDER SAUCE
- 1 tbsp cornstarch
- 2 cups cider

1 Preheat the oven to 375°F/190°C. Line a baking sheet with nonstick paper. Peel and core the apples and chop them into ½-inch/1-cm dice. Toss the pieces in a bowl, with the lemon juice, golden raisins, cinnamon, nutmeg, and sugar.

2 Lay out a sheet of phyllo pastry, spray with vegetable oil, and lay a second sheet on top. Repeat with a third sheet. Spread over half the apple mixture and roll up lengthwise, tucking in the ends to enclose the filling. Repeat to make a second strudel. Slide onto the baking sheet, spray with oil, and bake in the oven for 15–20 minutes.

3 For the sauce, blend the cornstarch in a pan with a little cider until smooth. Add the remaining cider and heat gently, stirring constantly, until the mixture boils and thickens. Serve the strudel warm or cold, dredged with confectioners' sugar and accompanied by the cider sauce.

DATE & APRICOT TART

THIS DRIED FRUIT TART IS RICH IN PROTEIN AND DIETARY FIBER, AND THEREFORE MAKES A HEALTHY CHOICE FOR A DESSERT. THERE IS NO NEED TO ADD ANY EXTRA SUGAR TO THIS FILLING BECAUSE THE DRIED FRUIT IS NATURALLY SWEET. THE TART CAN BE SERVED HOT OR COLD.

serves
8

preparation
15 minutes,
plus 30 minutes'
chilling

cooking
50 minutes

ingredients
- 1½ cups whole wheat flour, plus extra for dusting
- ⅓ cup mixed nuts, ground
- 7 tbsp margarine, cut into small pieces
- 4 tbsp water
- 1⅓ cups dried apricots, chopped
- 1⅓ cups chopped pitted dates
- scant 2 cups apple juice
- 1 tsp ground cinnamon
- grated rind of 1 lemon
- custard, to serve (optional)

1 Place the flour and ground nuts in a large bowl. Add the margarine and rub it in with your fingertips until the mixture resembles fine bread crumbs. Stir in the water and mix to a dough. Wrap the dough in plastic wrap and let chill in the refrigerator for 30 minutes.

2 Meanwhile, place the apricots and dates in a pan, with the apple juice, cinnamon, and lemon rind. Bring to a boil, cover, and let simmer over low heat for 15 minutes until the fruit softens. Mash to a purée.

3 Preheat the oven to 400°F/200°C. Set aside a small ball of dough for making lattice strips. Roll out the rest of the dough on a lightly floured counter to form a circle and use to line a 9-inch/23-cm loose-bottom quiche pan.

4 Spread the fruit filling evenly over the bottom of the pastry shell. Roll out the reserved dough and cut into strips ½ inch/1 cm wide. Cut the strips to fit the tart and twist them across the top of the fruit to form a decorative lattice pattern. Moisten the edges of the strips with a little water and seal them firmly around the rim of the tart.

5 Bake for 25–30 minutes until golden brown. Cut into slices and serve with custard, if liked.

9

BAKING

THERE IS NOTHING LIKE THE SMELL OF FRESHLY HOME-

BAKED BREAD AND PASTRIES TO GET EVERY MEMBER OF

THE HOUSEHOLD HOVERING AROUND THE KITCHEN.

IN THIS CHAPTER YOU WILL ENCOUNTER SOME TRULY

INSPIRITIONAL BREAD RECIPES, AND A WONDERFUL

SELECTION OF OTHER BAKED TREATS, INCLUDING

SAVORY PASTRIES AND SWEET, STICKY BUNS.

INTRODUCTION

THERE IS NOTHING LIKE THE AROMA OF FRESHLY BAKED BREAD, PIE DOUGH, CAKES, AND COOKIES TO STIMULATE THE APPETITE. BAKING THESE ITEMS FOR YOURSELF IS VERY SATISFYING, AND THE MOUTHWATERING AROMAS WILL PROVE TO BE AN IRRESISTIBLE TEMPTATION FOR YOUR FAMILY AND FRIENDS.

Making bread at home

Making your own bread does not have to be difficult—anyone can make delicious loaves and rolls with the minimum of effort. The key to making perfect bread is to use the right ingredients at the right temperature. Always use white bread flour rather than ordinary flour: bread flour has a higher gluten content than ordinary flour, which increases the elasticity of the dough. You can use any of the different kinds of yeast, but each has a different method for breadmaking. You will also need to use the correct quantities: 1/2 oz/15 g fresh yeast or 1 tbsp dried yeast is enough to make 1 lb 10 oz/750 g strong bread flour rise. When you add water, make sure it is tepid, because if it is too hot, it will kill the yeast.

Fresh yeast
Crush this in a pitcher with a little warm water, then cover and let it stand until the surface starts to bubble.

Dried yeast
Sprinkle the dried yeast over a little warm water in a pitcher, then stir in a pinch of sugar. Cover and let stand until it froths.

Active dry yeast
Mix this yeast straight into the flour before the warm water is added.

Yeast

Key techniques for making dough

Making the perfect dough can be straightforward, but it is important to follow a certain procedure to achieve good results every time.

MIXING

❶ To mix the dough, sift the flour and salt into a mixing bowl. Make a well in the center, then add the yeast. Pour in hand-hot water, then gradually pull in the flour from the edges and mix together, adding more hand-hot water as necessary in order to form a soft dough.

KNEADING

❷ This process is necessary in order to make the dough smooth and increase its elasticity. To knead the dough, push your hand into it, then stretch it away from you. Pick up the furthest end of the dough and pull it back to the top, then turn the dough 45° and repeat the kneading action away from you. Keep turning the dough 45° and repeating the kneading action. The kneading process usually takes about 5 minutes. To save time and effort, you could use a free-standing mixer or food processor with a dough hook to mix and knead the

Bread

dough for you. Kneading will take about 3 minutes if you do it this way.

RISING

③ After the dough has been kneaded, place it in an oiled bowl, cover it with plastic wrap, and put it in a warm place, such as an airing cupboard. Leave it rise to about double its original size.

KNOCKING BACK

This process is also known as "punching down." Simply punch your fist into the risen dough so that it collapses and releases the air. Then turn the dough out onto a floured counter (some of it may need scraping out) and knead it for about 1 minute until it has lost its cold feel and has an even temperature.

PROVING

This stage literally means proving that the yeast is still active. To do this, after knocking back the dough, divide and shape it as required (see below). Cover as before and leave it to rise for a second (but shorter) time, until the dough has doubled in size.

SHAPING

④ To shape the dough correctly for a loaf pan, use your hands to form the dough into an oval, then bring over the two short sides to the center, turn the dough over, and transfer, seam-side down, to a greased loaf pan. To make rolls, simply use your hands to roll even-size pieces of the dough into balls, and place on a greased baking sheet.

Baking and storing bread

The dough will keep, covered, in the refrigerator for up to a day before baking. To bake the bread, you will need a hot oven, so make sure you preheat it beforehand. Underbaked bread has a moist, doughlike consistency and flavor, so it is always better to overbake if necessary. To test if the bread is properly baked, remove it from the oven, turn it out of its pan, and use your knuckles to give it a sharp tap on the bottom. If it sounds hollow, the bread is done. It it does not, return it to the oven and bake for another 5 minutes, or until the bread is properly baked. When it is done, remove from the oven, and let cool on a wire rack. If you want a soft crust, cover the loaf with a clean dish towel while it is cooling. Freshly baked bread will keep, covered, for 2–3 days at room temperature, but no longer because it has no added preservatives. You can also keep it wrapped in the refrigerator for up to a week, or wrap it in a freezer bag and freeze it for up to a month.

Making pie dough

Pie dough is very versatile and lends a professional finish to a wide range of savory and sweet dishes. Choose your pie dough to match the occasion: unsweetened pie dough for savory or sweet pies, tarts, and tartlets; choux pastry for profiteroles and eclairs; paper-thin phyllo pastry for savory pancake rolls or sweet apple strudel; or puff pastry for sausage rolls and a wide range of desserts.

Unsweetened pie dough

This recipe will make enough pie dough to line an 8-inch/20-cm tart pan.

scant 1¼ cups all-purpose flour
6½ tbsp butter, diced
2–3 tbsp cold water

❶ To make the pie dough, sift the all-purpose flour. ❷ Use your fingertips to rub in the butter until the mixture resembles fine bread crumbs. Gradually mix in enough water to make a soft dough. ❸ Use your hands to shape the dough into a ball. Cover with plastic wrap and refrigerate before use. When you are ready to use it, turn it out onto a clean counter lightly dusted with flour. ❹ Use a rolling pin to roll it out to the desired thickness.

Variation: To make a sweet pie dough, stir 1 tablespoon of superfine sugar into the flour after sifting, and replace half the water with 2 beaten egg yolks.

Choux pastry

This quantity will make about 24 round choux buns.

generous ¾ cup water
5¾ tbsp butter
generous ¾ cup all-purpose flour
½ tsp salt
½ tsp confectioners' sugar
3 eggs, plus a little beaten egg to glaze

Preheat the oven to 400°F/200°C. Pour the water into a pan and add the butter. Gently bring to a boil. Sift the flour and salt into a bowl, then mix in the confectioners' sugar. In a separate bowl, beat the eggs.

When the butter is just beginning to boil, remove from the heat and stir in the flour mixture. Continue to stir until smooth, then return to the heat and stir until the mixture begins to pull away from the sides of the pan. Remove from the heat and gradually beat in the eggs until the mixture forms a thick, glossy paste.

Put 24 round spoonfuls of the mixture onto greased baking sheets and brush the tops with a little beaten egg. Bake in the preheated oven for 20 minutes, or until golden. Remove from the oven and cool.

Serving suggestion: Split the cooled buns in half horizontally and sandwich with whipped cream. You can also brush melted chocolate over the tops and let cool, or serve with a chocolate sauce.

Making cakes and cookies

You can make cakes of varying densities depending on the ingredients you use and the method of mixing. For cakes and cookies there are four basic methods of mixing, as follows:

CREAMING

This is a good method for making light sponge cakes. Simply beat the butter and sugar together until light, then beat in the eggs and fold in the flour. Use softened butter or margarine for this method.

ALL-IN-ONE

This method saves time and effort when making light sponge cakes, and can be done manually or in a machine. Put all the ingredients into a bowl and beat well until smooth. Alternatively, put the ingredients into a free-standing mixer or food processor and beat on slow speed for 2–3 minutes until smooth.

RUBBING IN

This method is ideal for biscuits and teabreads. Use your fingertips to rub the butter into the flour until it resembles fine bread crumbs. Mix in the sugar, egg, and other liquid ingredients. Stir in the flour from the sides of the bowl.

MELTING

Use this method for moist cakes and cookies. Melt the butter in a pan along with the sugar and any other dissolvable ingredients. Remove from the heat and let cool slightly. Meanwhile, sift the flour into a bowl and make a well in the center. Beat together the eggs and milk and pour into the well, then add the egg mixture. Stir in the flour from the sides of the bowl.

Basic sponge mixture
This recipe will make enough for two 8-inch/20-cm greased and lined sandwich pans.

1 cup unsalted butter, softened, or soft margarine suitable for baking
1⅛ cups superfine sugar
4 eggs
1⅝ cups self-rising flour, sifted
2 tsp baking powder
pinch of salt

Preheat the oven to 375°F/190°C. Grease and line the sandwich pans. Place the butter in a large bowl, then add the sugar and use a wooden spoon to beat together until the mixture is smooth and light. Gradually beat in the eggs, making sure that the mixture stays smooth throughout.

In a separate bowl, sift together the flour, baking powder, and salt, then fold into the egg mixture in a figure-eight movement. Divide the batter between the sandwich pans and bake for about 25 minutes until golden and risen. Remove from the oven and let cool in the pans for about 5 minutes before turning out on a wire rack to cool completely.

Variation: To make a chocolate version of this sponge, replace 1 tablespoon of the self-rising flour with 1 tablespoon of unsweetened cocoa.

Butter shortbread
This recipe makes 8 large pieces of shortbread or 16 smaller pieces.

9 tbsp unsalted butter, softened, plus extra for greasing
scant 1¼ cups all-purpose flour
scant ⅓ cup rice flour
¼ cup superfine sugar, plus extra for sprinkling

Preheat the oven to 325°F/160°C. Grease an 8-inch/20-cm loose-bottom tart pan. Sift the all-purpose and rice flours into a large bowl.

In a separate bowl, cream together the butter and superfine sugar, then stir in the sifted flours. Put the mixture into the prepared tart pan and smooth the surface. Lightly sprinkle over some superfine sugar, then prick all over the surface with a fork. Using a sharp knife, score the surface into 8 wedges (or 16 smaller wedges, if preferred), then bake in the preheated oven for 30 minutes, or until lightly golden.

Remove from the oven and let cool in the pan for 5 minutes. Slide the shortbread out of the pan, then use a sharp knife to cut along the score marks and divide the shortbread into wedges. Cool on a wire rack, then serve immediately or store in an airtight container for up to a week.

CRUSTY WHITE BREAD

THERE IS A LOT OF MYSTIQUE THAT SURROUNDS BREADMAKING, BUT IN REALITY ANYONE CAN BAKE THEIR OWN BREAD AT HOME. THIS RECIPE IS EASY TO DO, AND WILL MAKE YOU WANT TO BAKE YOUR OWN BREAD AGAIN AND AGAIN.

makes
1 medium loaf
preparation
30 minutes, plus
1¾ hours' rising
cooking
30 minutes

ingredients
- 1 egg
- 1 egg yolk
- hand-hot water, as required
- 1 lb 2 oz/500 g white bread flour, plus extra for dusting
- 1½ tsp salt
- 2 tsp sugar
- 1 tsp active dry yeast
- 2 tbsp butter, diced

1 Place the egg and egg yolk in a pitcher and beat lightly to mix. Add enough hand-hot water to make up to 1¼ cups. Stir well.

2 Place the flour, salt, sugar, and yeast in a large bowl. Add the butter and rub it in with your fingertips until the mixture resembles bread crumbs. Make a well in the center and add the egg mixture and work to a smooth dough.

3 Turn the dough out onto a lightly floured counter and knead for 10 minutes, or until the dough is smooth and elastic. Place the dough in an oiled bowl, cover with plastic wrap, and leave in a warm place to rise for 1 hour, or until it has doubled in size.

4 Oil a loaf pan. Turn the dough out onto a lightly floured counter and knead for 1 minute until smooth. Shape the dough the length of the pan and three times the width. Fold the dough into three lengthwise and place it in the pan with the join underneath. Cover and leave in a warm place for 30 minutes until it has risen above the pan.

5 Preheat the oven to 425°F/220°C. Bake in the oven for 30 minutes, or until firm and golden brown. Test that the loaf is cooked by tapping it on the bottom—it should sound hollow. Transfer to a wire rack to cool completely before serving.

WHOLE WHEAT HARVEST BREAD

THIS WHOLE WHEAT LOAF IS FULL OF HEALTHY FIBER AND NATURAL GOODNESS. IT NEEDS VERY LITTLE PREPARATION AND IS VERY EASY TO MAKE. SIMPLY FOLLOW THE INSTRUCTIONS GIVEN HERE, POP THE DOUGH IN THE OVEN, AND WAIT FOR THE DELICIOUS AROMA TO PERVADE YOUR KITCHEN.

makes
1 small loaf
preparation
30 minutes, plus
1½ hours' rising
cooking
30 minutes

ingredients
- 1⅝ cups whole wheat bread flour
- 1 tbsp skim milk powder
- 1 tsp salt
- 2 tbsp brown sugar
- 1 tsp active dry yeast
- 1½ tbsp sunflower-seed oil
- ¾ cup hand-hot water

1 Place the flour, milk, salt, sugar, and yeast in a large bowl. Pour in the oil and and add the water then mix well to make a smooth dough.

2 Turn the dough out onto a lightly floured counter and knead for 10 minutes, or until the dough is smooth. Place the dough in an oiled bowl, cover with plastic wrap, and leave in a warm place to rise for 1 hour, or until it has doubled in size.

3 Oil a 2-lb/900-g loaf pan. Turn the dough out onto a lightly floured counter and knead for 1 minute until smooth. Shape the dough the length of the pan and three times the width. Fold the dough into three lengthwise and place it in the pan with the join underneath. Cover and leave in a warm place for 30 minutes until it has risen above the pan.

4 Preheat the oven to 425°F/220°C. Bake in the oven for 30 minutes, or until firm and golden brown. Test that the loaf is cooked by tapping it on the bottom—it should sound hollow. Transfer to a wire rack to cool completely before serving.

MIXED SEED BREAD

THIS SEEDED BREAD IS DELICIOUSLY AROMATIC, TASTES WONDERFUL, AND IS RICHER IN CALCIUM AND PROTEIN THAN A PLAIN LOAF. IT IS ALSO RICH IN OMEGA-3 ESSENTIAL FATTY ACIDS, WHICH NUTRITIONISTS SAY CONTRIBUTE TO GOOD HEALTH AND OVERALL WELL-BEING.

makes
1 medium loaf
preparation
30 minutes, plus
1½ hours' rising
cooking
30 minutes

ingredients
- 2⅝ cups white bread flour
- 1⅜ cups rye flour
- 1½ tbsp skim milk powder
- 1½ tsp salt
- 1 tbsp brown sugar
- 1 tsp active dry yeast
- 1½ tbsp sunflower-seed oil
- 2 tsp lemon juice
- 1¼ cups hand-hot water
- 1 tsp caraway seeds
- ½ tsp poppy seeds
- ½ tsp sesame seeds

TOPPING
- 1 egg white
- 1 tbsp water
- 1 tbsp sunflower or pumpkin seeds (pepitas)

1 Place the flours, milk, salt, sugar, and yeast in a large bowl. Pour in the oil and add the lemon juice and water. Stir in the seeds and mix well to make a smooth dough.

2 Turn the dough out onto a lightly floured counter and knead for 10 minutes, or until the dough is smooth and elastic. Place the dough in an oiled bowl, cover with plastic wrap, and leave in a warm place to rise for 1 hour, or until it has doubled in size.

3 Oil a 2-lb/900-g loaf pan. Turn the dough out onto a lightly floured counter and knead for 1 minute until smooth. Shape the dough the length of the pan and three times the width. Fold the dough into three lengthwise and place it in the pan with the join underneath. Cover and leave in a warm place for 30 minutes until it has risen above the pan.

4 Preheat the oven to 425°F/220°C. For the topping, lightly beat the egg white with the water to make a glaze. Just before baking, brush the glaze over the loaf, then gently press the sunflower or pumpkin seeds (pepitas) all over the top.

5 Bake in the oven for 30 minutes, or until firm and golden brown. Test that the loaf is cooked by tapping it on the bottom—it should sound hollow. Transfer to a wire rack to cool completely before serving.

OLIVE & SUN-DRIED TOMATO BREAD

THIS DELICIOUS BREAD CONJURES UP AROMAS AND FLAVORS OF THE WARM MEDITERRANEAN, WITH PLUMP, JUICY OLIVES AND RIPE, FLAVORFUL TOMATOES DRIED IN THE HOT MIDDAY SUN. THE TASTE IS IRRESISTIBLE—IT WILL LEAVE YOUR HOUSEHOLD AND YOUR GUESTS LONGING FOR MORE.

serves
4

preparation
20 minutes, plus
2¼ hours' rising

cooking
40 minutes

ingredients
- generous 2¾ cups all-purpose flour, plus extra for dusting
- 1 tsp salt
- 1 sachet active dry yeast
- 1 tsp brown sugar
- 1 tbsp chopped fresh thyme
- scant 1 cup warm water (heated to 122°F/50°C)
- 4 tbsp olive oil, plus extra for oiling
- ⅓ cup black olives, pitted and sliced
- ⅓ cup green olives, pitted and sliced
- ⅜ cup sun-dried tomatoes in oil, drained and sliced
- 1 egg yolk, beaten

1 Place the flour, salt, and yeast in a bowl and mix together, then stir in the sugar and thyme. Make a well in the center. Slowly stir in enough water and oil to make a dough. Mix in the olives and sun-dried tomatoes. Knead the dough for 5 minutes, then form it into a ball. Brush a bowl with oil, add the dough, and cover with plastic wrap. Let rise in a warm place for about 1½ hours, or until it has doubled in size.

2 Dust a baking sheet with flour. Knead the dough lightly, then cut into two halves and shape into ovals or circles. Place them on the baking sheet, cover with plastic wrap, and let rise again in a warm place for 45 minutes, or until they have doubled in size.

3 Preheat the oven to 400°F/200°C. Make 3 shallow diagonal cuts on the top of each piece of dough. Brush with the egg. Bake for 40 minutes, or until cooked through—they should be golden on top and sound hollow when tapped on the bottom. Transfer to wire racks to cool. Store in an airtight container for up to 3 days.

BANANA & ORANGE BREAD

THE SWEETNESS OF THE BANANA AND THE CITRUS TANG OF THE ORANGE MAKE A WONDERFUL
COMBINATION IN THIS BREAD. IT IS DELICIOUS SPREAD WITH CREAMY UNSALTED BUTTER, BUT
YOU CAN ALSO USE A LOWER-FAT MARGARINE TO KEEP THE FAT CONTENT LOW.

makes
1 medium loaf
preparation
30 minutes, plus
1½ hours' rising
cooking
30 minutes

ingredients
- 1 lb 2 oz/500 g white bread
  flour, plus an extra 1–2 tbsp
  for sticky dough
- 1 tsp salt
- 1 tsp active dry yeast
- 3 tbsp butter, diced
- 2 medium ripe bananas
  or 1 large ripe banana,
  peeled and mashed
- 4 tbsp orange juice
- scant 1 cup hand-hot
  buttermilk or water
- 1½ tbsp skim milk powder
  (if using water)
- 3 tbsp runny honey
- milk, to glaze (optional)

1 Place the flour, salt, sugar, and yeast in a large bowl. Rub in the butter and add the mashed bananas and honey. Make a well in the center and gradually work in the the orange juice and buttermilk or water to make a smooth dough. If using water, add the skim milk powder to the mixture.

2 Turn the dough out onto a lightly floured counter and knead for 5–7 minutes, or until the dough is smooth and elastic. If the dough looks very sticky, add an additional 1–2 tablespoons of white bread flour. (The stickiness depends on the ripeness and size of the bananas.) Place the dough in an oiled bowl, cover with plastic wrap, and leave in a warm place to rise for 1 hour, or until it has doubled in size.

3 Oil a 2-lb/900-g loaf pan. Turn the dough out onto a lightly floured counter and knead for 1 minute until smooth. Shape the dough the length of the pan and three times the width. Fold the dough into three lengthwise and place it in the pan with the join underneath. Cover and leave in a warm place for 30 minutes until it has risen above the pan.

4 Preheat the oven to 425°F/220°C. Just before baking, brush the milk over the loaf to glaze, if desired.

5 Bake in the oven for 30 minutes, or until firm and golden brown. Test that the loaf is cooked by tapping it on the bottom—it should sound hollow. Transfer to a wire rack to cool completely before serving.

FRESH CROISSANTS

PREPARE THIS RECIPE THE NIGHT BEFORE. MAKE THE DOUGH AND ROLL INTO CROISSANT SHAPES, THEN BRUSH WITH THE GLAZE, COVER WITH PLASTIC WRAP, AND REFRIGERATE OVERNIGHT. THE NEXT MORNING, LET RISE FOR 30–45 MINUTES, THEN PLACE ON A BAKING SHEET AS PER THE RECIPE.

makes
12 croissants
preparation
40 minutes, plus
2 hours' rising
and chilling
cooking
15–20 minutes

ingredients
- 1 lb 2 oz/500 g white bread flour, plus extra for dusting
- scant ¼ cup superfine sugar
- 1 tsp salt
- 2 tsp active dry yeast
- 1¼ cups milk, heated until just warm to the touch
- 1¼ cups butter, softened, plus extra for greasing
- 1 egg, lightly beaten with 1 tbsp milk, to glaze
- jelly, to serve (optional)

1 Stir the dry ingredients into a large bowl, make a well in the center, and add the milk. Mix to a soft dough, adding more milk if too dry. Knead on a lightly floured counter for 5–10 minutes, or until smooth and elastic. Let rise in a large, greased bowl, covered, in a warm place until doubled in size. Meanwhile, flatten the butter with a rolling pin between 2 sheets of waxed paper to form a rectangle ¼-inch/5-mm thick, then let chill.

2 Knead the dough for 1 minute. Remove the butter from the refrigerator and let soften slightly. Roll out the dough on a well-floured counter to 18 x 6 inches/46 x 15 cms. Place the butter in the center, folding up the sides, and squeezing the edges together gently. With the short end of the dough toward you, fold the top third down toward the center, then fold the bottom third up. Rotate 45° clockwise so that the

fold is to your left and the top flap toward your right. Roll out to a rectangle and fold again. If the butter feels soft, wrap the dough in plastic wrap, and let chill. Repeat the rolling process twice more. Cut the dough in half. Roll out one half into a triangle ¼ inch/5 mm thick (keep the other half refrigerated). Use a cardboard triangular template, base 7 inches/18 cm and sides 8 inches/20 cm, to cut out the croissants.

3 Brush the triangles lightly with the glaze. Roll into croissant shapes, starting at the base and tucking the point underneath to prevent unrolling while cooking. Brush again with the glaze. Place on an ungreased baking sheet and let double in size. Preheat the oven to 400°F/200°C. Bake for 15–20 minutes until golden brown. Serve with jelly, if liked.

CHELSEA BUNS

SWEET AND STICKY CHELSEA BUNS, WITH A HINT OF SPICE, ARE AN IRRESISTIBLE ADDITION TO A TRADITIONAL AFTERNOON TEA, OR AN EXCELLENT SNACK AT ANY TIME OF DAY. THEY ARE ALSO WONDERFULLY PORTABLE. WHY NOT TAKE A FEW ALONG TO FINISH A PICNIC IN STYLE?

makes
9
preparation
30 minutes, plus
1¾ hours' rising
cooking
30 minutes

ingredients
- 2 tbsp butter, plus extra for greasing
- 1⅝ cups white bread flour, plus extra for dusting
- ½ tsp salt
- 2 tsp active dry yeast
- 1 tsp golden superfine sugar
- ½ cup tepid milk
- 1 egg, beaten
- vegetable oil, for brushing
- ¾ cup confectioners' sugar, to glaze

FILLING
- ¼ cup packed brown sugar
- ¾ cup luxury mixed dried fruits
- 1 tsp pumpkin pie spice
- 4 tbsp butter, softened

1 Grease a 7-inch/18-cm square cake pan. Sift the flour and salt into a warmed bowl, stir in the yeast and sugar, and rub in the butter. Make a well in the center. Mix the milk and egg together in a separate bowl and pour into the dry ingredients. Beat to make a soft dough.

2 Turn out onto a floured counter and knead for 5–10 minutes, or until smooth. Brush a clean bowl with oil, place the dough in the bowl, cover with oiled plastic wrap, and leave in a warm place for 1 hour, or until doubled in size.

3 Turn the dough out onto a floured counter and knead lightly for 1 minute. Roll out into a 12 x 9-inch/30 x 23-cm rectangle.

4 To make the filling, place the brown sugar, fruit, and spice in a bowl and mix. Spread the dough with the softened butter and sprinkle the fruit mixture on top. Roll up from a long side, then cut into 9 pieces. Place in the prepared pan, cut-side up. Cover with oiled plastic wrap and leave in a warm place for 45 minutes, or until well risen.

5 Preheat the oven to 375°F/190°C. Bake the buns in the oven for 30 minutes, or until golden. Let cool in the pan for 10 minutes, then transfer, in one piece, to a wire rack to cool. Sift the confectioners' sugar into a bowl and stir in enough water to make a thin glaze. Brush over the buns and let set. Pull the buns apart to serve.

cook's tip

When you place the buns in the prepared cake pan, place them close to each other in three rows, so that they join up into one single piece as they expand during cooking.

BLINIS

BLINIS COME FROM RUSSIA. TRADITIONALLY THESE SMALL YEAST PANCAKES ARE MADE WITH BUCKWHEAT FLOUR, WHICH GIVES THEM A TASTY AND UNUSUAL FLAVOR. THIS RECIPE PRESERVES THAT TRADITION. YOU CAN ALSO SERVE THESE PANCAKES WITH CAVIAR.

makes
8
preparation
20 minutes, plus
1 hour's standing
cooking
20 minutes

ingredients
- ¾ cup buckwheat flour
- ¾ cup white bread flour
- ⅙-oz/7-g sachet active dry yeast
- 1 tsp salt
- scant 1¾ cups tepid milk
- 2 eggs, 1 whole and 1 separated
- vegetable oil, for brushing

TO SERVE
- sour cream
- smoked salmon

1 Sift both flours into a large, warmed bowl. Stir in the yeast and salt. Beat in the milk, whole egg, and egg yolk until smooth. Cover the bowl and let stand in a warm place for 1 hour.

2 Place the egg white in a spotlessly clean bowl and whisk until soft peaks form. Fold into the batter. Brush a heavy-bottom skillet with oil and set over medium–high heat. When the skillet is hot, pour enough of the batter onto the surface to make a blini about the size of a saucer.

3 When bubbles rise, turn the blini over with a spatula and cook the other side until light brown. Wrap in a clean dish towel to keep warm while cooking the remainder. Serve the warm blinis with sour cream and smoked salmon.

variation
If buckwheat flour is unavailable, use whole wheat bread flour instead.

LEEK & ONION TARTLETS

THESE FLAVORSOME TARTLETS ARE RATHER LIKE MINI QUICHES. THEY ARE RICH IN PROTEIN AND VERY VERSATILE. YOU CAN SERVE THEM WARM OR COLD, AND THEY MAKE AN EXCELLENT CHOICE FOR A LUNCH BOX OR A PICNIC, ACCOMPANIED BY A CRISP SALAD.

serves
6

preparation
30 minutes, plus
1 hour's chilling
and cooling

cooking
40 minutes

ingredients
- butter, for greasing
- 8 oz/225 g ready-made unsweetened pie dough
- all-purpose flour, for dusting

FILLING
- 2 tbsp unsalted butter
- 1 onion, thinly sliced
- 1 lb/450 g leeks, thinly sliced
- 2 tsp chopped fresh thyme
- 2 oz/55 g Gruyère cheese, grated
- 3 eggs
- 1¼ cups heavy cream
- salt and pepper

1 Lightly grease 6 x 4-inch/10-cm tartlet pans with butter. Roll out the dough on a lightly floured counter and stamp out 6 circles with a 5-inch/13-cm cutter. Ease the dough into the pans, prick the bottoms, and let chill for 30 minutes.

2 Preheat the oven to 375°F/190°C. Line the pastry shells with foil and baking beans, then place on a baking sheet and bake for 8 minutes. Remove the foil and beans and bake for an additional 2 minutes. Transfer the pans to a wire rack to cool. Reduce the oven temperature to 350°F/180°C.

3 Meanwhile, make the filling. Melt the butter in a large, heavy-bottom skillet. Add the onion and cook, stirring constantly, for 5 minutes, or until softened. Add the leeks and thyme and cook, stirring, for 10 minutes, or until softened. Divide the leek mixture between the tartlet shells. Sprinkle with Gruyère cheese.

4 Lightly beat the eggs with the cream and season to taste with salt and pepper. Place the tartlet pans on a baking sheet and divide the egg mixture between them. Bake in the preheated oven for 15 minutes, or until the filling is set and golden brown. Transfer to a wire rack to cool slightly before removing from the pans and serving.

variation
For a slightly milder version of these tartlets, substitute 1 lb/450 g of sliced zucchini for the leeks.

STEAK & KIDNEY PUDDING

STEAK AND KIDNEY STEAMED IN A SUET CRUST PIE DOUGH, FLAVORED WITH MUSHROOMS AND PARSLEY, MUST BE THE MOST BRITISH OF BRITISH MEAT DISHES. ALSO GOING BY THE AFFECTIONATE COCKNEY NAME OF "KATE & SYDNEY," THIS PUDDING IS TRADITIONAL ALL OVER THE BRITISH ISLES.

serves
4

preparation
40 minutes

cooking
4–5 hours

ingredients
- butter, for greasing
- 1 lb/450 g top round steak, trimmed and cut into 1-inch/2.5-cm pieces
- 2 lamb's kidneys, cored and cut into 1-inch/2.5-cm pieces
- ³/₈ cup all-purpose flour
- 1 onion, finely chopped
- 4 oz/115 g large portobello mushrooms, sliced (optional)
- 1 tbsp chopped fresh parsley
- about 1¼ cups stock, or a mixture of beer and water
- salt and pepper

SUET PIE DOUGH
- 2³/₈ cups self-rising flour
- 6 oz/175 g suet
- 1 cup cold water
- salt and pepper

1 Lightly grease a 5-cup ovenproof bowl with butter.

2 Place the prepared meat with the flour and salt and pepper in a large plastic bag and shake well until all the meat is well coated. Add the onion, mushrooms, if using, and the parsley and shake again.

3 Make the suet dough by mixing the flour, suet, and a little salt and pepper together. Add enough of the cold water to make a soft dough.

4 Keep a quarter of the dough to one side and roll the remainder out to form a round large enough to line the ovenproof bowl. Line the bowl, making sure that there is a good ½ inch/1 cm hanging over the edge.

5 Place the meat mixture in the bowl and pour in enough of the stock to cover the meat.

6 Roll out the remaining dough to make a lid. Fold in the edges of the dough, dampen them, and place the lid on top. Seal firmly in place.

7 Cover with a piece of waxed paper and then foil, with a pleat to allow for expansion during cooking, and seal well. Place in a steamer or large pan half-filled with boiling water. Simmer the pudding for 4–5 hours, topping off the water occasionally.

8 Remove the bowl from the steamer and take off the coverings. Wrap a clean cloth around the bowl and serve at the table.

MUSHROOM & SPINACH PUFF PASTRY

THESE PUFF PASTRY PACKAGES HAVE A MOUTHWATERING FILLING OF GARLIC, MUSHROOMS, AND
SPINACH. THEY ARE EASY TO MAKE AND DELICIOUS TO EAT, AND MAKE A SUPERB SNACK, LUNCH, OR
SUPPER. SERVE THEM HOT, OR LET THEM COOL AND POP THEM INTO LUNCH BOXES FOR A PICNIC.

serves
4

preparation
20 minutes

cooking
30–35 minutes

ingredients
- 2 tbsp butter
- 1 red onion, halved
  and sliced
- 2 garlic cloves, crushed
- 8 oz/225 g open-cap
  mushrooms, sliced
- 3⅜ cups baby spinach
- pinch of nutmeg
- 4 tbsp heavy cream
- 8 oz/225 g prepared
  puff pastry
- all-purpose flour,
  for dusting
- 1 egg, beaten
- 2 tsp poppy seeds
- salt and pepper

1 Preheat the oven to 400°F/200°C.
Melt the butter in a skillet. Add the
onion and garlic and sauté for 3–4
minutes until the onion has softened.

2 Add the mushrooms, spinach, and
nutmeg and cook for an additional
2–3 minutes. Stir in the cream,
mixing well. Season to taste with salt
and pepper and remove the skillet
from the heat.

3 Roll the pastry out on a lightly
floured counter and cut into
4 x 6-inch/15-cm circles. Spoon a
quarter of the filling onto one half of
each circle and fold the pastry over
to encase the filling. Press down to
scal the edges of the pastry and brush
with the beaten egg. Sprinkle with
the poppy seeds.

4 Place the packages onto a
dampened baking sheet and cook in
the preheated oven for 20 minutes
until risen and golden brown.

5 Transfer the mushroom and
spinach puff pastry packages to
serving plates and serve immediately.

cook's tip
The baking sheet is dampened so that steam
forms with the heat of the oven and helps
the pastry to rise and set.

VEGETABLE JALOUSIE

A JALOUSIE IS A SMALL FRENCH LATTICED CAKE MADE WITH PUFF PASTRY AND AN ALMOND AND JELLY FILLING. THIS JALOUSIE IS A SAVORY VERSION. IT LOOKS IMPRESSIVE, BUT IS REALLY VERY EASY TO MAKE. THE MIXTURE OF VEGETABLES GIVES IT A WONDERFUL COLOR AND FLAVOR.

serves
4

preparation
30 minutes

cooking
45–50 minutes

ingredients
- 1 lb/450 g prepared puff pastry
- all-purpose flour, for dusting
- 1 egg, beaten, to glaze

FILLING
- 2 tbsp butter or margarine
- 1 leek, shredded
- 2 garlic cloves, crushed
- 1 red bell pepper, sliced
- 1 yellow bell pepper, sliced

- 1 3/4 oz/50 g mushrooms, sliced
- 2 3/4 oz/75 g small asparagus spears
- 2 tbsp all-purpose flour
- 6 tbsp vegetable stock
- 6 tbsp milk
- 4 tbsp dry white wine
- 1 tbsp chopped oregano
- salt and pepper

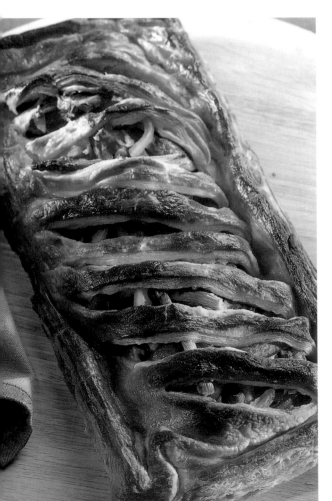

1 Preheat the oven to 400°F/200°C. To make the filling, melt the butter in a pan. Add the leek and garlic and sauté for 2 minutes. Add the remaining vegetables and cook, stirring, for 3–4 minutes.

2 Add the flour and cook for 1 minute. Remove the pan from the heat and stir in the stock, milk, and white wine. Return the pan to the heat and bring to a boil, stirring, until thickened. Stir in the oregano and season to taste with salt and pepper.

3 Roll half of the pastry out on a lightly floured counter to form a rectangle 15 x 6 inches/ 38 x 15 cm.

4 Roll out the other half of the pastry to the same shape, but a little larger. Place the smaller rectangle on a baking sheet lined with dampened parchment paper.

5 Spoon the filling on top of the smaller rectangle, leaving a 1/2-inch/1-cm clean edge. Cut parallel slits across the larger rectangle to within 1 inch/2.5 cm of each edge.

6 Brush the edge of the smaller rectangle with egg and place the larger rectangle on top, sealing the edges well.

7 Brush the whole jalousie with egg and cook in the preheated oven for 30–35 minutes until risen and golden. Serve immediately.

POTATO, BEEF & LEEK PASTIES

THESE MOUTHWATERING PASTIES ARE FILLED WITH POTATOES, SUCCULENT CUBES OF BEEF,
CARROTS, AND LEEKS. THEY MAKE A SATISFYING MEAL AT ANY TIME OF DAY. SINCE YOU CAN
SERVE THEM COLD AS WELL AS HOT, THEY ARE IDEAL FARE FOR LUNCH BOXES AND PICNICS.

makes
4

preparation
35 minutes

cooking
50 minutes

ingredients
- butter, for greasing
- 8 oz/225 g waxy
  potatoes, diced
- 1 small carrot, diced
- 8 oz/225 g beef
  steak, cubed
- 1 leek, sliced
- 8 oz/225 g ready-made
  unsweetened pie dough
- all-purpose flour,
  for dusting
- 1 tbsp butter
- 1 egg, beaten
- salt and pepper
- green salad or onion
  gravy, to serve

1 Preheat the oven to 400°F/200°C.
Lightly grease a baking sheet with
butter. Mix the potatoes, carrots,
beef, and leek together in a
large bowl. Season well with salt
and pepper.

2 Divide the pie dough into 4 equal
portions. Roll each portion out on a
lightly floured counter into an
8-inch/20-cm circle.

3 Spoon the potato mixture onto
one half of each circle, to within
½ inch/1 cm of the edge. Top the
potato mixture with the butter,
dividing it equally between the
circles. Brush the dough edge with
a little of the beaten egg.

4 Fold the dough over to encase the
filling and crimp the edges together.
Transfer the pasties to the prepared
baking sheet and brush them with
the beaten egg.

5 Cook in the preheated oven
for 20 minutes. Reduce the oven
temperature to 325°F/160°C and
cook the pasties for an additional
30 minutes until cooked through.
Serve the pasties with a crisp salad or
onion gravy.

variation
*Use other types of meat, such as pork or
chicken, in the pasties and add chunks of
apple in Step 2, if preferred.*

PROFITEROLES

WHO CAN RESIST THE RICH, BUTTERY TASTE OF PROFITEROLES, WITH THEIR SUMPTUOUS CREAMY CENTERS? THESE PROFITEROLES HAVE A LUXURIOUS CHOCOLATE AND BRANDY SAUCE POURED OVER THEM—THE ULTIMATE EXPERIENCE FOR THE HOPELESSLY INFATUATED CHOCOLATE LOVER.

serves
4
preparation
25 minutes
cooking
35 minutes

ingredients

CHOUX PASTRY
- 5 tbsp butter, plus extra for greasing
- scant 1 cup water
- ¾ cup all-purpose flour
- 3 eggs, beaten

CREAM FILLING
- 1¼ cups heavy cream
- 3 tbsp superfine sugar
- 1 tsp vanilla extract

CHOCOLATE & BRANDY SAUCE
- 4½ oz/125 g semisweet chocolate, broken into small pieces
- 2½ tbsp butter
- 6 tbsp water
- 2 tbsp brandy

1 Preheat the oven to 400°F/ 200°C. Grease a large baking sheet with butter.

2 To make the pastry, place the water and butter in a pan and bring to a boil. Meanwhile, sift the flour into a bowl. Turn off the heat and beat in the flour until smooth. Cool for 5 minutes.

3 Beat in enough of the eggs to give the mixture a soft, dropping consistency. Transfer to a pastry bag fitted with a ½-inch/1-cm plain tip. Pipe small balls onto the baking sheet. Bake for 25 minutes.

4 Remove from the oven. Pierce each ball with a skewer to let the steam escape.

5 To make the filling, whip the cream, sugar, and vanilla extract together. Cut the pastry balls across the middle, then fill with cream.

6 To make the sauce, gently melt the chocolate, butter, and water together in a small pan, stirring constantly, until smooth. Stir in the brandy. Pile the profiteroles onto individual serving dishes or into a pyramid on a raised cake stand. Pour over the sauce and serve.

CHERRY BISCUITS

THESE ARE AN APPEALING ALTERNATIVE TO TRADITIONAL BISCUITS, USING SWEET CANDIED
CHERRIES, WHICH NOT ONLY CREATE COLOR BUT ADD A DISTINCT AND PLEASURABLE FLAVOR,
AS WELL AS ADDED CHEWINESS. THESE ARE SURE TO PLEASE THE MOST DISCERNING PALATE.

makes
8
preparation
10 minutes
cooking
30 minutes

ingredients
- 6 tbsp butter, cut into small pieces, plus extra for greasing
- 1⅝ cups self-rising flour, plus extra for dusting
- scant ⅛ cup superfine sugar
- pinch of salt
- ¼ cup candied cherries, chopped
- ¼ cup golden raisins
- 1 egg, beaten
- ¼ cup milk

1 Preheat the oven to 425°F/220°C. Lightly grease a baking sheet with a little butter.

2 Sift the flour, sugar, and salt into a mixing bowl. Add the butter and rub it in with your fingertips until the mixture resembles bread crumbs.

3 Stir in the candied cherries and golden raisins. Add the egg.

4 Set aside 1 tablespoon of the milk for glazing, then add the remainder to the mixture. Mix well together to form a soft dough.

5 Roll out the dough on a lightly floured counter to a thickness of ¾ inch/2 cm and cut out 8 biscuits, using a 2-inch/5-cm cutter.

6 Place the biscuits on the prepared baking sheet and brush the tops with the reserved milk.

7 Bake in the preheated oven for 8–10 minutes, or until the biscuits are golden brown.

8 Let cool on a wire rack, then serve split and buttered.

cook's tip
These biscuits will freeze very successfully but they are best thawed within 1 month and eaten immediately.

TREACLE TART

THIS IS A TRADITIONAL DESSERT THAT NEVER SEEMS TO GO OUT OF FASHION: IT STILL DELIGHTS
PEOPLE TIME AFTER TIME. IT IS ALSO VERY QUICK TO MAKE IF YOU USE READY-MADE DOUGH, WHICH
YOU CAN BUY FROZEN FROM MOST SUPERMARKETS. SIMPLY THAW IT AND IT IS READY TO USE.

serves
8

preparation
25 minutes,
plus 30 minutes'
chilling

cooking
35–40 minutes

ingredients
- 9 oz/250 g ready-made
  unsweetened pie dough
- all-purpose flour,
  for dusting
- 1½ cups corn syrup
- 2¼ cups fresh white
  bread crumbs
- ½ cup heavy cream
- finely grated rind of
  ½ lemon or orange
- 2 tbsp lemon or
  orange juice
- custard, to serve

1 Preheat the oven to 375°F/190°C.
Roll out the pie dough on a lightly
floured counter and use to line an
8-inch/20-cm loose-bottom tart
pan, reserving the dough trimmings.
Prick the bottom of the pie dough
with a fork and let chill in the
refrigerator.

2 Cut out small shapes from the
reserved dough trimmings, such as
leaves, stars, or hearts, to decorate
the top of the tart.

3 Mix the corn syrup, bread crumbs,
heavy cream, and grated lemon
rind and lemon juice together in a
small bowl.

4 Pour the mixture into the pastry
shell and decorate the edges of the
tart with the dough cut-outs.

5 Bake in the preheated oven for
35–40 minutes, or until the filling is
just set.

6 Let the tart cool slightly in the
pan before turning out and serving
with custard.

variation

*Use the dough trimmings to create a lattice
pattern on top of the tart, if preferred.*

RICH FRUIT CAKE

THIS MOIST, FRUIT-LADEN CAKE LOOKS VERY IMPRESSIVE, YET IT IS DECEPTIVELY SIMPLE TO MAKE.
SERVE IT FOR A SPECIAL OCCASION—IT WOULD MAKE AN EXCELLENT TREAT FOR CHRISTMAS OR
THANKSGIVING, OR A MEMORABLE BIRTHDAY CAKE IF YOU ADD A FEW SMALL CANDLES.

serves

4

preparation

25 minutes,
plus 40 minutes'
cooling

cooking

1³/₄ hours

ingredients

- butter, for greasing
- 1 cup pitted unsweetened
  dates
- ³/₄ cup no-soak
  dried prunes
- scant 1 cup unsweetened
  orange juice
- 2 tbsp molasses
- 1 tsp finely grated
  lemon rind
- 1 tsp finely grated
  orange rind
- 1⁵/₈ cups whole wheat
  self-rising flour

- 1 tsp pumpkin pie spice
- ³/₄ cup seedless raisins
- ³/₄ cup golden raisins
- generous ³/₄ cup currants
- ³/₄ cup dried cranberries
- 3 large eggs, separated
- 1 tbsp apricot jelly, warmed

FROSTING

- 1¹/₈ cups confectioners' sugar,
  plus extra for dusting
- 1–2 tsp water
- 1 tsp vanilla extract
- orange rind strips, to decorate
- lemon rind strips, to decorate

1 Preheat the oven to 325°F/160°C.
Grease and line a deep 8-inch/20-cm
round cake pan. Chop the dates and
prunes and place in a pan. Pour over
the orange juice and let simmer for
10 minutes. Remove the pan from
the heat and beat the fruit mixture
until puréed. Add the molasses and
citrus rinds and cool.

2 Sift the flour and spice into a bowl,
adding any bran that remains in the
strainer. Add the dried fruits. When
the date and prune mixture is cool,
whisk in the egg yolks. Whisk the egg
whites in a separate, clean bowl until
stiff. Spoon the fruit mixture into the
dry ingredients and mix together.

3 Gently fold in the egg whites.
Transfer to the prepared pan and
bake in the preheated oven for
1¹/₂ hours. Let cool in the pan.

4 Remove the cake from the pan
and brush the top with jelly. To make
the frosting, sift the sugar into a
bowl and mix with enough water
and the vanilla extract to form a
soft frosting. Lay the frosting over
the top of the cake and trim the
edges. Decorate with orange and
lemon rind.

CHOCOLATE & ALMOND LAYER CAKE

THIS CAKE IS UTTERLY IRRESISTIBLE. IT BOASTS THIN LAYERS OF DELICIOUS LIGHT CHOCOLATE CAKE SANDWICHED TOGETHER WITH A CHOCOLATE FROSTING. IT SHOULD CARRY A WARNING, BECAUSE IT WILL SERIOUSLY AFFECT THE RESTRAINT OF THE MOST STRONG-WILLED IN YOUR HOUSEHOLD.

serves
10–12

preparation
40 minutes,
plus 40 minutes'
cooling

cooking
30–35 minutes

ingredients
- butter, for greasing
- 7 eggs
- 1 cup superfine sugar
- 1 cup all-purpose flour
- ½ cup unsweetened cocoa
- 3½ tbsp butter, melted

FILLING
- 7 oz/200 g semisweet chocolate
- 9 tbsp butter
- ⅜ cup confectioners' sugar

TO DECORATE
- ⅔ cup toasted slivered almonds, lightly crushed
- small chocolate curls or grated chocolate

1 Preheat the oven to 350°F/180°C. Grease a deep 9-inch/23-cm square cake pan and line the bottom with parchment paper.

2 Whisk the eggs and superfine sugar together in a mixing bowl with an electric whisk for 10 minutes, or until the mixture is very light and foamy and the whisk leaves a trail that lasts a few seconds when lifted.

3 Sift the flour and cocoa together and fold half into the mixture. Drizzle over the melted butter and fold in the rest of the flour and cocoa. Pour into the prepared pan and bake in the preheated oven for 30–35 minutes, or until springy to

the touch. Let cool slightly, then remove from the pan and let cool completely on a wire rack. Wash and dry the pan and return the cake to it.

4 To make the filling, melt the chocolate and butter together, then remove from the heat. Stir in the confectioners' sugar, let cool, then beat until thick enough to spread.

5 Halve the cake lengthwise and cut each half into 3 layers. Sandwich the layers together with three-quarters of the chocolate filling. Spread the remainder over the cake and mark a wavy pattern on the top. Press the almonds onto the sides. Decorate with chocolate curls or grated chocolate before slicing and serving.

JEWEL-TOPPED MADEIRA CAKE

BRIGHTLY COLORED CRYSTALLIZED FRUITS MAKE A STUNNING AND UNUSUAL TOPPING FOR THIS
CLASSIC MADEIRA CAKE. IT WILL GO DOWN A TREAT WITH TEA, COFFEE, OR A GLASS OF SHERRY, OR
WHY NOT BRING IT OUT AS A SPECTACULAR FINALE TO A DINNER PARTY?

serves
8

preparation
25 minutes, plus
30 minutes'
cooling

cooking
1¼–1½ hours

ingredients
- 1 cup butter, softened, plus
  extra for greasing
- 1⅛ cups golden
  superfine sugar
- finely grated rind of
  1 lemon
- 4 eggs, beaten
- 2 cups self-rising flour,
  sifted
- 2–3 tbsp milk

FRUIT TOPPING
- 2½ tbsp honey
- 8 oz/225 g crystallized fruit

1 Preheat the oven to 325°F/160°C.
Grease and line the bottom of a deep
8-inch/20-cm round cake pan. Place
the butter, sugar, and lemon rind in a
bowl and beat together until light
and fluffy. Gradually beat in the eggs.
Gently fold in the flour, alternating
with enough milk to give a soft,
dropping consistency.

2 Transfer the mixture to the
prepared pan and bake in the
preheated oven for 1¼–1½ hours,
or until risen and golden and a
skewer inserted into the center
comes out clean.

3 Let cool in the pan for 10 minutes,
then turn out onto a wire rack and
remove the lining paper. Let cool
completely. To make the topping,
brush the honey over the cake and
arrange the fruit on top.

variation
*Traditionally, a Madeira cake is simply
decorated with a slice of candied peel on
top, which is placed on the cake after it
has been cooking for 1 hour.*

GINGERBREAD

THIS WONDERFULLY SPICY GINGERBREAD IS MADE BEAUTIFULLY MOIST BY THE ADDITION OF
CHOPPED FRESH APPLES. IT MAKES A PERFECT AFTER-DINNER TREAT, OR A DELICIOUS SNACK AT
ANY TIME OF THE DAY. IT IS VERY POPULAR WITH CHILDREN, SO GET YOUR SHARE WHILE YOU CAN.

makes

12 bars

preparation

25 minutes, plus
50 minutes'
cooling

cooking

35 minutes

ingredients

- generous ⅔ cup butter, plus extra for greasing
- ¾ cup packed brown sugar
- 2 tbsp molasses
- 1⅝ cups all-purpose flour
- 1 tsp baking powder
- 2 tsp baking soda
- 2 tsp ground ginger
- ⅔ cup milk
- 1 egg, beaten
- 2 eating apples, peeled, chopped, and coated with 1 tbsp lemon juice

1 Preheat the oven to 325°F/160°C. Grease a 9-inch/23-cm square cake pan and line with parchment paper.

2 Melt the butter, sugar, and molasses in a pan over low heat and let the mixture cool.

3 Sift the flour, baking powder, baking soda, and ginger into a mixing bowl. Stir in the milk, beaten egg, and cooled buttery liquid, followed by the chopped apples coated with the lemon juice.

4 Mix everything together gently, then pour into the prepared pan and smooth the surface.

5 Bake in the preheated oven for 30–35 minutes, or until the cake has risen and a fine skewer inserted into the center comes out clean.

6 Let the cake cool in the pan before turning out and cutting into 12 bars.

variation

If you enjoy the flavor of ginger, try adding 1 oz/25 g finely chopped preserved ginger to the batter in Step 3.

CHOCOLATE CHIP MUFFINS

MUFFINS ARE ALWAYS POPULAR AND ARE SO VERY SIMPLE TO MAKE. THEY MAKE FABULOUS BITE-SIZE TREATS FOR CHILDREN AND ADULTS ALIKE—AND ARE PERFECT FOR PARTIES TOO. OR WHY NOT POP THEM INTO LUNCH BOXES OR A PICNIC? THEY ARE SURE TO DELIGHT THE LUCKY RECIPIENTS.

makes
12

preparation
15 minutes,
plus 30 minutes'
cooling

cooking
25 minutes

ingredients
- 7 tbsp soft margarine
- 1⅛ cups superfine sugar
- 2 large eggs
- ⅔ cup whole-milk plain yogurt
- 5 tbsp milk
- scant 2 cups all-purpose flour
- 1 tsp baking soda
- 1 cup semisweet chocolate chips

1 Preheat the oven to 375°F/190°C. Line a 12-hole muffin pan with paper liners.

2 Place the margarine and sugar in a mixing bowl and beat with a wooden spoon until light and fluffy. Beat in the eggs, yogurt, and milk until combined.

3 Sift the flour and baking soda together and add to the mixture. Stir until just blended.

4 Stir in the chocolate chips, then spoon the batter into the paper liners and bake in the preheated oven for 25 minutes, or until a fine skewer inserted into the center comes out clean. Let cool in the pan for 5 minutes, then turn out onto a wire rack to cool completely before serving.

variation

The batter can also be used to make 6 large or 24 mini muffins. Bake mini muffins for 10 minutes, or until springy to the touch.

MANHATTAN CHEESECAKE

THIS IS AN ABSOLUTELY STUNNING EXAMPLE OF A CLASSIC AMERICAN BAKED CHEESECAKE. THE TRADITIONAL FRUITY BLUEBERRY TOPPING GIVES IT A WONDERFULLY DRAMATIC SPLASH OF COLOR. IT IS EASY TO PREPARE AND YOU CAN KEEP IT IN THE REFRIGERATOR UNTIL YOU NEED IT.

serves
8–10

preparation
20 minutes, plus
10 hours' cooling
and chilling

cooking
none

ingredients
- sunflower-seed oil, for brushing
- 6 tbsp butter
- 7 oz/200 g graham crackers, crushed
- 1¾ cups cream cheese
- 2 large eggs
- ¾ cup superfine sugar
- 1½ tsp vanilla extract
- 2 cups sour cream

BLUEBERRY TOPPING
- generous ¼ cup superfine sugar
- 4 tbsp water
- 1⅝ cups fresh blueberries
- 1 tsp arrowroot

1 Preheat the oven to 375°F/190°C. Brush an 8-inch/20-cm springform pan with oil. Melt the butter in a pan over low heat. Stir in the crackers, then spread in the pan. Place the cream cheese, eggs, ½ cup of the sugar, and ½ teaspoon of the vanilla extract in a food processor. Process until smooth. Pour over the cracker base and smooth the top. Place on a baking sheet and bake for 20 minutes until set. Remove from the oven and leave for 20 minutes. Leave the oven switched on.

2 Mix the cream with the remaining sugar and vanilla extract in a bowl. Spoon over the cheesecake. Return it to the oven for 10 minutes, let cool, then chill in the refrigerator for 8 hours, or overnight.

3 To make the topping, place the sugar in a pan with 2 tablespoons of the water over low heat and stir until the sugar has dissolved. Increase the heat, add the blueberries, cover, and cook for a few minutes, or until they begin to soften. Remove from the heat. Mix the arrowroot and remaining water in a bowl, add to the fruit, and stir until smooth. Return to low heat. Cook until the juice thickens and turns translucent. Let cool.

4 Remove the cheesecake from the pan 1 hour before serving. Spoon the fruit topping over and let chill until ready to serve.

cook's tip

If possible, it is best to leave the cheesecake to chill in the refrigerator overnight at the end of Step 2.

CRUNCHY PEANUT COOKIES

THESE RICH, CRUNCHY COOKIES WILL BE POPULAR WITH CHILDREN OF ALL AGES, SINCE THEY
CONTAIN ONE OF THEIR FAVORITE FOODS—PEANUT BUTTER. THEY ARE ALSO VERY NUTRITIOUS
BECAUSE THE PEANUTS ARE AN EXCELLENT SOURCE OF PROTEIN.

makes
20
preparation
15 minutes
cooking
15 minutes

ingredients
- 9 tbsp butter, softened, plus extra for greasing
- ½ cup chunky peanut butter
- 1⅛ cups granulated sugar
- 1 egg, lightly beaten
- generous 1 cup all-purpose flour
- ½ tsp baking powder
- pinch of salt
- ½ cup unsalted natural peanuts, chopped

1 Lightly grease 2 baking sheets. Beat the butter and peanut butter together in a large mixing bowl. Gradually add the granulated sugar and beat together well.

2 Add the beaten egg to the mixture, a little at a time, until it is thoroughly combined.

3 Sift the flour, baking powder, and salt into the peanut butter mixture. Add the peanuts and bring all of the ingredients together to form a soft

dough. Wrap in plastic wrap and let chill for 30 minutes. Preheat the oven to 375°F/190°C.

4 Form the dough into 20 balls and place them onto the prepared baking sheets about 2 inches/5 cm apart to allow for spreading. Flatten them slightly with your hand.

5 Bake in the preheated oven for 15 minutes, or until golden brown. Transfer the cookies to a wire rack and let cool.

cook's tip

For a crunchy bite and sparkling appearance, sprinkle the cookies with raw brown sugar before baking.

ALMOND BISCOTTI

BISCOTTI ARE HARD ITALIAN COOKIES THAT ARE TRADITIONALLY SERVED AT THE END OF A MEAL
FOR DIPPING INTO A SWEET WHITE WINE KNOWN AS VIN SANTO. THEY ARE EQUALLY DELICIOUS
SERVED WITH COFFEE OR ACCOMPANIED BY VANILLA OR ALMOND-FLAVORED ICE CREAM.

makes
20–24

preparation
20 minutes,
plus 20 minutes'
cooling

cooking
25 minutes

ingredients

- 1³/₄ cups all-purpose flour,
  plus extra for dusting
- 1 tsp baking powder
- pinch of salt
- ³/₄ cup golden
  superfine sugar

- 2 eggs, beaten
- finely grated rind of
  1 orange
- ⁵/₈ cup whole blanched
  almonds, lightly toasted

1 Preheat the oven to 350°F/180°C, then lightly dust a baking sheet with flour. Sift the flour, baking powder, and salt into a bowl. Add the sugar, eggs, and orange rind and mix to a dough. Knead in the toasted almonds.

2 Roll out the dough into a ball, cut in half, and roll out each portion into a log about 1¹/₂ inches/4 cm in

diameter. Place on the floured baking sheet and bake in the preheated oven for 10 minutes. Remove from the oven and let cool for 5 minutes.

3 Using a serrated knife, cut the logs into ¹/₂-inch/1-cm thick diagonal slices. Arrange the slices on the baking sheet and return to the oven for 15 minutes, or until slightly golden. Transfer to a wire rack to cool and crispen.

variation

*As an alternative to almonds, use hazelnuts
or a mixture of almonds and pistachio nuts.*

CHOCOLATE BROWNIES

YOU REALLY CAN HAVE A LOWFAT CHOCOLATE TREAT. THESE MOIST BARS CONTAIN A DRIED FRUIT PURÉE, WHICH ENABLES YOU TO BAKE WITHOUT ADDING FAT. SO THEY ARE THE PERFECT GUILT-FREE FOOD FOR THE AVID SLIMMER—AS LONG AS YOU HIDE THEM FROM THE REST OF YOUR HOUSEHOLD.

makes
12
preparation
55 minutes, plus
1 hour's cooling
and setting
cooking
35–40 minutes

ingredients
- butter, for greasing
- 1/3 cup unsweetened pitted dates, chopped
- 1/3 cup no-soak dried prunes, chopped
- 6 tbsp unsweetened apple juice
- 4 eggs, beaten
- 1 1/2 cups packed brown sugar
- 1 tsp vanilla extract
- 4 tbsp lowfat drinking chocolate powder, plus extra for dusting
- 2 tbsp unsweetened cocoa
- 1 1/4 cups all-purpose flour
- 1/3 cup semisweet chocolate chips

FROSTING
- 1 1/8 cups confectioners' sugar
- 1–2 tsp water
- 1 tsp vanilla extract

1 Preheat the oven to 350°F/180°C. Grease and line a 7 x 11 inch/ 18 x 28 cm cake pan with parchment paper. Place the dates and prunes in a small pan and add the apple juice. Bring to a boil, cover, and let simmer for 10 minutes until soft. Beat to form a smooth paste, then let cool.

2 Place the cooled fruit in a mixing bowl and stir in the eggs, sugar, and vanilla extract. Sift in 4 tablespoons of drinking chocolate, the cocoa, and the flour, and fold in along with the chocolate chips until well incorporated.

3 Spoon the batter into the prepared pan and smooth over the top. Bake in the preheated oven for 25–30 minutes until firm to the touch or until a skewer inserted into the center comes out clean. Cut into 12 bars and let cool in the pan for 10 minutes. Transfer to a wire rack to cool completely.

4 To make the frosting, sift the sugar into a bowl and mix with enough water and the vanilla extract to form a soft, but not too runny, frosting.

5 Drizzle the frosting over the chocolate brownies and let set. Dust with the extra chocolate powder before serving.

cook's tip

Make double the amount, cut one of the cakes into bars and open freeze, then store in freezer bags. Take out pieces of cake as required—they'll take no time to thaw.

GLOSSARY

THIS GLOSSARY IS NOT INTENDED TO BE EXHAUSTIVE BUT TO PROVIDE A CONCISE GUIDE TO KEY TERMS WITH WHICH A BEGINNER MAY NOT BE FAMILIAR. SOME OF THE BASIC COOKING TECHNIQUES AND INGREDIENTS, INCLUDING SEVERAL OUTLINED EARLIER IN THIS BOOK, ARE LISTED HERE FOR EASE OF REFERENCE.

A

Agar-agar Thickening and setting agent made from seaweed. It is vegetarian alternative to gelatin.

Al dente Italian term, literally meaning "at the teeth," indicating desired texture of cooked pasta, soft on the outside but still firm and not overcooked inside.

Antipasto Italian term, literally meaning "before pasta," denoting a hot or cold appetizer, or "hors d'oeuvres."

Arborio rice Medium- to long-grain type of rice, from Northern Italy, which is ideal for risotto because it absorbs liquid while retaining a firm texture.

Arrowroot Starch extract of maranta root used to thicken sauces.

Aspic Clear jelly made from clarified meat, fish, or vegetable stock mixed with gelatin. It is used to glaze or protect meat or fish and other foods, or for savory dishes set in a mold.

B

Bain-marie Method of cooking ingredients where they are placed in a dish, which is in turn placed in a shallow container of water and is gently heated in an oven or on a stove. This is used to melt ingredients, such as chocolate, without burning them.

Baking powder Raising agent used in baking cakes, cookies, and breads. It usually contains baking soda, tartaric acid, and dried starch or flour for absorbing moisture.

Balsamic vinegar Dark brown vinegar from Italy, made from fermented, reduced white grape juice, and aged in wooden barrels.

Basmati rice Small but long-grain type of rice grown in the Himalayan foothills. It is a creamy yellow with a nutty a flavor and aroma.

Basting Spooning or brushing food during cooking with melted fat or stock to add flavor, color, and to prevent the food from drying out.

Bay leaf Aromatic herb used for flavoring meat, casseroles, and soups, often in a bouquet garni.

Béarnaise sauce French sauce made from reduced vinegar, white wine, tarragon, black peppercorns, and shallots, finished with egg yolks and butter.

Béchamel sauce Basic French, smooth white sauce made from flour stirred into a mixture of milk and butter.

Beurre manié French term meaning "kneaded butter," a mixture of flour and softened butter, used to thicken sauces.

Bisque Thick, rich soup, made with cream and usually including shellfish.

Black butter Butter cooked over low heat until brown and usually flavored with vinegar or lemon juice, capers, and parsley.

Black pepper Dried whole peppercorn, which is often crushed or ground to add flavor to food.

Blanching Technique of plunging food into boiling water then placing in cold water to stop the cooking process. This is used to loosen skins, or preserve color and flavor.

Blind baking Partially cooking a pastry shell before the filling is added. This involves cooking the pie dough with a foil or paper lining and weighing down with cooking weights (such as baking beans). It avoids overcooking the dough or making its bottom too moist when the filling is added.

Borsch or borscht Eastern European soup made with beet, cabbage, and/or other vegetables and served hot or cold with sour cream.

Bouillabaisse Fish stew from southern France.

Bouquet garni Small group of herbs, usually parsley, bayleaf, and thyme, tied together, and used to flavor soups, casseroles, and stocks in cooking, but removed before serving.

Brochette Cubes of meat or fish and vegetables cooked on a skewer.

Buttermilk Sour-tasting liquid remaining when milk has been churned to butter. It is often used in biscuits and soda breads.

C

Calvados Northern French dry spirit made from distilled cider and used to flavor meat dishes.

Canapés Small appetizers, often served with drinks.

Capers Sun-dried flower buds of a shrub from the Mediterranean and parts of Asia. They need to be rinsed to remove excess salt or brine, and are used to provide a piquant flavor to sauces or condiments, or as a garnish.

Caramelizing Heating sugar until it melts and turns brown, resetting as a hard glaze, or cooking chopped fruit or vegetables in water and sugar until they brown and glaze.

Cayenne pepper Ground spice powder with a hot flavor, made from the flesh and seeds of chili pepper.

Chantilly cream Sweetened heavy whipped cream, often flavored with vanilla, used as a topping for desserts, or folded into custards or cream for fillings.

Chiffonade Thin strips of shredded vegetables (usually sorrel or lettuce), used raw or lightly sautéed, often as a garnish.

Chili Chili peppers are small, come in many varieties, and are characterized by their extremely hot seeds and flesh. Their potency can be reduced by removing their seeds, but this must be done carefully. It is important to avoid touching sensitive skin or eyes when handling chilies and to wash your hands thoroughly immediately afterward.

Chinois Conical, fine-meshed strainer used to strain soups and sauces.

Choux pastry Light, double-cooked dough used to make cakes and buns. It has a hard, crisp exterior and a hollow inside.

Clarified butter Unsalted butter heated slowly to evaporate the water content, and then strained to separate the milk solids. The clarified butter can then be used for cooking at higher temperatures than normal butter without burning.

Compote Dish of fruit, slowly cooked whole or in sugar.

Cornstarch Fine, white, powdered starch extract of corn, used to thicken sauces. To avoid it forming lumps, the cornstarch should be mixed with twice its amount of cold liquid before being added to the sauce, which should be constantly stirred until it boils.

Coulis Thick and smooth fruit or vegetable sauce. It may be served hot or cold.

Court-bouillon Spiced stock commonly used for cooking fish, seafood, or vegetables.

Crêpe French term for pancake. Crêpes can be made from plain or sweetened batters with different flavors and for savory and dessert dishes.

Crème fraîche French term for a thickened, tangy-flavored cream made from pasteurized cow's milk.

Croutons Small cubes of broiled, toasted, or fried bread, which then drained and cooled. Used to garnish salads or soups.

Crudités Raw seasonal vegetables, sometimes sliced or grated, usually served as an appetizer with a dipping sauce.

Custard A smooth mixture of eggs and milk that can be used as the basis for a savory or sweet sauce or dish.

D
Dariole Small, steep-sided cylindrical mold for shaping dough, or the dough cooked in it.

Daube French dish of red meat, vegetables, and seasoning, slowly braised in a red wine stock. It can also refer to the method of cooking meat, some vegetables, or fish in a similar way.

Dauphinoise (à la) French term referring to the method of slowly baking in an oven with cream and garlic (such as potatoes).

Descaling Removing the scales from a fish by scraping the back of a knife along its surface, from the tail to the head.

Dropping consistency Required consistency of cake batter, where it falls reluctantly from the spoon.

E
Emulsifying Combining fats (for instance, butter or oil) and vinegar or citric juices together with a binding agent such as egg yolk.

Entrecôte French term, meaning "between the ribs," referring to a tender beef joint, cut from the sirloin.

Escalope French term for a very thin slice of meat or fish, often flattened for quick cooking.

Extract Concentrated extract or oil from foods such as fish, almonds, vanilla, coffee beans, or various plants, and used to flavor foods.

F
Fines herbes French term referring to a mixture of chopped aromatic herbs, usually chervil, tarragon, parsley, and chives, used to flavor dishes.

Florentine In the style of a dish from Florence, usually referring to dishes served on a bed of cooked spinach. Also a small cookie of dried fruit and nuts, coated in chocolate on one side.

Fond French term for stock.

French dressing Cold sauce, made from olive oil and wine vinegar, seasoned with herbs, and salt and pepper, and used to dress salads.

Fricassée Stew made from lightly frying white meat, such as chicken, and then cooking it in a white sauce with vegetables.

Fritter Piece of meat, fish, or vegetable coated in batter and deep-fried until crisp and cooked.

Fromage frais Fresh, soft, cream cheese that has the consistency of sour cream.

G
Galangal Spice related to ginger and used in south-east Asian cooking for flavor.

Garam masala Mixture of dry-roasted, ground spices, including cumin, coriander, and turmeric, mixed to form a paste, or added to a dish for flavor just before the end of cooking.

Gelatin Setting agent derived from the protein of animal bones, used to set sweet or savory jellies or thicken soups. Agar-agar is a vegetarian alternative, derived from red algae.

Ghee Type of clarified butter with a nutty, caramel-like flavor, created by simmering butter until the milk solids turn brown. It can be used for sautéing or frying at higher temperatures than normal butter without burning.

Gluten Flour protein, which gives dough elasticity and strength when mixed with water.

Granita Italian sherbet made from sweetened syrup flavored with coffee or liqueur and often served as a refreshment.

Gratin Any dish topped with cheese or bread crumbs, mixed with pieces of butter and heated until crisp and brown.

Gravy Sauce made from meat juices, mixed with a stock, wine, or milk and thickened with flour. Also refers to the juices remaining in the pan after meat, fish, or poultry has been cooked.

Griddle Flat, shallow, cast-iron pan, usually with ridges, for cooking food on a stove.

H
Harissa North African paste with a very hot flavor, made from chilies, garlic, cumin, coriander, mint, and oil. It is usually served with couscous, and is used to flavor soups and stews.

Herbes de Provence Mixture of herbs traditionally used in the Provence region of southern France, usually consisting of

basil, bay, marjoram, oregano, parsley, rosemary, tarragon, and thyme.

Hoisin sauce Thick, reddish-brown, sweet and spicy Chinese sauce, made from a mixture of soybeans, garlic, chili peppers, and spices, commonly used as a table condiment or flavoring.

Hollandaise Rich, creamy, and smooth sauce made from egg yolks, butter, and lemon juice, and usually served on vegetables, fish, or egg dishes.

Horseradish Herb grown for its leaves (for salads) and root. The pungent and spicy root is peeled and grated, and used to flavor sauces.

I
Infusing Imbuing a liquid (usually hot or boiling) with the flavors of herbs, spices, tea, or coffee, by letting them stand in the liquid.

J
Jambalaya Spicy Creole rice dish traditionally including ham, sausage, chilies, and tomatoes, but can also consist of any kind of meat, poultry, or shellfish.

Julienne Shredded or thinly cut vegetables or citrus zest, commonly used as a garnish.

Jus French term for "juice," referring to fruit or vegetable extract, or juice from meat.

K
Kedgeree Traditional British breakfast dish, originally deriving

from India, consisting of rice, flaked fish (usually smoked haddock), and hard-cooked eggs.

Kneading Stretching and mixing dough by hand or mechanically, to make it smoother, softer, more elastic and pliable. The movement helps the gluten strands in the dough to stretch and enables the dough to retain gas bubbles and rise when cooked.

L
Lardons Small chunks of fat bacon or pork fat used to flavor dishes.

Lemon grass Root used in south-east Asian (especially Thai) cooking to impart a lemon flavor to sweet or savory dishes.

Lyonnaise (à la) French term describing dishes including chopped onions. Lyonnaise sauce is made with sautéed onions and white wine and is then strained. It is usually served with meat or poultry dishes.

M
Mace Pungent spice made from the outer membrane of nutmeg, used to flavor various sweet and savory dishes.

Macerating Soaking fruit in a liquid, such as brandy, to soften and add flavor.

Madeleine Small, buttery sponge cake, made with sugar, flour, butter, and eggs, usually flavored with lemon or almonds.

Marinating Soaking food in a seasoned liquid mixture, or

marinade (usually containing oil, lemon, or wine, herbs, and spices), to tenderize and add flavor.

Marinière (à la) French term meaning "in the style of a mariner," referring to cooking shellfish, or other seafood, in white wine and herbs. It can also refer to a dish garnished with mussels.

Mascarpone Thick, creamy, and soft Italian cheese used in savory and sweet dishes.

Mayonnaise Thick, creamy dressing made from oil, egg yolks, vinegar or lemon juice, and seasoning.

Meringue Light, sweet dessert made by stiffly beating egg white and sugar together and baking.

Meunière (à la) French term meaning "in the style of a miller's wife," referring to the method of cooking where the food (usually fish) is coated in flour, then shallow-fried in butter.

Mille-feuille French term for "a thousand leaves," referring to a dessert made from puff pastry, whipped cream, jelly, or fruit.

Miso Paste made from soybeans and used as a flavoring in Japanese cooking, including soups, sauces, and dressings.

Molasses By-product of refining sugar, molasses is a thick, dark brown syrup with a slightly bitter flavor.

Mornay sauce Béchamel sauce with grated cheese (usually Gruyère or Parmesan) added, often served with fish, egg, or vegetable dishes.

Mustard Plant with piquant-tasting seeds which are used whole, ground, or powdered form as a flavoring for seasoning, dressings, sauces, and accompaniments.

N

Navarin French stew made from lamb or mutton, potatoes, and other vegetables.

Noodles Thin pasta strips, made with flour, water, and egg or egg yolk.

O

Olive oil Rich oil, extracted from pressed olives, used for shallow-frying, dressings, marinades, and baking. Extra virgin olive oil is the purest form of the oil, taken from the first pressing of the olives.

P

Pancetta Italian bacon cured with salt and spices and used to flavor pasta, rice, soup, or salad dishes.

Panna cotta Italian term meaning "cooked cream," referring to a cold dessert made from a set custard of cream and gelatin, often flavored with vanilla or caramel.

Papillote (en) French term meaning "in a parcel," referring to a method of cooking food in a folded parcel of waxed paper, to protect it from the high heat of the oven and help it retain moisture and flavor.

Parboiling Boiling food until half-cooked, in preparation for adding to other ingredients with shorter cooking times or to tenderize the food before roasting (as with potatoes).

Parmesan Hard, dry cheese, made from skim cow's milk, with a rich, sharp taste and used grated, usually after cooking, to flavor a dish, especially pasta and sauce.

Pasta Italian for "paste," referring to the dough made from durum-wheat semolina, water, and sometimes egg. Pasta comes in a wide variety of shapes and sizes and is served with sauces or soups.

Pectin Natural gelling agent extracted from ripe fruit and vegetables, and used in making preserves and jellies.

Pesto Italian term meaning "pounded," referring to a green sauce made from a blend of pine nuts, fresh basil, Parmesan cheese, garlic, and olive oil. It is most commonly served with Pasta or as a dressing.

Phyllo pastry Very thin layers of pie dough, often used in Greek or Middle Eastern dishes, which dry out and cook very quickly.

Pita bread Middle Eastern flat, hollow bread made from flour or whole wheat flour and usually served with fillings or to accompany spicy dishes and dips.

Polenta Italian cornmeal porridge, which can be eaten hot or, when cooled and firm, fried.

Prosciutto Italian term for a ham that has been seasoned, salt-cured, and air dried, and served very thinly sliced, traditionally as an appetizer.

Puréeing Grinding or mashing fruit or vegetables to form a very smooth paste, manually by pressing the food through a strainer, or mechanically.

Q

Quenelle Small dumpling made from seasoned ground meat, fish, or ground vegetables, bound with eggs and usually poached in stock.

Quiche Open pie-dough tart, usually filled with an egg and milk custard and savory ingredients.

Quinoa Small, beadlike grain, very rich in protein and mild in taste, which is cooked and served like rice.

R

Ragoût Thick, well-seasoned French stew consisting of meat, poultry, fish, or vegetables, flavored with wine.

Ratatouille French vegetable stew consisting of eggplants, zucchini, tomatoes, onions, sweet bell peppers, and garlic simmered in olive oil.

Reducing Boiling a liquid, such as stock, wine, or sauce, quickly to reduce its volume by evaporation, thicken it and concentrate the flavors.

Relaxing Leaving dough to "rest" after rolling in order to prevent it shrinking.

Ricotta Rich, creamy, and smooth Italian cheese made from the curd of ewe's milk, used in many Italian dishes and as a stuffing for pasta.

Rissole Sweet or savory round pastry, filled with chopped meat or fish and bread crumbs and cooked by frying or baking.

Risotto Italian rice dish, made by gradually mixing hot stock and rice during cooking to ensure that the rice absorbs the liquid. Traditionally, arborio rice is used because of its capacity to absorb liquid and retain a firm texture.

Rösti Swiss term meaning "crisp and golden," referring to a flat, round pancake of shredded potato, shallow-fried on both sides until crisp and brown.

Rouille French term meaning "rust," referring to a hot, chili-flavored red sauce usually served as a garnish with fish or fish stews.

Roulade French term, referring to a sweet or savory rolled dish. The savory dish may be a slice of meat, poultry, or fish rolled around a filling, while the sweet dish is a filled and rolled sponge.

Roux Mixture of flour and fat, slowly cooked over low heat, and used as a base for soups and sauces to thicken them.

S

Saffron Pungent and aromatic spice, yellow in color, and available in whole or powdered form, which is used for coloring and flavoring dishes. The spice is derived from the stigmas of the saffron crocus and is very expensive.

Salsa Spanish term meaning "sauce," and specifically referring to a spicy, hot-flavored, thick relish made from chilies and fruit, and served cold.

Salt Sodium chloride crystals, used for seasoning and preserving food. It is available in various forms, including sea salt and rock salt, from which cooking and table salt are derived.

Samosa Indian triangle-shaped pastry, filled with spiced meat or vegetables, and deep-fried.

Satay Indonesian speciality, consisting of meat, fish, or poultry cubes, broiled on a skewer, and usually served with a spicy sauce.

Sherbet Smooth, semifrozen water ice mixed with fruit juice or liqueur, and sometimes egg white or Gelatin, and commonly served as a dessert.

Shucking To remove the edible part of food from its outer casing, such as removing an oyster from its shell, using a small, thick-bladed knife.

Sirloin Premium cut of tender beef, from the back, available as tenderloin steaks or joints for roasting.

Slaking Mixing a thickening agent with a liquid.

Smoothie Thick, smooth, and cold drink made from blending fruits or vegetables, often with liquids, such as water, milk, or ice cream.

Soy sauce Sauce commonly used in Chinese and Japanese cooking, made from fermented and boiled soybeans. It is used to flavor sauces, soups, marinades, meat, fish, and vegetables.

Stock Flavored, strained liquid made by cooking meat, fish, poultry, and vegetables, with seasoning, in water, used for flavoring sauces, soups, stews, or braised dishes.

Strained canned tomatoes Smooth Italian-style tomato sauce.

Sweating Method of cooking ingredients, usually vegetables, in a little fat, slowly over low heat so that they cook in their own steam without browning.

T

Tabasco sauce Hot-flavored, spicy sauce made from Tabasco chili peppers, vinegar, and salt, and used to add flavor to sauces, meat or cocktails.

Tapenade Thick French paste made from black olives, capers, anchovies, lemon juice, olive oil, and herbs, used to flavor sauces, marinades, stews, pasta, or meat.

Tarte Tatin French apple tart made in a shallow dish by covering butter, sugar, and apples with a pie-dough topping and baking until the ingredients caramelize. The tart is served upside down.

Terrine Pâté cooked in a small, fat-lined, deep-sided dish (also called a terrine), and usually made from pieces of fish or meat.

Timbale Dish cooked in a mold (also called a timbale), consisting of layers, usually of rice and vegetables.

Tisane Infusion of herbs in boiling water, drunk hot.

Tofu Curd of the soybean, pressed into firm cheeselike blocks, which is bland in flavor but rich in iron and protein. Commonly used in Asian dishes, it can be cooked in soups, stir-fries, casseroles, or sauces.

Turmeric Spice derived from root of a ginger-related plant, with a yellow color and bitter taste, used in Asian cooking to add color and flavor.

U

Unsweetened pie dough Crumbly pie dough used for sweet or savory pies and tarts.

V

Vanilla Sweet and fragrant flavoring extracted from the dried beans and seeds of the vanilla orchid, used to flavor sweet and savory foods.

Vichyssoise Rich and creamy soup, served cold, made from potatoes, leeks, and cream, and garnished with chopped chives.

Vinaigrette Cold sauce made from a mixture of vinegar, oil, and seasoning, normally used as a dressing for leaf salads or other cold dishes.

W

White sauce Basic smooth sauce, also known as Béchamel, made from flour stirred into a mixture of milk and butter.

Y

Yeast Microscopic, live fungus that converts its food, through fermentation, into carbon dioxide and alcohol and is therefore used in bread-making to make dough rise, or in brewing to make alcohol.

Z

Zabaglione Italian frothy dessert made by whisking egg yolks, wine, and sugar together, while heating gently, is served slightly warm.

Zest Fragrant outer rind of a citrus fruit, grated or shredded and used to add flavor or as a garnish to a dish.

INDEX

agar-agar 312
alcohol 13, 47
al dente 312
allspice 214
almonds 43, 301, 309
anchovies 204
antipasto 312
apple corer 17
apples 250
    apple strudel 268
    in braised red cabbage 200
    in gingerbread 304
    golden baked pudding 265
    in roast chicken salad 205
    with roast duck 167
    stuffed baked 261
    traditional apple pie 260
apricots 225, 251, 261, 269
arrowroot 312
artichokes 91, 198
aspic 312
avocado 180
azuki beans 42, 230

bacon 119, 126, 150, 191, 238
bain-marie 312
bakeware 18
baking 34
    blind 35, 312
    bread 272–3, 276–85
    cakes/cookies 274–5, 300–11
    pastry/pie dough 274, 288–94, 298
baking powder 312
bananas 252, 266, 281
barbecue 37, 143, 172
barding 24
barley 231
basil 44, 212, 218
basins 19
basting 24, 312
batter 102, 103
bay 213, 222, 245, 312
beans
    cassoulet 245
    chili con carne 246
    crispy noodle stir-fry 196
    dried 230
    French 242
    fresh 180
bean sprouts 196
beating 24–5
béchamel sauce 133, 203, 312
beef 116–27, 130–3
    bourguignon 119
    broiled steak with tomatoes & garlic 125
    chili con carne 246
    Chinese noodles 247

choosing cuts 112, 113
    fajitas 122
    goulash, Hungarian 121
    moussaka 133
    potato & leek pasties 293
    roasting 114, 115, 116
    shepherd's pie 130
    spaghetti bolognese 232
    steak & kidney pudding 289
    steak, in mixed grill 126
    stroganoff 120
beet 176, 182
bell peppers 180
    ratatouille 187
    roast summer vegetables 192
    peeling 37
    stuffed red, with basil 199
    in vegetable jalousie 292
    in vegetable lasagna 235
berries, dried 47
berry yogurt ice 254
beurre manié 140, 312
biscotti, almond 309
biscuits, cherry 297
bisque 312
blackberries 252, 254, 266
black-eye peas 42, 230
blanch 32, 312
blend 26
blenders 22
blinis 286
blow torch 37
blueberries 252, 307
boil 32, 52–3
bok choy 178
borscht 182, 312
bottled food 47
bottle opener 21
bouillabaisse 312
bouillon cubes 47
bouquet garni 212, 245, 312
bowls 19
braising 35, 150, 200
brassicas 178
bread
    baking 40, 272–3
    banana & orange 281
    Chelsea buns 285
    croissants 282
    croûtes 184
    croutons 204, 313
    crusty white 276
    mixed seed 279
    olive & sun-dried tomato 280
    pantry essential 47
    pita 315
    recipes using 97, 265, 298
    sauce 168
    whole wheat harvest 277

broccoli 178
brochette 312
broil 37
Brussels sprouts 178
buckwheat flour 286
bulgar wheat 41, 231, 243
buns, Chelsea 285
butter
    black 312
    buying/storing 47, 54–5
    clarified 25, 313
butterfly 26, 112
buttermilk 312

cabbage 178, 200, 247
Caesar salad 204
cakes 274–5, 296–307
Calvados 312
canapés 312
canned food 47
cannellini beans 42, 230
can opener 17
capers 312
carambola 253
caramelize 33–4, 312
caraway 214
carbohydrates 10
cardamon 214
carrots 176, 196
carving 114, 152–3
cashew nuts 43
casserole 36
cassoulet 245
cauliflower 178
cayenne pepper 214, 312–13
celery root 176
cellophane noodles 228
cereals, in diet 10, 12, 13
Chantilly cream 313
chargrill 36–7, 172
cheese
    buying/storing 47, 55
    fondue 63
    sauce 235
cheesecake, Manhattan 307
Chelsea buns 285
cherries 251, 266, 297
chervil 213, 221
chicken
    biryani 156
    buying/storing 150
    fricassée 159
    and ginger stir-fry 163
    in paella 95
    potato & leek pasties 293
    preparation/cooking 152–3
    roast 152, 155
    salad with orange dressing 205
    spaghetti bolognese 232

tarragon 219
    Thai red curry 157
chickpeas 42, 230
chiffonade 26, 313
chili con carne 246
chilies 108, 180, 313
chili powder 45, 214
Chinese fried rice 238
Chinese noodles 247
Chinois 313
chives 213, 221
chocolate 47
    and almond layer cake 301
    and brandy sauce 294
    brownies 310
    chip ice cream 75
    chip muffins 305
    fudge sauce 75
    milk shake 78
    sponge cake 275
cholesterol 11, 12
chop 27
chops 112, 113, 142
chorizo 95
cilantro 213, 225, 242
cinnamon 45, 214, 225, 260, 265, 268, 269
clams 85
clarify 25, 313
cloves 44, 215
cocoa 47
coconut milk 47
cod 83
    and french fries 103
    seafood gratin 97
    smoked fish pie 107
coffee 13
compote 313
condiments 45, 46
conversion charts 23
cooked food, reheating 14
cookies 274–5, 308–11
cooking methods 30–7
cooling racks 21
coriander seeds 44, 215
corkscrew 21
corn 47, 181
cornmeal 41, 231, 237, 315
cornstarch 40, 313
coulis 313
court-bouillon 313
couscous 41, 225, 231, 242
crab 84
cranberries 252, 300
cranberry beans 42, 230
cream 28, 55, 294
crème anglaise 313
crème brûlée tarts 37, 70
crème caramel 73

crépes 67
crimp 29
croissants 282
cross-hatch 29
croûtes 184
croutons 204, 313
crudités 313
crushing 24
cucumber 181, 205
cumin 44, 215
cure 28
currants
    dried 300
    white/red/black 252
curry
    paste 46
    powder 45, 215
    shrimp & pineapple 99
    Thai red chicken 157
custard 73, 313
cut 28
cutting boards 14, 21

dairy products
    buying/storing 47, 54–5
    in diet 12
    recipes 60–79
dariole 313
dates 253, 266, 269, 300, 310
daube 313
dauphinoise 313
deep-fryer 22
deep-fry 30
deglaze 25
degorge 29
descaling 313
dice 29
dill 44, 213, 222
dredge 28
dressing 28, 205, 206, 313, 316
dried fruit 47, 265, 285
drinking 13
drinks, milk shakes 78–9
dropping consistency 313
dry-fry 31
duck 151
    breasts with chili & lime 164
    Peking duck 165
    roast 153, 167

egg noodles 228, 247
eggs 56–60, 67–75
    benedict 56
    buying/storing 47, 52
    cooking methods 52–3
    florentine 57
    separating 53
    Spanish tortilla 59
    sweet soufflé omelet

whisking whites 52, 68
electric utensils 22
emulsify 27, 313
enrich 27
entrecôte 313
equipment 16–22
eggplants 180
    baked 203
    gratin 64
    mixed vegetable gratin 198
    moussaka 133
    ratatouille 187
    roast summer vegetables 192
    vegetable lasagna 235
exotic fruits 253
exotic vegetables 181
extract 313

fat, in diet 11, 12, 13
fennel
    bulb 192, 222
    herb 213
    seeds 214
feta cheese 206
figs 253
fines herbes 221, 313
fire 14, 15
first aid kit 15
fish 86–109
    buying/storing 82
    cakes 87
    canned 47
    cooked with dill 222
    Greek baked 96
    oily 13, 82, 83
    pie 107
    sauce 46
    smoked 82, 107
    types 82–3
five spice 45, 215
flageolet beans 230
flambé 34
florentine 57, 313
flounder 83, 104
flour 40
folding 24
fond 313
food
    buying 15
    preparation 14, 24–9
    storage 15
food mixer 22
food processor 22
freezer
    essentials 47
    open freeze 28
French dressing 313
fricassée 159, 313
fritter 313

fromage frais 313
fruit 254–69
    buying/storing 250
    crystallized 302
    in diet 12, 13
    dried 47, 265, 285
    poaching 34
    types 250–3
fruit cake, rich 300
fruit salad, tropical 258
frying 30–1, 53

galangal 313
game
    buying/storing 150
    pheasant 151, 170
    quail 151, 171
    venison 150, 151, 172
garam masala 215, 313
garlic 179, 189, 192
garlic press 21
gelatin 47, 314
ghee 25, 314
ginger 44, 215, 225, 260, 261
gingerbread 304
glaze 27
gluten 314
gnocchi 236
golden raisins 265, 268, 297, 300
goose 151
gooseberries 252
grains
    in diet 10, 12, 13
    types 41, 231
granita 314
grapefruit 251
grapes 252
grate 17, 29
gratin dishes 64, 97, 198, 314
gravy 314
grease 28
Greek salad 206
griddle 36, 314
grind 22, 24, 29
grouse 151
guinea fowl 150

haddock 83, 107
hake 83
ham, steaks 128
halibut 83
haricot beans 230
harissa 46, 314
hazelnuts 43
health and safety 14–15, 20, 52, 55
healthy eating 10–13
herbes de Provence 314
herbs and spices 216–25
    buying/storing 212

dried 44
    types 212–15
herrings 83
hoisin sauce 46, 165, 314
hollandaise sauce 56, 314
horseradish 46, 314
hygiene 14–15
ice cream
    berry yogurt ice 254
    chocolate chip 75
    orange sherbet 257
    rich vanilla 74
ice-cream scoop 21
infusing 24, 314

jambalaya 314
julienne 27, 314
juniper 214
jus 314

kabobs, lamb 129
kedgeree 314
kidney beans 42, 230, 245, 246
kiwifruit 253, 266
knead 26, 272, 314
knives 16–17
knock back 25, 273

lamb 126, 129–39
    biryani 156
    choosing cuts 113
    kabobs 129
    kidneys, in mixed grill 126
    preparation techniques 112
    Provençal barbecued 136
    rack of 112, 134
    roasting 114, 115
    rogan josh 139
    shanks with roasted onions 137
    shepherd's pie 130
    tagine 225
lard 27
lardons 314
lasagna, vegetable 235
leafy vegetables 177
leeks 179, 183, 288, 292, 293
lemon 251
    meringue pie 69
    tarte au citron 262
lemon grass 314
lemon squeezer 21
lentils 42, 230, 241
lettuce 177, 204
lima beans 42, 230
limes 251, 266
line 25
litchis 253
lobster 84, 95
lyonnaise 314

mace 44, 214, 314
macerate 28, 314
mackerel 82, 83
Madeira cake, jewel-topped 302
madeleine 314
mandarin family 251
mango 253, 258, 266
marble 26
marinades 14, 126, 136, 143, 160, 164, 172
marinate 25, 314
marinière 314
marjoram 213
marscapone 314
mash 27, 130
mayonnaise 314
mealtimes 13
measurements, conversion 23
measuring equipment 16
meat
    bacon/ham recipes 126–8
    beef recipes 116–27, 130–3
    buying/storing 14, 15, 112, 113
    cooking/carving 114–15
    lamb recipes 126, 129–39
    pork recipes 126–8, 140–3
    preparation techniques 112
    roasting 114–15
    stuffing 112
    thawing 14
    veal recipes 144–7
melon 253
meringue 68, 69, 314
meunière 314
milk 47, 54, 78
mille-feuille 314
millet 231
minerals 11
mint 134, 213, 216, 243
miso 46, 314
mixed herbs 44
molasses 315
mornay sauce 315
molds, decorative 21
mortar and pestle 21
moussaka 133
muffins, chocolate chip 305
mushrooms 181
    crispy noodle stir-fry 196
    and spinach packages 290
    in vegetable jalousie 292
    vegetable lasagna 235
mustard 46, 214, 315

Napa cabbage 178, 196
navarin 315
nectarines 79, 250
noodles 315
    see also pasta

Chinese 247
    types 41, 228
    and vegetable stir-fry 196
nutmeg 44, 215, 268
nuts, types 43
oiling 28
oils 38–9
olive oil 38, 206, 315
olives 47, 206, 243, 280
omelets 58–9, 221
onions 179
    Greek salad 206
    and leek tartlets 288
    les Halles soup 184
    roasted 137, 192
orange 251
    and banana bread 281
    dressing 205
    sherbet 257
    tropical fruit salad 258
oregano 44, 213, 292
organic produce 13
oven temperatures 23, 115, 152
ovenware 18
oysters 85

paella 95
pancakes
    blinis 286
    potato 171
pancetta 315
pan-fry 31
panna cotta 315
pantries 38–47
papaya 253, 258, 266
papillote 315
paprika 45, 214
parboil 315
Parmesan cheese 315
parsley 213, 221, 242, 243, 245, 247
parsnips 176, 198
partridge 151
passion fruit 253, 266
pasta
    buying/storing 228
    cooking 228, 229
    machine 22
    making 229
    spaghetti bolognese 232
    types 41, 228–9, 315
    vegetable lasagna 235
paste, types 46
pasties, potato, beef & leek 293
pastry 288–94, 298
    bags/tips 21
    brush 21
    choux 274, 294, 313
    cutters 17

phyllo 268, 313
    puff 290, 292
    suet crust 289
peaches 251
peanuts 43, 308
pears 250
peas 180, 216
pecan nuts 43
peel 29
peppercorns 45, 214
pesto 46, 218, 315
pheasant 151, 170
pickled foods 47
pie dough 288–94, 298
    handling 70
    savory 60
    sweet 69, 70, 274
    unsweetened 260, 262, 274, 293, 316
pie funnel 21
pilaf, brown rice vegetable 241
pineapple 253
    barbecued 143
    and ham steaks 128
    and shrimp curry 99
    tropical fruit dessert 266
    tropical fruit salad 258
pine nuts 43, 218
pistachio nuts 43
pita bread 315
plums 251
plum sauce 46
poach 34, 53
pod vegetables 180
polenta 315
pork 126–8, 140–3
    buying/storing 112
    cassoulet 245
    choosing cuts 112, 113
    citrus chops 142
    crackling 114
    potato & leek pasties 293
    pot-roast 140
    roasting 114, 115
    sweet-&-sour ribs 143
potatoes 176
    beef & leek pasties 293
    dauphinois 190
    French fries 103
    garlic mashed 189
    gnocchi with quick tomato sauce 236
    and leek soup 183
    mashed 130
    pancakes 171
    roast 188
    storage 15
    stuffed baked 191
potato masher 21

pot-roast 36, 140
pots and pans 18
poultry 154–71
    buying/storing 15, 150
    jointing 153
    preparation/cooking 152–3
    thawing 14
    types 150–1
preparation techniques 24–9
pressure cooker 22
processed foods 13
profiteroles 294
prosciutto 315
protein 10, 12
prunes 300, 310
pulses 42, 47, 230
pumpkin 181
pumpkin pie spice 45, 215, 260, 285, 300
purée 29, 46, 315

quail 151, 171
quenelle 315
quiche lorraine 60, 315
quinoa 315

rabbit 150, 151
radishes 176
ragoût 315
raisins 300
ramen noodles 228
raspberries 252, 254
ratatouille 187, 315
red cabbage 178, 200
red snapper 96
reduce 32, 315
refrigerators 14, 15, 47
relaxing 315
rhubarb 253
rice
    arborio 240, 312
    basmati 312
    brown, vegetable pilaf 241
    buying/storing 231
    Chinese fried 238
    cooking 231
    flour 40
    keeping cooked rice 14
    noodles 228
    paella 95
    risotto Milanese 240
    stuffed red bell peppers 199
    types 41, 231
ricotta cheese 315
risotto 240, 315
rissole 315
roasting 35, 114
    beef 113, 114, 115, 116
    chicken 152, 154–5

duck 153, 167
  garlic 189
  lamb 113, 114, 115
  onions 137
  pheasant 170
  pork 113, 114, 115
  squab chicken 160
  summer vegetables 192
  turkey 152, 168
  veal 113
rogan josh 139
rolling pin 21
root vegetables 176
rosemary 44, 213, 222
rösti 315
rouille 315
roulade 315
roux 316
rub in 25
rutabaga 176

saffron 44, 215, 316
sage 44, 213
salad
  Caesar 204
  dressings 205, 206, 313, 316
  Greek 206
  roast chicken with orange
    dressing 205
  spicy tomato 209
salad greens 177
salmon 83, 86, 222, 286
salsa 108, 122, 316
salt 12, 13, 45, 316
samosa 316
sardines 83, 90
satay 316
sauce
  apricot 167
  béarnaise 312
  béchamel 133, 203, 312, 316
  bread 168
  brown 46
  cheese 235
  chocolate & brandy 294
  chocolate fudge 75
  hollandaise 56, 314
  mint 134
  mornay 315
  spaghetti bolognese 232
  tomato 46, 203, 237
  types 46
  warm cider 268
  white 316
sausages 95, 126, 245
sauté 33
scallions 179, 196, 243, 247
scallops 85, 97
scissors 17

score 26
scrambling eggs 52
sea bass 91, 96
seafood gratin 97
sear 34
seasonings 44— 5
seaweed 181
seeds, types 43
sesame-seed paste 46
shallots 179, 198, 199, 216
shallow-fry 31
shellfish 84, 95, 97, 99
shepherd's pie 130–1
sherbet 257, 316
shrimp
  buying/storing 84, 85
  in fish pie 107
  in paella 95
  and pineapple curry 99
  seafood gratin 97
shortbread 275
shred 25
shuck 29, 316
sift 29
simmer 32
sirloin 316
skewers 21
skim 26
slaking 316
slow cooker 22
smoke alarms 15
smoothie 316
snip 29
soba noodles 228
soft fruits 252
sole 83, 92
soup
  borscht 182, 312
  leek and potato 183
  les Halles onion 184
  pea and mint 216
soybeans 42, 230
soy sauce 46, 316
spaghetti bolognese 232
Spanish tortilla 59
spatchcock 28, 152
spatulas 20
spices 44–5, 214–15
spinach 177, 205, 290
split peas 42, 230
sponge cake 275
spoon measurements 23
spoons 20
sprats 83
squab chicken 150, 160
squash 181
squid 85, 100
star anise 214
steak

beef 125, 126, 247, 289, 293
  ham 128
  preparation 27, 112
  venison 172
steam 33
steep 27
stew 36
stir-fry 31–2, 100, 163, 196, 247
stock 313, 316
  chicken 152
strained canned tomatoes 46, 315
strain 19, 29, 313
strainers 19
strawberries 252, 254, 258, 266
stuffing 112, 168
sugar
  in diet 10, 13
  types 45
summer fruit fool 266
sweat 34, 316
sweet-&-sour pork ribs 143
syrups 45

tabasco sauce 46, 316
tabbouleh 243
tablespoon 23
tagine of lamb 225
tapenade 136, 316
tarragon 212, 219, 221
tarte au citron 262
tarte tatin 316
tarts 60–1, 262, 269, 288, 298
tea 13
tempura whitebait 102
tenderize 27, 112
terrine 316
thermometers 21, 114
thyme 44, 212, 222, 245, 280
timbale 316
timers 21
tiramisù 76
tisane 316
toast 34
tofu 47, 316
tomatoes 180
  canned/bottled 47
  chili con carne 246
  Greek salad 206
  oven-dried 195
  paste 46
  ratatouille 187
  roast summer vegetables 192
  sauce 46, 203, 237
  spaghetti bolognese 232
  spicy salad 209
  sun-dried 47, 280
  vegetable lasagna 235
treacle tart 298
tropical fruit dessert 266

tropical fruit salad 258
trout 83, 88
truss 28
tuna 83, 108
turbot 83
turkey 150–1, 152–3, 168
turmeric 44, 215, 316
turnips 176, 242

udon noodles 228

vanilla 47, 316
veal
  braised in red wine 144
  choosing cuts 113
  osso bucco 147
vegetable peeler 17
vegetables 182–209
  brown rice vegetable pilaf 241
  buying/storing 176
  chargrilled 36
  choice 176–81
  couscous 242
  and crispy noodle stir-fry 196
  in diet 12, 13
  jalousie 292
  lasagna 235
  mixed vegetable gratin 198
  roast summer 192
vegetarian diet 12, 47
venison 150, 151, 172
vichyssoise 316
vinaigrette 316
vinegar 39, 312
vitamins 11

walnuts 43
water chestnuts 47
weight, conversion chart 23
whisking 26, 52
whisks 21, 22
whitebait 83, 102
Worcestershire sauce 46

yeast 272, 316
yogurt 47, 54, 254
Yorkshire pudding 116

zabaglione 316
zest 26, 316
zester 17
zucchini 181
  crispy noodle stir-fry 196
  and onion tartlets 288
  ratatouille 187
  roast summer vegetables 192
  vegetable couscous 242
  vegetable lasagna 235